Julia D Carrothers

The sunrise kingdom

Or life and scenes in Japan, and woman's work for woman there

Julia D Carrothers

The sunrise kingdom
Or life and scenes in Japan, and woman's work for woman there

ISBN/EAN: 9783742840547

Manufactured in Europe, USA, Canada, Australia, Japa

Cover: Foto ©Andreas Hilbeck / pixelio.de

Manufactured and distributed by brebook publishing software (www.brebook.com)

Julia D Carrothers

The sunrise kingdom

WAYSIDE TEA-HOUSE.

THE SUNRISE KINGDOM;

OR,

LIFE AND SCENES IN JAPAN,

AND

WOMAN'S WORK FOR WOMAN THERE.

BY

Mrs. JULIA D. CARROTHERS.

PHILADELPHIA:
PRESBYTERIAN BOARD OF PUBLICATION,
No. 1334 CHESTNUT STREET.

Copyright, 1879, by
THE TRUSTEES OF THE
PRESBYTERIAN BOARD OF PUBLICATION.

WESTCOTT & THOMSON,
Stereotypers and Electrotypers, Philada.

TO

THE MEMBERS OF

THE WOMAN'S FOREIGN MISSIONARY SOCIETY

OF THE

PRESBYTERIAN CHURCH,

IN REMEMBRANCE OF THEIR EARNEST PRAYERS FOR JAPAN
AND THEIR FAITHFUL CO-OPERATION IN "WOMAN'S
WORK FOR WOMAN THERE,"

THIS BOOK IS AFFECTIONATELY DEDICATED BY

ONE OF THEIR MISSIONARIES.

PREFACE.

If they who walk beside me as seven years of missionary life are retraced, find the Master near as I find him; if they who stand beside me as the seed is sown over Japan realize the care of the Father, the power of the Spirit, the preciousness of the seed and the blessedness of the sower as I do; if any, being themselves "heirs of the kingdom," are led to seek with redoubled zeal to lead others to the same heritage,—then shall I feel that my work has not been in vain.

To the members of the society with which I was most nearly connected, and under whose care my work was done and is still carried on, this book is dedicated. But it goes forth with greetings to ALL SOCIETIES, MISSION CIRCLES and BOARDS, and to all MISSIONARIES who in any clime and among people of any tongue are laboring to sow the *seed of the kingdom.*

J. D. C.

CHICAGO, Sept., 1878.

INTRODUCTION.

The following pages are a picture of seven years of missionary-life in Japan.

Looking upon the incidents and events here recorded, the reader may enter in some degree into the experiences of such a life, and understand, dimly at least, the richness and beauty which may be found in it. The simplicity and steadfast adherence to the one aim and purpose of mission-work, turning aside neither to the right hand nor the left for earthly pleasure or reward, may have seemed to some like a monotonous treading of the mill of duty. This little book will perhaps show to such that there are endless sources of delight and interest ever open to the earnest missionary in the minds and souls of those among whom he is laboring.

And as we go in and out with the writer of

this familiar account of her own knowledge of the Japanese people and intercourse with them, we shall see fresh evidence of the ever-new power of the old gospel, and realize the silent yet wonderfully transforming influence which it carries with it wherever it takes possession of the heart of man.

The writer's hope is that the simple story of what she saw and heard during her residence in Japan, when she had unusual opportunities, which she diligently improved, of gaining access to the homes and hearts of the people, may answer the questionings of some doubters as to the benefit of mission-work, and may show what *present* reward the Master often gives his servants in the labor to which he calls them.

She trusts also that it will lead many who have never before done so to lift up heart and voice to God in prayer for this beautiful "Sunrise Kingdom," which is just beginning to turn its face toward the "Sun of righteousness," and to feel the blessed "healing in his wings."

M. H. P.

CONTENTS.

BOOK I.

CHAPTER I.

                                                           PAGE

" O-HAY-O "—" GOOD-MORNING "................... 17

    First Sight of Land.—Voyage.—General Appearance of Coast.—Junks, Fishing-Vessels, Sailors, Harbor, Sampans.—Yokohama.—" O-hay-O."

CHAPTER II.

A LOOK AT THE PEOPLE......................... 25

    Different Classes of Japanese.— Mikado.—Kugis.—Daimios.—Samurai.— Judges.—Priests.— Doctors.— Merchants.—Mechanics.—Barbers.—Coolies.—Beggars.— Religions of the Country.—Work of Missionaries.

CHAPTER III.

SUMMER DAYS IN YOKOHAMA..................... 37

    Climate. — Walks through the Rice-Paddies.— Trees.—Flowers.—Fruits.— Birds.— Animals.—Farmers.—A Pedestrian Tour.

CHAPTER IV.

A WINTER IN TOKIO.................................... 45

Tokio.—Its Situation.—The Castle.—Emperor's Garden.—O-hama-go-ten.—Temples.—A-sa-ku-sa.—Shi-ba.—Japanese Houses.—Large Fires.—The To-ri.—Canals.—Bridges.—The Foreign Concession.—Mu-ko-ji-ma.—Sku-da-ji-ma.—Winter Climate.—Flowers and Fruit.—Missionary Life in Tokio.

CHAPTER V.

HOME AND SCHOOL.................................... 59

Morning in Tokio.—Interior of a Japanese House.—Breakfast.—Going to School.—The Written Language.—What a Japanese Girl Learns.—The Baby O-ya-su-mi-na-sai.—Japanese Homes.—Position of Women.

CHAPTER VI.

GOING TO "SEE FLOWERS"............................ 75

Japanese Holidays.—A Letter.—Dressing the Hair.—The Bath-House.—A Little Girl's Dress.—Fans, Shoes and Umbrellas.—Meeting Friends.—Worship at the Temple.—Mu-ko-ji-ma.—The Feast.—Going Home.—Social Life.—Spoken Language.—May Days.

CHAPTER VII.

RO-KU-BAN... 91

The New Mission-House.—The Typhoon.—A Class of Boys.—Young Samurai.—The Bible Class.—The Ya-cu-nins.—Our New Year.

CHAPTER VIII.

PICTURES AND BOOKS.................................. 98

Ancient Warriors.—Court-Ladies.—Daimios.—Ha-ra-ki-ri.—Jo-ro-rei.—Japanese Books.—Religious.—Historical.—Encyclopædias.—Allegory.—Moral Teachings.—Poetry.—Novels.

CHAPTER IX.

GAMES AND TOYS...................................... 110

Japanese New Year.—Division of Time.—Mo-chi.—Ornaments.—O-mi-so-ka.—Money.—Driving away Evil Spirits.—New Year's Festivities.—The Dolls' Feast.—Games.—Toy-shops.—Japanese Children.

CHAPTER X.

WHAT LITTLE CHILDREN READ 120

The Names of their Books:—"The Ape and the Crab."—"The Rat's Wedding."—"Mo-mo-taro."—"Kin-ta-ro."—"The Tail-Cut Swallow."—"Story of Sho-set-su."—"The Treasure."

CHAPTER XI.

A JOURNEY FROM TOKIO TO O-DA-WA-RA............. 128

A Letter.—Political Divisions.—Postmen.—Setting out on a Journey.—The To-kai-do.—Tea-Houses.—Ka-gos.—No-ri-mo-no.—The Road to Fu-ji-sa-wa.—The Hotel.—A Day's Journey.—Night at O-da-wa-ra.

CHAPTER XII.

ON THE HA-KO-NES... 139

Sai-o-na-ra.—Mountain Scene.—Ha-ta-ji-ku.—Up to Ha-ko-ne.—The Lake.—The Temple.—Ji-go-ku.—A-shi-no-yu.—Mi-ya-no-shi-ta.— Yu-mo-to.

CHAPTER XIII.

PILGRIMS ON FU-JI... 146

Pilgrims come to Ha-ko-ne.—Descent of the Mountain.—Mi-shi-ma.—Yo-shi-wa-ra.—The Base of Fu-ji.—The Cinder Cone.—The Huts.—Going up to the Crater.—The Storm.

BOOK II.

CHAPTER I.

AN OPEN DOOR... 153

CHAPTER II.

MIDSUMMER HOLIDAYS... 163

CHAPTER III.

THE GOSPEL IN JAPANESE....................................... 172

CHAPTER IV.

LOAVES AND FISHES.................. 181

CHAPTER V.

THE HOLY SPIRIT ALONE.................. 190

CHAPTER VI.

CHRISTMAS AT RO-KU-BAN.................. 197

CHAPTER VII.

THE "PEEP OF DAY".................. 204

CHAPTER VIII.

THE WOMAN AT THE WELL.................. 210

BOOK III.

CHAPTER I.

"THE CHURCHES OF ASIA SALUTE YOU".............. 219

CHAPTER II.

ENO-SHIMA 227

Contents.

CHAPTER III.
THE STRAIT GATE AND THE NARROW WAY............ 234

CHAPTER IV.
A JIN-RI-KI-SHA JOURNEY............................ 246

CHAPTER V.
THE TWO CAPITALS IN 1875........................ 254

CHAPTER VI.
"THE POOR HAVE THE GOSPEL PREACHED TO THEM".. 267

CHAPTER VII.
COMING INTO THE KINGDOM........................ 278

CHAPTER VIII.
"OUR FATHER WHICH ART IN HEAVEN"............. 287

CHAPTER IX.
LITTLE CHILDREN.................................. 294

CHAPTER X.
THE HEM OF THE GARMENT........................ 302

BOOK IV.

CHAPTER I.
	PAGE
WOMEN'S WORK FOR WOMEN	307

CHAPTER II.
"THE CHRISTIAN'S SHINING LIGHT" 341

CHAPTER III.
THE REGIONS BEYOND 365

CHAPTER IV.
"THE LORD SHOWED HIM ALL THE LAND" 379

CHAPTER V.
SAI-O-NA-RA 403

THE SUNRISE KINGDOM.

BOOK I.

CHAPTER I.

"O-HAY-O!"—"GOOD-MORNING!"

FIRST SIGHT OF LAND—VOYAGE—GENERAL APPEARANCE OF COAST—JUNKS, FISHING-VESSELS, SAILORS, HARBOR, SAMPANS—YOKOHAMA—"O-HAY-O!"

THE sun was just rising over the islands of Japan when we saw them for the first time. It was a beautiful hour in which to arrive in ZI-PAN-GU, "The Sunrise Kingdom."

The voyage across the Pacific Ocean had been long and dreary. Day after day sea and sky were of the same dull and leaden hue. Only once or twice did the mists roll away to disclose the blue sky and the still bluer sea. One evening the breeze freshened a little, and there were white caps on the waves. The Chinese in the steerage threw out square pieces of paper with strange characters printed on them to appease the gods of the storm. But the wind soon died away, the sea became as smooth as ever, and there was not even a gale to vary the monotony of our voyage.

The people on shipboard were not favorable to missionary enterprise in Japan. They said that it was contrary to the treaty, and that missionaries had no right to go, as such, to Japan at all. We thought differently, and looked above the treaty to One who has commanded his disciples to go into all the world.

The Japanese have a pretty legend concerning the origin of their country. They say: "A god once dipped his spear into the sea, and as he lifted it again the drops which fell from it congealed, and Japan's four thousand isles were formed."

But we, in our Western wisdom, cannot admit any such poetic and peaceful origin to these islands. Our science rather suggests that they were broken off from the great Asiatic continent in some violent convulsion of Nature, and frequent earthquakes still proclaim the existence of restless internal fires.

The coast-line of the Japan islands is broken and irregular, with many bays and inlets. There is little of the sublime to mark the scenery, but the islands are fair and sunny, and diversified by mountain and valley and wide-extended plains. Over the plains broad, shallow rivers flow peacefully in their channels, and down from the mountain-sides, into the pleasant valleys, come wild little streams, making up in swiftness and impetuosity what they lack in size.

As you travel among the mountains the murmur and gurgle of waterfalls hidden from sight fall upon the ear as they tumble over the rocks and down the precipices. Mountains, valleys and plains are clothed in the richest green, and exhibit in pleasing combination the productions of both temperate and semi-tropical climes.

Japan bears traces of the curse in the earthquake and the tempest, the brier and the thorn, but there is little here that is hurtful; few poisonous plants or reptiles are found. The Japanese are justly proud of their land, whose beauty they celebrate in many a song and poem.

All around the islands sweeps the Pacific Ocean, dashing in white foam upon the rocks and murmuring against the low shores. Sometimes it grows rough and angry, and appears as if threatening to submerge the whole land. But it is only a threat, for even the tiniest isles are safe. After all, the sea loves the land, and delights in whispering to it pleasant stories and in casting its lovely treasures upon its shores.

As we neared our port we passed some Japanese junks. These clumsy, ill-contrived vessels do not often venture far from land, but are used in transporting manufactures and products from one part of the country to another through rivers and inland seas. Nearer the shore were smaller fishing-vessels, in whose construction and the shape of the sails you would observe a wide difference from those dotting our own waters.

The Japanese are very dependent upon their supply of fish ; as they eat no meat, it forms a principal article of their diet. In the morning, when the wind is fair, the fishing-boats go out to sea, and all day long their white sails glitter far out upon the water. Usually the fish are plentiful and cheap. The smaller ones are eaten by the poorer classes, while the rich choose the delicious *tai* and *bora*. Sometimes the fishermen bring home sharks and enormous cuttle-fish.

Japanese sailors are very expert in the management of their boats, seldom meeting with accidents. They are good swimmers and divers, and this renders them all the more fearless in the water.

The harbors are very shallow. Ships are obliged to anchor far from the shore, and passengers and freight are landed by means of small open boats, called *sampans*. These are worked by a single oar, as in sculling, and the boat is rapidly propelled with a peculiar hissing on the part of the oarsman.

When our steamer dropped anchor in the harbor of Yokohama, we were immediately surrounded by these sampans. From the deck we saw the small, frail vessels and the almost naked boatmen, with their skin bronzed by constant exposure to the sun and wind. The first view of the Japanese is not prepossessing, nor are the tones of their voices, when first heard, agreeable to the ear. But we could not dwell upon these early impressions, as we were anxious to reach the city of Yokohama, that lay just a mile from us. So bidding adieu to the officers of the Great Republic and to our fellow-passengers, whose destination was still farther on —to China, the Flowery Kingdom—we descended the ladder by the side of the steamer, stepped cautiously into a sampan, and with our baggage were soon landed on the shore.

Yokohama was not the first foreign settlement on this side of the island. The name of the city signifies "opposite shore," as it lies directly opposite Kanagawa, where foreigners were first allowed to live. English and French troops are stationed here, each nation striving to gain the ascendency and to obtain a monopoly of trade with a people so recently opened to commerce. In speaking of the city, foreigners use the terms *native town, settlement* and *bluff*. In the "settlement," houses are mostly built in the European style, and in its stores you can purchase almost anything in the way of clothing and furniture. Here also are the various churches, mission-houses, hotels, consulates and many residences belonging to the foreign population, now numbering about five thousand.

The most beautiful part of the city is the bluff. Across the bridge, near the mission-house, the road leads along the bank of a canal for a few steps, and then, making a sudden turn, takes its course up the hill, which rises gradually to about two hundred feet above the level of the ocean and extends several miles. This road is very pretty, with embankments on one side, and on the other views of the Buddhist cemeteries, and occasional glimpses of the sea. The foreign residences on the bluff are very pleasant, and some are even elegant. Here also are tea-houses, where we can sit and enjoy the view of the settlement and the harbor whilst drinking the cup of tea which is always offered to the casual visitor by the smiling Japanese girl.

The foreign cemetery on the bluff is a sweet, quiet spot, more home-like than anything else in this strange land.

In the native city the principal street is called Curio street by the foreigners, and To-ri by the natives. Here the curious China *lacquer* and native woodenware are temptingly arranged.

We have already learned a few words of their language, such as *i-ku-ra* ("how much?"), *arigato* ("thank you!"), *yo-ro-shiu* ("all right"), and others. But *o-hay-o* ("good-morning!") has the clearest, most winning sound of all, and is the word we oftenest hear. "*O-hay-o!*" say the servants early in the morning; "*O-hay-o!*" call out the children in the streets; "*O-hay-o de goza-i masu,*" politely say the men and women we meet on the hillside and in the native city.

All this means simply "early," but to us is something more than a mere salutation. And how strange it all seems to us! It is indeed *o-hay-o* — "good-morning" — with this people. For many centuries they have lived in seclusion, and in a state of somnolence with regard to the rest of the world. Ever following the same customs, with fashion of dress unchanged, they have pursued the same beaten track of national habit. But now they are just waking from their sleep; and stepping forth into the light of a new morning, they are pleasantly and happily saying to the world at large, "*O-hay-o!*"

And the prayer of God's children is, "That this land, which catches the first beams of the morning sun when it comes to light up the eastern hemisphere, may soon rejoice in the light of the Sun of righteousness." And thus do the people of the West hold out the hand to this newly-awakened land, and with earnest congratulations call out to them in the same cheering tones,

"*O-hay-o!*" ("Good-morning!")

CHAPTER II.

A LOOK AT THE PEOPLE.

Different Classes of Japanese—Mikado—Kugis—Daimios—Samurai—Judges—Priests—Doctors—Merchants—Mechanics—Barbers—Coolies—Beggars—Religions of the Country—Work of Missionaries.

WHENEVER we stop to examine any object, a crowd collects around us. We soon learn to distinguish the different classes of people by their dress. Although there has been a great revolution in Japan, and the distinctions of *caste*, hitherto so marked, are passing away, we still observe great differences in the appearance, manners and dress of the people we meet. It may be well just here to note the various classes that gradually became known to us.

At the summit stands the Mikado, or *emperor*. His person was formerly considered very sacred. He was kept almost in seclusion. No one was permitted to look upon him except the very highest nobles. It is said that he had to submit to many tiresome forms, such as sitting motionless for hours on his throne, with a heavy crown upon his head. He wears richly-embroidered robes of silk, on which is stamped the chrysanthemum, the emblem of royal sovereignty. No one but members of the royal family or those nearest his person is allowed to wear this badge. It is probable that the use of this emblem grew out of this flower's resemblance to the sun, which was once an object of worship among this people, traces of which worship are to be seen in relics of Sintooism still existing.

Next to the emperor come the great lords, or *Kugis*. They wait in the sacred presence of the Mikado and kneel around the throne. In the pictures they are represented as wearing very high hats and robes with long trains. They are but few in number, and their places in the empire or exact prerogatives are not distinctly defined.

The *Daimios* are the feudal chiefs, whose authority was very great until the revolution, when the progressive party, led by the Mikado (legitimate emperor), drove from his castle the Tycoon (usurping emperor) and completely broke up the feudal system, which had for many centuries prevailed throughout the empire. These daimios, although deprived of their special prerogatives, still retain the names of their provinces. There is the prince of To-sa, of Sat-su-ma, the princes of Aid-zu, Su-ru-ga, and others.

Until the revolution the daimios had as their retainers the *Samurai*, or *Two-sworded men*. These men were supported by the government, and had no employment except that of war. They spent their idle hours in various pastimes —fishing, hunting, wrestling, reading and playing with their children. With their wives and children they occupied low houses around the daimio's residence, forming a large square enclosure, like barracks. Many of these still exist, and cover large spaces of ground.

Where there were so many independent chiefs there was, of course, much fighting, and the Samurai were expected to be always ready to go to war. They were devoted to the interests of their lords, often dying with them or for them.

Although the Samurai have been deprived of their support (except a small pension from the government for a limited term of years), and the wearing of the swords is no longer authorized, many of them retain their peculiar dress, which consists of a tunic and a wide skirt. They also retain their swords, wearing the long one on the left side and the short one concealed in their broad belts. They are the class with which we are brought most in contact. Our teachers and scholars, and even some of the servants, are Samurai. They are the gentry and the *literati* of the country, and walk the streets with an air of conscious superiority.

The judges (*ya-cu-nin*) are greatly feared and reverenced by the common people. They wear, in addition to the garments of the Samurai, a coat of peculiar cut, which comes high up over the shoulders, but without sleeves.

The priests (*bo-san*) form a large portion of the community. Their dress differs little in style from that of the Samurai, but their shaven heads give them an unmistakable appearance. Besides those in regular priestly office, there are monks and nuns, who live in and about the temples, and whose duty is to assist in the ministrations there. Also mendicant friars are numerous, who go about the country drawling their prayers in low, monotonous tones and waiting at the doors of the houses until a few coppers are given.

Japanese *doctors* traverse the streets in long robes, looking very solemn and wise. A boy walks behind them, carrying their boxes of medicines, consisting principally of powders and pills. They use blisters and the *moxa* to a very great extent. Their fees are very moderate.

Merchants are privileged to wear one sword.

COOLIES DRAWING CHARCOAL.

BUDDHIST PRIEST   SAMURAI.

Pages 27, 28 and 30.

They form the most solid and reliable part of the community. Silk-merchants occupy the largest stores. The beautiful silks and crapes manufactured in this country are not exposed to view like the more common cotton fabrics, but are kept shut up in the storerooms. At the other dry-goods stores the goods are displayed on the shelves, the floor, or are hung up by the door-post. There are shops where more trifling articles are kept for sale, such as hair-pins, combs, powders and paints, and articles used in worship. There are large tea and rice establishments, and groceries, where beans, eggs, etc., are sold. Confectioners' shops may be found, where children buy candy made of rice, beans and paste colored with seaweed. We see large china-stores, and are interested in the toy-shops filled with pretty things for the children, and in the book-stores, where the curious literature of the country is sold to those who wish to read.

We find, too, a class in which the merchant and the artisan mingle their callings—those employed in the manufacture and sale of umbrellas, shoes, fans, lamps, tables, chests of drawers, mats and other things, all exhibiting great skill and exquisite neatness. There are carpenters and smiths, masons, stone-cutters, lapidaries, and carvers in wood and ivory. Many are employed in making the beautiful lacquered articles, turning bronzes and manufacturing china-ware in every conceivable style.

Barbers form a numerous class, and do an extensive work in keeping the faces of the men smooth and a bald place on the top of the head, while the heads of priests, old women and babies are often completely shorn.

In the cities are jugglers, who perform wonderful tricks, and acrobats, who amuse the people by tumbling and wrestling, and *geishas*, or girl-minstrels, who sing and play upon the *samisen*, a species of guitar, and a popular instrument in Japan. At night blind men, called *a-mas*, blow their shrill whistles in the streets, and are called on to rub sick or tired people. They profess to cure diseases by manipulation, in the same way that magnetic physicians have undertaken to do in our land, and they have a regular school for instruction,

Nin-so-kus (*coolies*) are the most numerous, and form the lowest, class in the social life of Japan. These are they who bear the heavy burdens, draw the carts and perform the most menial occupations. Even among them, however, distinctions may be found, as those who work in hides and leather are looked upon by the coolie race itself with great disdain, and are kept separate from all others. We presume this is owing to the fact of their coming in contact with the dead bodies of animals and being thus defiled, according to the strict rules of Buddhism.

Beggars.—Beggary is a profession in Japan. The beggar is doomed to beg all his life long, and to do nothing else. He besets the traveler on the highways, and waits about the temple-gates to receive alms from those who are going up to worship. He sleeps where he can, and when death comes lies down by the roadside, few hearing or pitying his dying groans.

Such is a description of the people we meet in Japan. Let us now look at the *religions* of the people. There are two principal religions in the land, BUDDHISM and SINTOOISM.

BUDDHISM is an imported religion, coming through China from India. It was at first very simple in its details. Its founder, the first BUDDHA—the *Sha-ka-sa-ma* of the Japanese—taught mercy and tenderness. The first Buddha died, and his followers said that a great many wonderful scenes took place at his death. He and his five hundred disciples were deified, and images of them were made and worshiped. These are beautiful statues with mild, placid countenances, touchingly suggestive of mercy. Some of them are represented with three heads and six arms, that "they might better help men," says a Japanese.

Some of these images are called *Ho-to-kes*, a name applied to such as are not yet deified, but are on the calendar for that high distinction and retain all the elements proper to such a result. The gods *Bin-dzu-ru*, whose image we see in the temples as the *Pain-god*, and *Gi-zo*, who is in shrines by the wayside as the special protector of travelers, and in the cemeteries as the god who cares for the souls of the dead, are Ho-tokes. Mothers believe that the god Gi-zo watches over their dead infants in paradise.

The Buddhist priests talk of abstractions, contemplations, absorptions and annihilations. Many sects have arisen, and the whole system has become very complicated. It is hard for the women and children to understand anything about it. And yet Buddhism is a wonderful system, and has a powerful influence over the human mind. Sometimes it appears in a refined and cultivated form and its votaries are scholarly men. Even Christian missionaries cannot fail to commend the humanizing influences of this system.

Sintooism is the native religion of Japan. Its probable origin is in the worship of the sun (*O-Ten-to-sama*.) The moon (*Tsu-ki-sama*) is also an object of worship. The emperor (*Ten-shi-*

THE SEVEN HAPPY GODS.

Page 33.

sama) is regarded as the direct descendant of the sun. Some deity must have made Japan, they say, and thus their fables and stories of gods were invented and images formed. Japan is filled with these images. We see them in the temples and in shrines by the wayside, on the tops of the highest mountains and in the farthest recesses of the caves. Every house has its shrine, and the people carry about with them pictures or exceedingly small images of the gods. There is *Ha-chi-man-sama*, the god of war, and *I-na-ri-sama*, the god of rice, and *Ye-be-su-sama* and *Dai-ko-ku-sama*, the gods of riches, and many others. The image of the fox is worshiped as a servant of *I-na-ri*, because the animal is a devourer of the insects that are apt to feed upon the rice. The snake is one form under which the god *Ben-ten* appears. The horse, the image of which is seen in many temples, is the servant of *Ha-chi-man-sama*. These images are of all sizes, from the tiny *Dai-ko-ku-sama*, which we can scarcely hold in our fingers, to the colossal *Dai-Butsu*, on whose thumb we can sit with ease.

Some of these gods are merry-looking fellows. There are seven who are called the "happy gods" of Japan, and they all have smiling faces; while others are hideous in their appearance, such as the red and green monsters who stand at the gates of the temples to protect the other gods, and the frightful representations of Satan and his attendants.

Now, the people say that these gods are in Paradise, and these images are only used as aids in worship. The most intelligent among the people deny that they are idolaters at all. However this may be, we find in Japan a mingling of sentiments and ideas drawn from these two religions, so that Buddhism and Sintooism often blend in the eyes of the worshiper. In one respect both sects agree. *They all worship their ancestors*, and thus show a Mongolian origin in common with the vast neighboring nation, the Chinese.

The writings of Confucius are much read in the empire. Confucianism is a system of moral teaching.

Long years ago some Roman Catholic missionaries were in Japan, and a great many people heard of God and of the Lord Jesus. For a time the missionaries were allowed to teach and the people to believe and worship as they pleased. But one of the Roman priests was foolish enough to tell of the power of his lord the pope, whose aim was universal sovereignty of civil as well as spiritual power. Upon this the government, fearing that the pope would come with a great army and take possession of the country, entered upon a course of the severest persecution. They banished from the land all foreign priests and tortured the native Christians, putting men, women, and even little children, into the prisons, or, still worse, pitching them into the crater of a burning volcano. They threw the converts from the great rock *Shima-bara*, which rises almost perpendicularly out of the water in the harbor of Nagasaki.

The Christian religion was prohibited, and the edicts to that effect, written in large characters and nailed to high boards, were placed in conspicuous localities throughout the whole empire. A large cross of wood was made, and every year was brought out for the people to trample upon. Some of the earliest ideas we have connected with Japan are drawn from pictures in which mothers are represented as bringing their children forward to trample upon this cross. Such was the effect of Jesuitical intrigue on the one hand and governmental jealousy on the other that Japan for three centuries became closed to all Christian efforts, and held herself aloof from all civilized intercourse.

But since the visit of Commodore Perry of the U. S. Navy in 1854 the gates of Japan have been thrown open once more, and foreigners are again allowed to dwell here. Following upon the soldiers, the sailors and the merchants came the missionaries, ready to spread the truths of the gospel, and to tell the Japanese, not of the power of the pope, but of the power of the Lord Jesus, whose kingdom, though not of this world, is yet an everlasting kingdom whose dominion hath no end.

These missionaries are learning the manners and customs of the natives, and gradually winning their confidence. Much of their time is occupied in studying the difficult language and preparing grammars and dictionaries; also in translating the Bible and other books for popular use. They are now distributing Bibles in the Chinese tongue, and also teach English to those who apply, using Christian books, and sometimes the Scriptures themselves, for that purpose. The missionary doctor treats the physical diseases of his patients and tries to lead them to the GREAT PHYSICIAN. The missionaries are watching, praying and waiting for the time to come when the gospel may be publicly proclaimed in Japan, and its people allowed full liberty to worship as they please.

CHAPTER III.

SUMMER DAYS IN YOKOHAMA.

CLIMATE—WALKS THROUGH THE RICE-PADDIES—TREES—FLOWERS—FRUITS—BIRDS—ANIMALS—FARMERS—A PEDESTRIAN TOUR.

THE August days pass rapidly in this new, strange land. The weather is warm, but we have usually a pleasant breeze from the sea. Some days the rain comes down in torrents, for this is the rainy season in Japan. The dampness and heat make the vegetation very rank, and everything is fresh and bright and green as in early spring. There is little danger here of long-continued drought, and consequent famine.

We often take long walks over the bluff to the rice-paddies and the fields where the farmers labor. The country immediately around Yokohama is rolling, and green bottoms and high grounds are beautifully variegated by clumps of trees and small forests, among which we recognize firs, cedars and oaks. In some places on the hillside the shade is so dense that the rays of the sun never penetrate. In the low, damp places fern and moss and ivy hide, and quantities of tiny wild flowers carpet the ground. Groves of graceful bamboo, their leaves stirring in the slightest breeze, give a peculiar charm to the landscape.

Just now the beautiful white lilies are blooming far up on the mountain-side, and we see the hydrangea with its great flowers of pale pink and blue. The lotus-flowers of red and white lie on their immense umbrella-like leaves upon the frequent ponds. These flowers are sacred to the Japanese; the Buddhas are represented as sitting upon them, and golden lotus-flowers are found in the temples. We have many varieties of the chrysanthemum, which blooms from the early part of July until far into the mild Japan winter. While these flowers are beautiful to the eye, they are, for the most part, odorless.

The summer fruits are pears, peaches and plums, also apples and apricots, but all of these, unless, it may be, the plum, are very inferior to the same in our own country, being hard and tasteless; cooking alone brings out the distinguishing flavor of the pears and peaches. Later in the season we shall have grapes, figs and pomegranates, and in the winter mandarin-oranges and persimmons. These fruits are more decided in flavor. The oranges are small, but sweet, while the persimmons are large, and hang upon the trees in the autumn like great golden balls. Why foreigners should call this fruit "persimmon" is not evident, for it in no way resembles the fruit of that name in America.

Rice is to be found here, as in every country, in low, wet lands, and where the water is not on the ground and the fields are irrigated from the nearest springs. It is cultivated with great care, being the chief object of agricultural labor and the principal staple of food for the entire population. On the high ground we see millet, wheat, barley, buckwheat and other grains, mostly of an inferior quality. They are raised solely for the support of such animals as may be in use among them. The Japanese do not eat bread, but there are now bakers who make a good article for the use of foreigners, and it is apparent, from the name they give to it (*pan*), that the French must have given them the first idea of so doing. They get their flour from California.

There is a great variety of native potatoes besides the "Irish," the latter being very small, but palatable, while the native kinds are mucilaginous, and not acceptable to foreigners. Roots of the lily, lotus and bamboo are largely used by the natives. The radish (*dai-kon*) grows to a remarkable size, and is eaten by all classes of the people. Often it is hung up until it begins to decay, and is then salted down for use. Egg-plants, onions and pumpkins are known, but the Japanese do not use vegetables as freely as we do, rice, the dai-kon and fish being their chief articles of diet.

Grass, in this land, is of a very coarse quality, unfit for animal use, and we are not surprised, therefore, at seeing no sheep browsing upon the hillsides nor cattle feeding in the meadows. Owing to this, all attempts at grazing have hitherto failed, sheep and cattle dying from throat-disease produced by the coarseness of the grass. Still, we may hope that in the future even this great drawback may be overcome, and the time arrive when all over this green and lovely island flocks and herds will rejoice the eye.

Tea (*cha*) forms the principal export of Japan, and is the universal beverage of the people. It is a low shrub, whose cultivation requires great care; and when the time of picking comes, it is leaf by leaf, close selection being required. Cotton grows on the southern plains of good quality, but it is only manufactured into coarse cloths, owing to imperfect native machinery.

Tobacco of a mild quality is cultivated and largely used. The mulberry and the silkworm are found in profusion. The silks of Japan are very beautiful and durable, and its crapes are unsurpassed.

Animals.—In a country of so limited an area, with over thirty millions of people, it is not to be expected that many wild animals would be found. Cultivation often extends to the highest hilltops, terrace rising above terrace, the land being tilled in the high places wholly by hand and without the plough. But sometimes bears, wolves and monkeys are seen. A wretched breed of dogs, small, scrubby horses and a few bullocks, with *tailless* cats, are the only domestic animals of the land.

Birds twitter in the branches of the trees, but do not sing. Pheasants and cranes are here. The latter bird is national, and is considered a sacred emblem; their pennons, lacquer-work, china-ware and fans are all emblazoned with its figure. In the dense shade of the thickets we sometimes hear the plaintive notes of the *un-gui-so*, the Japanese nightingale. There are a few parrots, while swallows, robins and crows are numerous.

Farmers.—The farmers are a simple-hearted and industrious race. They have rakes, spades and ploughs of rude construction. Sometimes the ploughs are drawn by oxen, but just as frequently by men, women or children. They show their kindness to animals by constructing awnings over their heads to protect them from the rays of the sun. Tea, tobacco, cotton and the various grains are packed in strong bags by the farmers, and sent to the cities on packhorses.

Work in the rice-fields is no easy task, for the men and women are obliged to stand in the water, while the sun beats down upon them, causing intense headaches.

The rice-plant has a bright, peculiar green of its own, and from the time the young rice (*i-ne*) springs up until the ripened grain (*ko-me*) bends the stalk, the fields are very beautiful. The thatched farmhouses in the valleys and on the hillsides, the roofs sometimes scarcely distinguishable from the hill itself, with trees and shrubs hiding their want of beauty, make pretty pictures. In the summer evenings the farmers sit on benches at the doors of their houses and smoke pipes, tell stories and exchange greetings with the passers-by. These farmers are very heavily taxed, and often rebel, causing much trouble to the princes and the general government.

Some of the missionaries have lately returned from a short pedestrian tour, and give a pleasant account of their trip. They have much to say concerning the beauties of the land—its mountains and valleys, green fields and bright waters; but our interest is chiefly centred in speaking and hearing of the people, especially with reference to their preparation for the reception of the gospel which is to be given them. Much of interest and encouragement has been obtained. Bibles in the Chinese for the upper classes, all of whom read in this language, are being circulated throughout the country. Many are inquiring for them, and are anxious to study them. The teacher of one of the missionaries, who has just come from the capital, brings word that one of the Japanese there has a school of ninety persons expressly for the purpose of teaching the Bible, and that he is determined to teach it even at the risk of his life. He is constantly armed and prepared to resist any attack. He also tells us that a man high in authority expressed a wish to have a Bible, and that he presented one to him.

For these things especially are we praying— viz., that the laws against Christianity may be repealed, that the native converts may prove faithful, that the reading of the word may be blessed to the people, and that the work of translation may progress rapidly. We ask God's people at home to unite with us in these petitions. Starting forth with these hopeful views in the very beginning of our missionary efforts among this interesting people, and encouraged by what has already been accomplished, we wait upon our heavenly Father, asking him to crown our future labors with great success, that Japan may yet be the Lord's.

CHAPTER IV.

A WINTER IN TOKIO.

TOKIO—ITS SITUATION—THE CASTLE—EMPEROR'S GARDEN—O-HAMA-GO-TEN — TEMPLES—A-SA-KU-SA — SHI-BA—JAPANESE HOUSES—LARGE FIRES—THE TO-RI—CANALS—BRIDGES—THE FOREIGN CONCESSION—MU-KO-JI-MA—SKU-DA-JI-MA—WINTER CLIMATE—FLOWERS AND FRUIT—MISSIONARY LIFE IN TOKIO.

COMING into Japan is like going back a few centuries in the world's history. Especially has it so appeared since our home has been this little Japanese house, right among the people. We are glad to live in the great capital, although cut off from the privilege of intercourse with our own people enjoyed in Yokohama.

The city of Tokio—the old Yedo or Jeddo—is on the east coast of the island of Niphon, the largest and most important of the Japan group, about eighteen miles north of Yokohama. The latitude of the city is 36° N. (about that of Raleigh, N. C., and Nashville, Tenn.), and longitude 138° E. from Greenwich; its mean annual temperature being 42° Fahrenheit, it is subject to no extremes of heat or cold. Except when, during some parts of the months of June and July, the heat and rain bring dampness and mould and swarms of mosquitoes, or occasionally in the winter, when cold and snow send the people in-doors to wrap themselves in thickly-wadded garments and shiver over charcoal braziers, the climate is remarkably pleasant, and the inhabitants can live most of the time in the open air.

Yedo Bay lies to the east of the city. From the water the land rises into tolerably high wooded hills on the west. The river *Su-mi-da* comes over the plains from the north, and flows through the city to the bay. The river intersects the city, but the largest and most important part is on its west bank. Mountains bound the horizon on every side. To the south-west, just where the sun sets in the winter, rises *Fu-ji*, the pride of the Japanese, the grandest thing the people know. Every one who possesses Japanese pictures, fans or vases is familiar with the peculiar truncated cone of *Fu-ji-yama*. It is an object of special reverence, and the shrine to which thousands of pilgrims resort every year to pay their devotions at its summit.

Below Fu-ji is the *Ha-ko-ne* range, and still farther to the west the mountains of *O-i*. Across the bay are *Ka-dzu-sa's* hills, and farther to the north, when the day is very clear, we can see the sacred mountains of *Nik-ko*.

The emperor's palace or castle, surrounded by a moat and three walls, stands on the high ground in the western part of the city. Within the two outer walls are the low, unsightly houses of the princes. Here we see kugis and daimios riding on gayly-caparisoned horses, and occasionally a retainer (*Samurai*) running by their side, calling out loudly for all to make way as the master rides.

Inside the third wall lives the Emperor, or Mikado, surrounded by his high officers. The house is built in the general style of all the houses, but is much larger and more elegantly finished. But to foreign eyes it is almost invisible. Sentinels keep watch at some distance, and none are allowed to approach the sacred threshold but the favored princes and great dignitaries of the empire.

There are a great many *ya-shi-kis* (residences of daimios) in Tokio, for the daimios were, until the time of the revolution, obliged to spend six months of the year in the capital. Most of these ya-shi-kis are now vacant, which is a great relief to foreigners, as we can go about the city with more freedom. There is less danger of meeting the trains of the daimios and the dreaded two-sworded men, who, under the influence of *sa-ki* (the national liquor), are ready at any moment to draw their swords upon the hated foreigner in the streets.

Near the castle are extensive pleasure-grounds for the exclusive use of the Mikado and his courtiers. Here he can hunt and fish without fear of intrusion or of being seen by unlicensed eyes.

Near the Foreign Concession is the sea-side palace, *O-Ha-ma-goten*, another delightful place of recreation for the Emperor. He passes from one to the other in a *no-ri-mo-no*, a close sedan-chair. In the same manner he is carried to the field to review his troops, so that no foreign eye can catch the slightest glimpse of majesty.

The finest buildings in Tokio, as indeed throughout all the empire, are the *te-ras*, or temples. These are large wooden buildings, usually painted red, with steep tiled roofs, turning up at the eaves with a peculiar curve. They are almost invariably built in groves, where the shade is very dense. This gives them an additional solemnity.

The gates of Buddhist temples are very large, and ornamented with dragons and serpents, flowers and leaves, in rude carving, while those of the Sintoo temples are plain and simple, with no attempt at ornament or decoration. It is only by this distinctive difference that one can tell the character of the temple he is approaching.

A-sa-ku-sa is one of the most noted of the temples in Tokio. It is quite near the river, in the north-eastern part of the city. The people throng its gates, and a broad stone walk which leads up to the temple resounds with the clatter of their wooden shoes. The way to the temple is lined with toy-shops, and the people who go up to worship stop to buy the frail playthings for the little ones they lead by the hand. We sometimes mingle with the crowds and watch the worshipers as they give alms to the beggars who crouch at the gates, then wash their hands in the stone basins near the steps of the main temple, throw their "cash" between the bars of a large contribution-box close by, pull a bell which hangs at the door, clap their hands and bow before the idols.

The whole scene, though one of pagan idolatry, cannot fail to remind us of the description given us of that greater temple originally designed as God's "house of prayer," but degenerated at the time of our Saviour's coming into a "house of merchandise" and "a den of thieves." There are the money-changers, the flocks of doves, the sellers of all kinds of merchandise, the same bartering and selling, and the ostentatious devotions of the worshipers, with the casting of gifts into the treasury over against the temple; in all this you could well imagine how similar the scene to that in our Lord's day, when, "eaten up" by zeal for his Father's house, he indignantly drove the sacrilegious crew from the sacred precincts. It will require the same divine Hand to cleanse these pagan counterfeits of a holy temple and make them truly houses for the Lord.

Within the building, taking off our shoes, we approach the altar, and are strikingly reminded of Roman Catholic churches by the gilded images of the Buddhas, the burning tapers and artificial flowers. A table stands before the altar, on which are pyramids of candies, with carrots and radishes cut so as to show the inside of these vegetables: these are offerings to the gods. Here we see the worshipers prostrate before the shrines, and mothers teaching their babes to clasp their little hands and bow before the idols. We watch the suffering ones going up to the Ho-to-ke Bin-dzu-ru (the "pain-god") and rubbing him for the purpose of obtaining relief from pain.

At A-sa-ku-sa is the only pagoda in Tokio. Around the larger building are small ones, called *mi-yas*, which are the shrines of particular deities. Within the temple-enclosure are exhibitions of dancing-bears, mountebanks, wax figures and feats of jugglery. There are also booths where story-tellers amuse the crowd with strange and marvelous tales, recited in a nasal, sing-song style. You can tell how deeply interested the people are by their applause and shouts of laughter greeting the ear.

Shi-ba, with its groves of magnificent trees and long avenues, lovely flowers, beautiful temples and mi-yas, is the most attractive spot in Tokio. This is a long distance from A-sa-ku-sa, being in the south-western part of the city. These two temples just mentioned are the most noted in the city, but there are many others.

Japanese houses are constructed of timbers from tolerably heavy wood, put together without nails and set right upon the ground. Instead of doors, windows or partitions, slides are used, the outer ones made of plain paper pasted only on one side of the framework, while the inner ones, which serve to make separate rooms, are made of beautifully-figured paper pasted on both sides of the framework. The whole house may be thrown into a single room by the removal, at pleasure, of these slides.

For protection against thieves and the inclemencies of the weather there are heavy wooden slides, which shut up the house effectually, making it close, dark and warm. The roofs of the houses are tiled or thatched, with projecting eaves. The rain runs easily from these roofs, which project so far as often to exclude the light. Around the houses are little verandas, the wood of which is very highly polished, and it is the pride of a good housekeeper to keep it bright and clean. The floors are covered with white mats, which the people call *ta-ta-mi*, to distinguish them from the ordinary matting (*go-za*). These houses are generally one story and a half high, or from twelve to fifteen feet. Back of the houses are pretty little gardens, with artificial lakes and rivers crossed by tiny bridges. The Japanese are real landscape-gardeners, and contrive, by making artificial hills on their grounds, to put a great deal in a small space.

The gardens, like the houses, are kept beautifully neat; but as they are all concealed from view, of course they add no beauty to the general appearance of the city. And it must be admitted that from the irregularity of the streets, the lowness of the houses and the entire want of artistic taste in their construction, Tokio cannot well be reckoned among the beautiful cities of the world. The light material out of which the houses are built ignites very rapidly; and as the Japanese have no means of

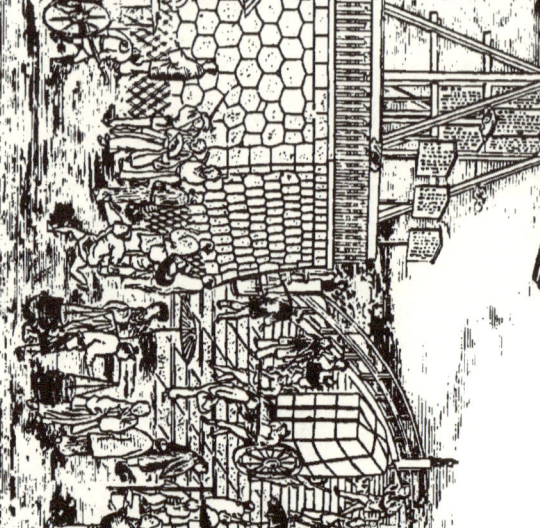

NIPHON BASHI.

Page 53.

extinguishing fire, almost every night we hear the clanging of the fire-bells, and look out to see the horizon red with the flames of some extensive conflagration.

All of the merchants have fireproof buildings, called *ku-ra*, in which their large stocks of goods are kept. These are made of adobe, or mud-plaster, and so smoothly polished as to resemble marble; and, though quite near the wooden houses, if a fire breaks out the light material quickly burns away, and the ku-ra remains untouched.

The principal street is called the *To-ri*, as in Yokohama. It runs through the centre of the city from north to south, and is part of the *To-kai-do*, or east sea-road, which connects the two capitals, Tokio and Kioto, a distance of three hundred miles, and may be called the great national road of the empire.

The city is intersected by canals, in which pass up and down boats loaded with rice, saki and charcoal. These canals are constantly crossed by arched bridges, in the construction of which great skill is exhibited. The most famous bridge in Tokio is *Ni-phon Ba-shi*, which crosses one of these canals on the To-ri. From this bridge all the distances throughout the empire are reckoned, and here the famous edicts against the Christians are posted.

Across the river Sumida are many long bridges—*Ye-tai Ba-shi*, *O-Ha-shi*, the great bridge, *Ri-yo-go-ku Ba-shi* and *A-dzu-ma Ba-shi*.

The Foreign Concession is in the eastern part of the city, lying along the bay. Its name (*Ts'kiji*) signifies "made land," and it has been conceded by the government for the use and residence of foreigners. At present the only European building there is the hotel, which is an object of great interest to the natives. It is of foreign construction, though built by native mechanics under the superintendence of a European architect.

On the east side of the river Sumida is Mu-ko-ji-ma, where the famous cherry trees grow along the bank. In the spring, when the bloom is out, crowds of Japanese go over the river to see the flowers, to drink tea made of the blossoms, and thus celebrate the return of the cheerful season. Opposite the city is *Sku-da-ji-ma*, a little island where the fishermen live who supply the great city with the products of their labor.

Our first winter in Tokio is quickly passing away, and yet we have never been without flowers, and the trees have been always green. Only once or twice has snow fallen, and then to melt away almost as soon as it touched the ground. The days are almost always bright, the sky of a deep soft blue, and the waters of the bay sparkle in the sunshine. Sometimes, however, the wind blows a perfect gale, the bay is rough and dark, the windows rattle, and the cold penetrates with chilling effect. The women in the streets have their heads wrapped up in their *dzukins*, or hoods, leaving only their eyes exposed, and hurry along to reach some place of shelter.

Watchmen patrol the foreign settlement all night, striking their staves upon the ground as they walk, making a jingling noise: they are expected to detect thieves or give warning in case of fire. A strong guard is placed at the gate of Ts'kiji. We have heard something of the guard being attacked and one of them killed by outsiders. Tales of *Ro-nins* (outlaws from the provinces) ready to do anything desperate to drive foreigners from the country have reached our ears.

Those who come into Ts'kiji have little blocks of wood with Chinese characters upon them hanging from their belts. These blocks answer to cards of admission, and no native can enter the lines without such blocks, which are given them by some official of the government.

In the midst of all these dangers and alarms

come pleasant little tokens of esteem from the few friends we have made among the people during the short time we have lived here. They bring the pretty winter flowers of the country—camellias and chrysanthemums and the bright red berry (*nan-ten*) which we admire so much. Then they bring also oranges in neat boxes and baskets ornamented with sprigs of evergreens, or boxes of eggs and native sweetmeats; and all these evidences of kindly feeling on their part are very gratifying to us, who are so recently come, and still are strangers in a strange land.

Our little house, which is rendered comfortable by outside doors and windows, a small stove and a few other articles of foreign furniture, is crowded every day with the pupils, who come to learn English. One of my pupils, a bright, pleasant boy of fifteen, has learned to read this winter, and on Sundays studies *Line upon Line*. He has a great many questions to ask concerning our religion, and seems much interested. One day, not long ago, he said, "God must be very angry with the Japanese because they worship idols."

One Saturday he said, "To-morrow I shall come to read the Bible." We asked him if the Japanese hated the Bible. "Oh no," he replied; "they did once, but not now."

With him comes a little boy about six years of age. He wears straw shoes, which he slips off when he enters the house, and a queer coat tied in front with a cord and with very wide long sleeves; these sleeves are his pockets. His books, when not using them, are carefully wrapped in a square cotton cloth which he calls a *fu-ru-shi-ki*. These fu-ru-shi-kis are sometimes made of crape or silk.

A few days ago his mother, with her little babe on the back of the nurse, came to call upon us. She was neatly dressed and of very ladylike deportment. We put the baby in a chair, and his black eyes danced as he lisped out in a clear, shrill voice, "*I-jin-san a-na-ta tai-san peg-gy!*" which means, "*You foreigner, go away!*" This he repeated over and over, greatly to the annoyance of his polite mother, whom we endeavored to reassure. We entertained the lady by showing her articles of dress and furniture, and she presented to us two handsome silk card-cases.

A late steamer from Nagasaki brings the news that seven hundred Roman Catholic Japanese have been banished from their homes. In spite of edicts and persecutions, sometimes very bloody, this faith has had its adherents in that part of the empire through these centuries past. We cannot refrain from sympathizing with these banished ones, although we know their creed is a sadly perverted one.

When we think of those who in years gone by have undergone all the tortures of Japanese prisons and suffered martyrdom for their faith, we are hopeful that all those who now profess Christianity among this people will prove faithful even to the end.

CHAPTER V.

HOME AND SCHOOL.

MORNING IN TOKIO—INTERIOR OF A JAPANESE HOUSE—BREAKFAST—GOING TO SCHOOL—THE WRITTEN LANGUAGE—WHAT A JAPANESE GIRL LEARNS—THE BABY O-YA-SU-MI-NA-SAI—JAPANESE HOMES—POSITION OF WOMEN.

NO one who has stood on the shore of the sea waiting for the sunrise, and has seen the water taking on a pale pink, then deepening into crimson as the grand luminary comes forth above the horizon, and waited still longer to see it mount higher and higher, pouring down floods of light, until the sea catches up the glory and breaks in golden waves against the shore, can wonder at the homage paid to an object so full of wondrous beauty. There are those who know not the One whose servant the sun is.

The worship of the heavenly bodies seems to us the purest, most natural form of idolatry; yet in the religion of the people around us we have evidence of the degrading effect of all worship of the creature instead of the Creator.

We have pictures of great sunrise-festivals where crowds of people are assembled, with banners and strange emblems held on high poles. Some are beating drums and some are praying, while others manifest their joy in songs and dances. Whether these festivals are still held in these islands we are not informed. Frequently, in our walks near the seashore, we see ropes stretched between two poles, to which long strips of paper are attached, and this seems to be connected somewhat with the old form of Sintoo worship. There is a story or legend of a *to-ri-ye* (Sintoo temple-gate) emitting a peculiar sound when the first beams of the morning sun fall upon it. The Mikado is supposed by the people to be the lineal descendant of the sun. His name (*Ten-shi-sa-ma*) signifies "child of the sun" or "son of Heaven."

This bright March morning in Tokio found very few people up to greet their *O-ten-to-sa-ma's* rising. The wind was from the north, and fishing-boats were coming down the river to go out on the bay. Some fishermen, standing up to their knees in water, were washing their nets. The To-ri was all quiet and deserted; the busy traffic of the day had not yet begun. In the temples a few devotees lay prostrate before the altars, while over the city at nearly regular intervals fell the deep rich tones of Shi-ba's bell.

But it made no difference to the sun whether

TEETH-BRUSHING.

OLD MAN AT WELL.

Page 61.

there were many or few to welcome him as he brightened Fu-ji's snow-crowned head, sent a long path of red light across the water, and shone upon the great city and on the house where our little neighbor O I-ne san lay asleep on her *futon* in a corner of a dark room. Her bed was made of blue cloth stuffed with cotton. These mattresses the people call *futons*. Her neck rested on a cushion on top of a wooden pillow.

Just outside of the house, in an open court, an old man was drawing water from a deep well. The water of Tokio is carried by pipes into cisterns or wells from a river near the city. It is tolerably good, but sometimes becomes brackish, from the salt water in the bay, which gets into the pipes. The old man drew the water slowly by means of buckets attached to each end of a long rope which ran over a pulley. Two crows kept flying about his head: these birds in Tokio are the great scavengers, carrying off all the refuse. They are very bold, and will snatch fish from a man's hand. They build their nests in the trees even by the palace, and look down unrebuked upon the emperor and his court. They have meetings upon the tops of the houses, and caw and clap their wings and twist their heads from side to side, until we look up to see what all the commotion is about.

They are not afraid of man, for man never injures them.

Near the well, O Cho ("Miss Butterfly") stood brushing her teeth. Her toothbrush was a straight stick made soft at one end, and she had a box of tooth-powder. She made a noise as if some one were choking her. Inside the house, O Kin ("Miss Gold") was opening the wooden slides, which run in grooves cut in the veranda. She began with the farthest one, and ran along, pushing it before her, until it was stopped by the end of the house. Then she started for the second, and disposed of that in the same manner, until all the slides were at one end of the small veranda.

The creaking of the well-rope, the caw-cawing of the crows, the toothbrushing process and the opening of the slides made noise enough to arouse any one, and O I-ne san opened her little almond-shaped eyes to see the sunshine pouring into the house. Then she remembered that she was going to school for the first time that day. O I-ne san was six years old, and it was time for her to begin to go to school.

She got up from her bed and went into the kitchen, which is in the front of the house and is the most completely furnished part. Beside the range are large kettles for rice and hot water. There are immense earthen jars for

JAPANESE KITCHEN.

1. Table. 2. Sauce-bottle. 3. Churn-jar. 4. Cupboard. 5. Shrine. 6. Fruit-bowl. 7. Sa-ki-bottle. 8. Large plate. 9 and 10. Rice-boxes. 11. Hot-water kettle. 12. Range. 13. Boiling-kettle. 14. Gridiron. 15. Salting-box. 16. Kettle. 17. Cutting radish. 18. Place where fire-wood is kept. 19. Water-jar. 20. Wash-basin. 21. Water-pail. 22. Dipper.

Page 62.

cold water, and wooden buckets, dippers and ladles. Where the earthen jars are kept the floor slants, so that the water is easily carried off into drains. Here, also, is usually found the shallow copper basin which serves as a wash-bowl for the whole family. On shelves are platters and bottles, and hanging on the wall, sieves and a variety of strainers.

When O I-ne san went into the kitchen, O Kin, with her cheeks all puffed out, was kneeling at the range, trying to make the charcoal burn by blowing. O Cho was cutting dai-kon (radishes) on a little table, using a large knife. When she saw O I-ne san she got up to take her some water in a basin, and handed her a toothbrush, with the pink powder. O I-ne san sat down on the veranda and washed her face and hands, wiping them with a little blue towel, and brushed her teeth. Then she slipped off her blue night-dress—Japanese always use blue where we prefer white—and O Cho helped her to dress. There were no buttons to fasten, no hooks and eyes, pins or strings, to render the process of dressing tedious. The loose garments of the Japanese are confined only by the broad belt.

When O I-ne san was ready, she went in to say "*O-hay-o*" ("Good-morning") to her father and mother. She found them sitting on the floor in a large room at the side of the house.

The best apartment in Japanese houses is always at the farthest side or the extreme rear, opening into the pretty garden. We have here, as in many other Japanese customs, the reverse of our own style—kitchen in front and parlor in the back. The clean white mats constitute the only furniture of a Japanese parlor. By way of ornament there are pictures in crayon, or long scrolls with poems written on them in Chinese or Japanese character. There are also vases for flowers. No chairs, ornamental tables, mirrors, book-cases, or anything of that sort, can be found in a purely native house.

The futons and pillows are carefully put away in the daytime. There are a great many little closets in these houses; the people have a wonderful way of economizing space, and even make drawers in their steep, narrow staircases. Tables which they use for meals, writing, or any other purpose, are small and only about a foot high from the ground. Some families have chests of drawers, and all possess baskets and boxes of all sizes and shapes.

The charcoal brazier, or *hi-ba-chi*, is the only stove used by the people. These are made in various shapes, some of them being highly ornamented. They are invariably made of copper. They give more heat than one would suppose; but the Japanese are very dependent

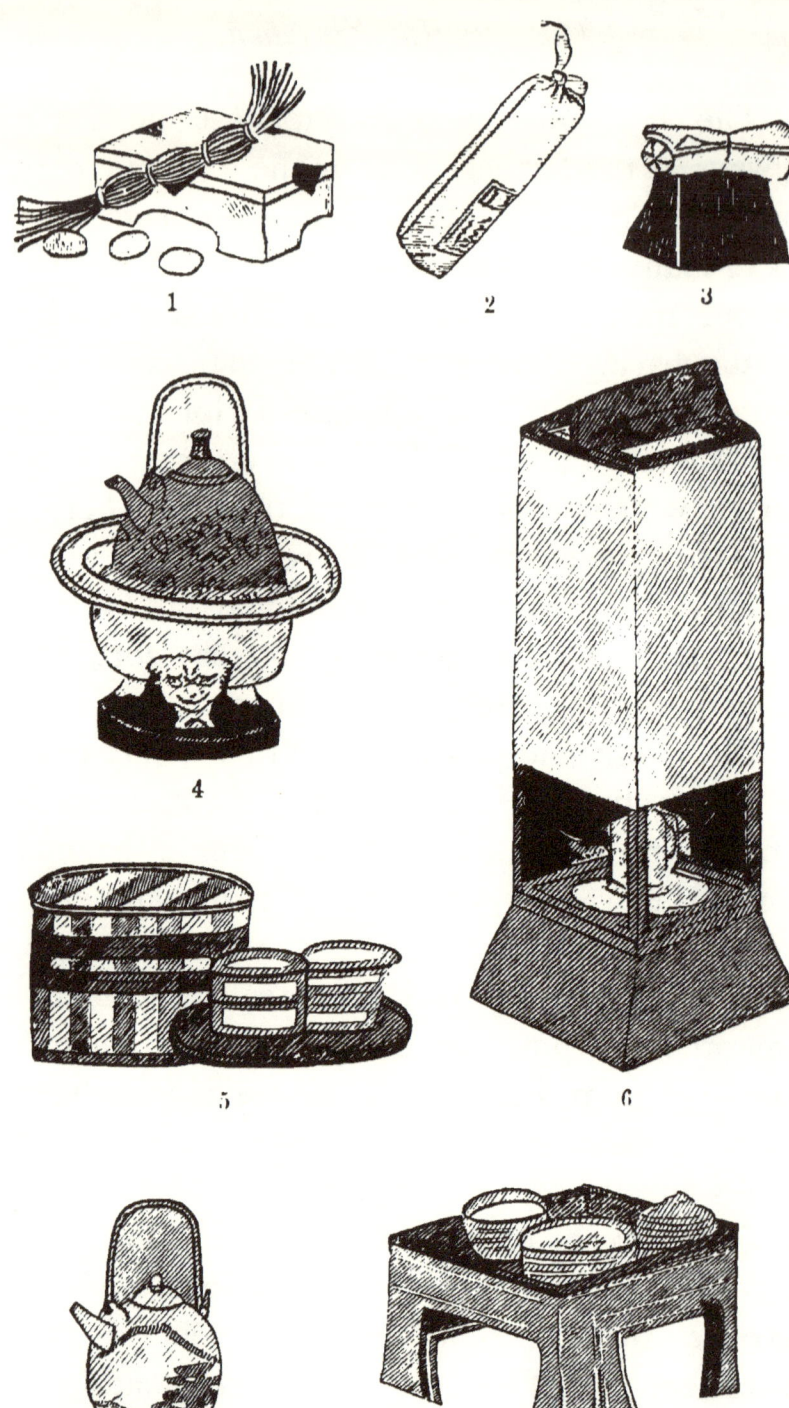

1. Egg box.
2. Paper of tea.
3. Pillow.
4. Hibachi.
5. Rice-boxes.
6. Lantern.
7. Tea-pot.
8. Breakfast-table.

upon the sunshine for warmth, and throw open their houses to admit it even in midwinter. It is only on damp, cloudy days that the people really suffer from the cold.

Were the houses like ours, these open charcoal fires would be dangerous, but the free ventilation here renders suffocation almost impossible. As it is, however, the constant inhalation of charcoal-fumes cannot be otherwise than injurious.

Even the paper slides were open in the sitting-room of the Ka-ji-ma family this morning, and the light and air poured through the house. On the veranda hung pieces of glass, which tinkled pleasantly as the wind swayed them to and fro. O I-ne san calls her father and mother O Tot san and O Ka san. *I-ne* means "young rice." It is a pretty name for a little girl, for young rice is something very tender and precious, and requires great care in its culture. *O* means "honorable," and *san*, "miss," so this little girl's name all signifies "Honorable Miss Young Rice." And this is no unusual designation. It is in accordance with the common habit of the land to give such.

O Cho and O Kin brought in the breakfast. O Cho carried the little tables—one for each of them—and tiny china cups and plates. On these tables they placed chopsticks, and blue bowls for the rice. O Kin brought the large wooden rice-box and the tea-pot. On a platter there were fish, cooked in the Japanese sauce, *sho-yu*, and some of the radish. O Kin helped to the rice with a wooden spoon, and poured tea into the little tea-cups. Then O Tot san and O Ka san and O I-ne san took their chopsticks in the right hand and pushed the rice into their mouths, eating as fast as they could swallow, washing down the food with cups of hot strong tea. The radish and the fish they also took up with their chopsticks. The radish had been cut into little pieces in the kitchen, and the fish was soft, so no knives were needed.

When the breakfast was over, O Cho and O Kin tied up their heads in kerchiefs. O Kin took a straight stick with long strips of paper at the end for a dusting-brush, and slapped away at the slides inside the house. O Cho carried away the breakfast-things, then got a broom to sweep the mats. Housekeeping in Japan is an easy matter compared to the care of our larger houses, filled with so much furniture, but perhaps it would be better for the women if they had more duties to employ their time.

It was now nearly nine o'clock. O Tot san went away to his business, and O Ka san and O I-ne san started for the school. O Cho walked a little way behind them, carrying some

WRITING A COPY.

SWEEPING AND DUSTING.

paper and the ink-box, which contains the camel-hair brushes and the India-ink. The school-house was just around the corner. Long before they reached it they heard the sound of children's voices as they all read together. The noise in a Japanese school is deafening to us, but they do not seem to mind it. The black *so-shi* were hanging up before the door, where the children had put them to dry. These are their copy-books, originally of white paper, but written over so often that they become perfectly black.

O Ka san called out at the door, "*O-go-men-na-sai!*" ("Beg pardon!") The schoolmaster opened the sliding door to admit his patron, and the noise suddenly ceased. O Ka san and O I-ne san made the usual courtesy, getting down upon their knees and touching the floor with their hands and foreheads. Their limbs are flexible, and from the power of habit they do this with perfect ease and grace.

O Cho went down in the same prostrate manner a little way behind them. O Ka san told the teacher that her little daughter was six years old; that she was very backward and had a very bad memory, but she wanted her to come to school. The teacher said, "I shall be very happy." Then O Ka san took the money, which was nicely folded up in a piece of paper, from O Cho, and gave it to the teacher. This was a private school, and the charge for tuition was only a few cents per month, paid in advance.

O Ka san then went back to the house, leaving O I-ne san with O Cho at the school. The scholars who were learning to write sat around the teacher with their copy-books on the floor. They held their brushes straight up in their hand and made long broad marks. O Cho untied the bundles she had, and gave O I-ne san some paper and her pen-brush. Then she got some water and poured it on the ink-stone, and rubbed the stick of India-ink in it.

The teacher sat by O I-ne san's side and showed her how to hold the pen. The little girl tried hard to copy the strange character given her. She felt lonely and a little frightened when she saw the other children gazing curiously at her. But a little girl whom she knew looked up and smiled at her, then crept to her side and said, "You have well come."

It is a difficult task even for Japanese children to master their own language. There are forty-eight letters in the Japanese alphabet, and two distinct sets of characters, the *ka-ta-ka-na* and the *hi-ra-ga-na*. Besides these, Chinese characters are extensively used. Some books are written almost entirely in Chinese.

The men among the higher classes all read this language, and even women and many of the lower orders are taught the particular characters most generally in use. All the signs about the shops and the proper names used are written in Chinese character, and we always see the same on lanterns and fans, and, indeed, upon almost everything that is used by the people.

The *written* language is entirely different from the *spoken*, so that it is almost like learning another language for a child to learn to read, even after it can talk with fluency. The words used in *letter*-writing differ both from the books and the colloquial, thus making another language for the children to learn; and if they do not, after all this is accomplished, attend the poetry-school, they cannot understand at all the poems of the country.

The girls are taught how to sew and embroider and make pretty little fancy articles, such as purses, chopstick-cases, bags and other things. Their needles are clumsy compared with ours, and they have thimbles open at both ends, and silk and cotton thread wound on pieces of wood. They also learn to play on the musical instruments of the country, the *samisen*, a three-stringed guitar, the *bi-wa*, a four-stringed guitar, and the *ko-to*, a thirteen-stringed harp; also they are taught to play on the fife and drum.

There are also *tea-schools*, where little girls are taught how to make tea and present it gracefully to guests. We will say more of these hereafter.

In the afternoon, when O Tot san had come home from his business and O I-ne san and O Cho had come from the school, O I-ne san was sitting idly on the floor by O Ka san's side. The mother was sewing in a way that appeared left-handed to us. The little girl heard voices at the door, and some one spoke out: " *O-ta-no-mo-shi-ma-su*" ("I call"). This practice of calling at the door is owing to the fact that no one can knock at these paper doors. It was a neighbor who had come in to have a little chat, and behind her was a servant with baby Kin-ta-ro on her back. The baby's hair was all shaved from his head, and his eyelashes and eyebrows plucked out. His eyes were bright and his little brown face clean. He wore a little red crape cap and a long silk dress with wide sleeves. He would have been a funny-looking little man to us, but O I-ne san thought him very pretty. She looked for his hands and feet, and he lay quietly and laughed at her. But soon the neighbor said it was late, and went away, after they had all drank tea and had *ku-wa-shi* ("sweetmeats"). Then the house was shut up for the night, and O Cho brought in the lamps.

These lamps (*an-don*) are quite high, with a drawer in the bottom, where wicks are kept. Over the drawer is a place for the oil-can, and above that still, and protected by paper slides, is the little saucer in which the oil is put and the wick for burning. They are rather cumbrous, and not handsome. They stand about two feet and a half from the ground, and are about fifteen inches square, all enclosed, with a sliding paper door which may be drawn up or down to increase or to subdue the light at pleasure. Besides these, the Japanese have tall wooden candlesticks with a sharp iron at the top, on which tallow candles are stuck.

The lamp in the sitting-room gave but little light, but the charcoal in the hi-ba-chi was red and glowing, O Ka san having just fanned it. O Cho and O Kin brought in supper, which is the principal meal in a Japanese family. O Cho had made some nice soup of fish, with rice and other things stirred in while it was boiling. After supper the futons were brought out, and O I-ne san was undressed and put on her own little bed. O Ka san covered her with another futon, said, "*O-ya-su-mi-ma-sai*" ("rest"), and O I-ne san was soon fast asleep.

Now the night has come, and O Tot san is writing at the little low table, occasionally reading aloud, and O Ka san is finishing the little garment she began to-day. What is she thinking about?

As we sometimes close our eyes and endeavor to realize the actual condition of the blind, so do I try to shut the eyes of my soul from the light of truth and form some conception of the darkness in which these heathen women are living. It has been said that Japan has "no home." Like the French, the language has no word corresponding to our "home;" it is simply "house" or "place of habitation." In a country where the houses are all so open, it is needless to look for such domestic life as we find in our more favored land. The early marriages contracted by the parents, or "go-betweens," and entered upon often without love or previous knowledge on the part of those married, must naturally produce more or less unhappiness.

Where the system of concubinage exists, and the children in a family scarcely know who is their own mother, and the women quarrel for the possession of the children, the picture of domestic life cannot but be far from pleasing. But there are some things in Japanese families which are very pleasant to us. The children are taught implicit obedience, and are polite and respectful to their parents. They are petted and seldom punished. Fathers carry their little babies very tenderly and soothe them when they cry, and when they come from their work or office often bring home pretty toys for their little ones.

Although the position of woman in Japan is superior to that in other heathen lands, it is by no means an enviable one. Woman in the family occupies an entirely subordinate place. A girl is subject to her father's wishes. There is no such thing as "coming of age" for a girl in Japan. She is all her lifetime a mere subject. When married she must obey her husband and father-in-law, and when a widow her son becomes her master. The baby-boy clings close to his mother's side, and lays his little cheek against hers, and talks a language which she alone can understand. But as he grows up, too often he learns to despise her. There are happy exceptions to these statements, where the family-life seems pure and peaceful, and woman appears to have her rightful place.

Yet with all this fathers seem to take great care of their little daughters. The best clothing they can afford is bought for them; they send them to school and are interested in their education, paying liberally whatever is required.

In Japanese history every woman who has distinguished herself in any way is given due credit, and mothers of great men are mentioned with praise. And I know that the little O I-ne san, who lies sleeping so quietly on her futon, is very tenderly loved and cherished, and that her education, as well as her comfort, occupies her mother's thoughts continually.

CHAPTER VI.

GOING TO "SEE FLOWERS."

Japanese Holidays—A Letter—Dressing the Hair—The Bath-House—A Little Girl's Dress—Fans, Shoes and Umbrellas—Meeting Friends—Worship at the Temple—Mu-ko-ji-ma—The Feast—Going Home—Social Life—Spoken Language—May Days.

THE Japanese knew nothing until lately of the Sabbath, the holy seventh day of rest, which our heavenly Father gave to the world, when he created it. But they know that it is necessary for man to rest, so they have always had a great many holidays. They celebrate the first day of the first month, the third of the third, the fifth of the fifth, the seventh of the seventh, and so on throughout the year.

Then there are the *I-chi-ro-ku*. *I-chi* means "one," and *ro-ku*, "six." Every day in the month which has a one or a six in it has been a rest-day. The first, sixth, eleventh, sixteenth, etc., are of that character. There are also the great religious festivals, which come principally in the summer.

The feast of *I-na-ri sama*, the "rice-god," is just over. It lasted three days, and in the temples drums were beaten without cessation. Once during the festival the god *I-na-ri* was brought out in his car, which was carried by people dressed in fantastic style, who were shouting, singing and dancing. Crowds followed the car, adding to the noise and confusion. If the god was really in the car, he must have been well shaken up, as it was rocked violently and turned almost upside down.

Now the warm spring days have come. The trees at *Mu-ko-ji-ma* are white and pink with blossoms. The camellias have just ceased blooming, and in their place azaleas cover the hillsides. Soon the wisteria and the purple iris will make the gardens beautiful. The people are all going out to "see flowers," and yesterday O Tot san, O Ka san and O I-ne san went with the others.

The Ka-ji-ma family belong to the merchant class—by far the most reliable part of the community. The father has an interest in extensive salmon and cod-fisheries at *Ha-ko-da-di*, a seaport-town of the island of Yeso, which lies a little to the north of Niphon. Besides the city home, they have a country-house at *O-ji*, a beautiful place in the suburbs of Tokio.

There O I-ne san's grandmother, O Ba san, lives, and with her several aunts and a little uncle, Sen-ki-chi.

A few days ago O Ka san sent a letter to O Ba san to ask if she and the aunts and Sen-ki-chi would meet them on the morning of the twenty-sixth (April) at a relative's house near A-sa-ku-sa, and go with them to Mu-ko-ji-ma. O Ka san sat down on the floor by a little table to write her letter, took from a drawer some strips of fine white paper, and with a delicate camel's-hair brush wrote in a fine hand the beautiful characters. There were a great many *yo-ro-shi-kus* and *so-ro-so-ros* and *so-ro-do-mos* in the letter—words which mean nothing, but which require great care in their use. These polite, meaningless words occupy much space, so that a letter may be two or three yards long without really containing much information.

When O Ka san had finished writing, she pasted the several strips of paper together, then folded them, turning down the corners in a peculiar way. Then she took from a little closet a lacquered box, put the letter inside, tied around the box a silken cord which had a pretty tassel at each end, and sent it by a messenger to O-ji. The answer soon came. O Ba san and all thanked O Ka san very much, and would be very happy to go with her. The answer came in the same box in which the letter was sent.

O I-ne san went to bed thinking of the pleasant time she would have going to "see flowers" with her little playmate and uncle, Sen-ki-chi. She was very anxious for fear it might rain, and the last thing at night looked out to see the stars shining in the sky, and the first thing in the morning to find the day bright and clear.

The hairdresser came early with little bottles of oil and wooden combs and strings and pads. She combed O I-ne san's long hair, oiled and twisted it, and rolled it over pads. O Ka san brought some red crape, all crinkled and dotted with white. It looked very pretty in O I-ne san's black hair. The little girl sat very still until the hairdresser had finished. Then O Cho took her to the bath-house, which was quite near. The steam poured through the roof, looking almost as if the house were on fire. Inside, people were in a large tank, laughing, talking and splashing the water. O Cho put O I-ne san into the tank with the women and children.

The Japanese use very hot water for their baths; we could not endure such heat. They have no soap, but depend entirely upon the hot water to make them clean. They are a very cleanly people in this respect, using the bath often. Yet the fact that many bathe in the same water no doubt may account for much of the cutaneous disease so prevalent.

When O Cho took O I-ne san to her home, she put on the little girl her pretty new clothes —a dark silk dress and a broad, long red sash. This sash was five or six yards long, and was wrapped round and round the girl's waist, and looped behind. Then O I-ne san's face was powdered until it was quite white. Her lips were stained a brighter red than their natural hue, and her finger-nails were colored brown.

Clean white stockings—or, rather, very low socks—made of cotton cloth, with a separation for the large toe, so as to be adapted to the shoe, were tied around the ankles. Pretty hairpins were stuck in her head, and a little bag, serving as an amulet or charm, was fastened to her belt.

O I-ne san's toilet was now complete. O Ka san's dress, except being plainer in color, was like her little daughter's. It is a remarkable thing that Japanese women wear no jewelry. The belt and the hairpins are the only ornaments they wear. Some of the hairpins are of amber and very costly, and the belts, or broad sashes, are of heavy brocade silk with gold and silver threads beautifully inwoven. No woman's toilet is complete without a fan, which they learn to use very gracefully. In their sleeves the women carry their paper handkerchiefs and purses made of silk, and sometimes little bags or cases for tobacco, snuff or chopsticks.

Fans, shoes or sandals, and umbrellas are an important part of out-door attire. They have two kinds of fans—*u-chi-wa*, answering to our palm-leaf, and *o-gi*, those which open and shut. They are mostly made of paper and bamboo, some very cheap (half a cent apiece); while others are of a much higher price, and some, made of silk, will cost two or three dollars. They are painted, ornamented with gold and silver paper, and embossed with fine silken figures, some very beautiful. All persons, men, women and children, carry fans.

Three pairs of shoes were waiting in the vestibule. Japanese never wear shoes in the house. O Tot san's were made simply of wood, with a plain strap for the toes. O Ka san's and O I-ne san's were made soft by straw-work on top, and had velvet straps. They wore no hats, but all carried umbrellas. There are two kinds of *ka-sa* (umbrellas)—the oiled, which are used to protect against the rain, and those not oiled, used only as sun-shades. The umbrellas for men and women are black and white, while those for little girls are often of bright, pretty colors.

O Cho and O Kin, in clothing made in the same style, but of plainer and coarser texture, walked a little behind them. So they all went away from the house, which was carefully shut and put under the charge of a neighbor, and went down a side street on to the To-ri, O I-ne san keeping tight hold of her mother's hand. They crossed *Niphon Bashi*, and saw the large boards which had written on them the edicts against Christianity. Then they turned off the To-ri, and went to the east, toward A-sa-ku-sa. It was warm, and O I-ne san was glad when they reached their relative's house. They found the party from O-ji waiting for them, and O Ba san came out to greet them. She wore a dark-gray dress and a black belt. She smiled pleasantly, and called O I-ne san "*Bo-ya*," which means "darling."

By this time all the party had gathered together, and they bowed many times and said: "Well come, compliments, pleasant weather; and for yesterday, day before yesterday, and the favors of long ago, thanks!"—words sounding very disconnectedly to our ears, and yet no doubt perfectly intelligible to the parties addressed, as conveying expressions of politeness and good-will.

Cups of tea were now brought, that all might refresh themselves before going to the temple. The crowd kept increasing as they neared A-sa-ku-sa—people of all classes, dressed in their best, going to Mu-ko-ji-ma. O Ba san bought a fan for O I-ne san. She took it and touched it to her forehead; this was her way of thanking her grandmother. They all went under the large red gate, up the broad walk to the steps of the temple. O I-ne san saw the bell and the idols and the flocks of doves. They threw money into the contribution-box, went up the steps into the temple, bowed low before the altar, and clapped their hands. This was doubtless to call the god's attention to the fact of their worship.

After they had performed their devotions, which were very brief, their only prayer being a repetition of the name of the god, they left the temple and went on down to the river. This they crossed in a low, flat-bottomed boat, in which were many fellow-passengers. The name Mu-ko-ji-ma signifies "opposite island," but it is really a part of the main land. The cherry and peach tree walk was lovely in the sweet spring sunshine. The trees were one mass of blossoms, and their branches interlaced over the broad avenue. O I-ne san looked up to see the pink and white flowers, catching

JAPANESE HOTEL.

occasional glimpses of the blue sky. She saw the river flowing peacefully along, and the sail-boats gliding swiftly by. She watched the crowds of men, women and little children like herself. Some of the women carried large dolls in their arms, dressed like real babies. Perhaps they had no children of their own, and so played with dolls to occupy the time. Many of the people carried branches of the trees. They laughed and talked and sang, and appeared to be very happy. It would all have been beautiful if they had sung and spoken sweet, pure words, but their language was often very low and obscene. So we see that flowers and beautiful things in nature do not lead people to holiness.

Our party now went into a large hotel upon the river-bank. The landlord came out to meet them with many bows, and told the servants to take them all up stairs. The servants asked what they would have for dinner, and they ordered *tai*, a kind of fish much prized, an omelette and eels. Some tea was brought, and candy made of rice and sugar, to eat while they were waiting for dinner. They opened the slides and sat where they could see the river and the boats.

In less than an hour the servant brought the little tables and the rice-box and some more tea. On an immense platter they had the fish and omelette, with side-dishes consisting of potatoes and red and yellow beans. The eels were served in lacquered boxes, with sharp skewers run through them, and dai-kon (radish) and horse-radish were brought on small plates.

They all ate, drank and talked, and had a happy time, after which O Tot san paid the bill— about a *boo* (twenty-five cents) for each member of the party—and then they all returned to the uncle's house. It was now growing dark, but the uncle said they must come in to hear O Tsuru san sing and play on the ko-to. They accepted the invitation, went in and listened to the song. It was called *E-no-shi-ma*, the name of a beautiful island on the coast, and was about the trees and mountains and little children.

And now it was time for O Tot san and O Ka san and their happy but tired little girl to go home. O Cho took O I-ne san on her back. She held flowers tightly in one hand, and the new fan she had carefully put away in her sleeve. The sun had gone down; O I-ne san saw the people carrying lanterns. No one is allowed to go out at night without a lantern. She heard the whistle of the blind a-mas, and looked at the lights in the houses as she passed. She was warm and comfortable, and tenderly carried because she was tired. She saw the stars in the sky, but did not know very well what they were. Long before they reached home she was fast asleep with her head on O Cho's shoulder and the pink blossoms still held in her hand.

It does not seem that the Japanese have anything corresponding to our large social in-door gatherings. The bath-houses are places of meeting and gossiping, and we see the people going in pleasure-boats on the Sumida or to the temples and public-gardens. The religious festivals give them frequent opportunities of meeting in a social way.

It is easy to tell when a festival is in progress, for the usually neglected children in the streets have their faces washed and powdered and hair smooth, and are neatly dressed. The babies have clean faces and look very smiling. The streets are ornamented with lanterns, and from the tops of high poles gayly-colored papers are flying, and the gates of the temples are thronged by crowds of worshipers dressed in their best.

The people appear to be very happy, but it is not pleasant to find that under the politeness and courtesy so lavishly displayed are hidden depths of corruption. They drink and quarrel, and the women have sore troubles, and bitter tears to shed, and often take their own lives to end the misery for which they know no remedy.

There is no such thing in Japan as plain, honest dealing between man and man. Everything must be done by means of a "go-between" (*na-ka*), through whom all bargains and sales on business, marriage, and everything else, are conducted.

The language itself discovers many peculiarities in the character of the people. It is syllabic, each syllable being distinctly pronounced. The distinctions of caste, and the relation of the speaker as a superior, inferior or equal of the person he addresses, are expressed by the use or omission of honorific prefixes and affixes. The humility, real or affected, professed by them is evinced by such expressions as "I reach it up to you" and "You reach it down to me," as expressive of "your superiority" compared with "my inferiority;" and then they add to this the free use of the honorific *O*.

Another peculiarity of the Japanese character is clearly brought out in the polite phrases and circumlocutions by which a disagreeable conclusion is reached. Those who have lived in the country know well the meaning of "I have had a bad cold," "My father is sick," as an excuse for absence or neglect of duty.

Such expressions, and many other expletives or redundant phrases commonly used, they do not consider as falsehoods, because they are in such common use, and not intended to be taken literally. Thus, "It is poison to my soul that I could not do more for you," and "I have made a great noise," said on leaving the house one has been visiting, are expressions that no one would accept as other than simple courtesy.

There are no abstract nouns and no words to express delicate shades of meaning. As an instance of the latter, the word *na-ku* ("to cry") is used for all the sounds made by dumb animals, as well as to express the crying of a human being. The word *ne-ru* means "to sleep," or merely "to lie down," and is used to convey the idea of grass being laid prostrate by the wind.

Words are merely arbitrary forms used to express our ideas. Where the idea is insignificant, there can be no depth of meaning in the word; and when we consider the comparative littleness of the things which Japanese words signify, we can gain some idea of their value. What are their ideas of truth, virtue and love? and what, consequently, do these words convey to them? In natural objects take, for instance, our word "star." Does their corresponding word *ho-shi* mean to them a great central sun with planets revolving around it, or merely a little taper in the sky? And apply their word for "god" (*ka-mi*) to the Sintoo deities, and consider the meaning it conveys to them. We have already seen how low and degraded that idea is, and "god" only represents that thought of their minds.

Although there is no special depth to the spoken language, it is like music in its sweetness and rhythm. There are no harsh combinations of syllables, and the words flow easily from the lips even of little children. And their manners correspond with their language; for when they meet, they bow low, and with profuse external ceremonies combine the most polite forms of speech. They never offend one another in word, and politeness never fails them in any circumstance.

Family names are derived from various sources. *Ta-ka-ha-shi, Ko-ba-ya-shi, Ha-ya-shi, A-ka-ba-ya-shi*, meaning respectively "high bridge," "little forest," "forest" and "red forest," are instances. It is well, in reading Japanese proper names, to remember that *ya-ma* means "mountain;" *ka-wa*, "river;" *ha-shi*, "bridge;" *ha-ya-shi*, "forest;" and *sa-ki*, "cape." The great mountain of Japan previously mentioned we call Fu-ji-ya-ma, but by the people is generally called Fu-ji only. The Sumida is spoken of to us as the Sumida-ga-wa ("river").

Boys' names always end in *ta-ro*, *ji-ro* and *ki-chi*, as *Mi-chi-ta-ro*, *Ta-ke-ji-ro* and *Sen-ki-chi*. And if we leave off the termination and prefix the honorific *O*, we have the girls' names—viz.: *O Mi-chi*, *O Ta-ke*, *O Sen*. *San* is a common termination to all names, meaning indiscriminately "Mr.," "Mrs.," "Miss" and "Master."

And now May has come to us in Tokio. It is a lovely month in Japan as well as at home. A few days ago we drove in a trap around the castle-walls. A perfect forest of trees surrounds the residence of the Mikado, and the beautiful green bank slopes from the outer wall down to the moat. On one side of the road are hedges, beautiful now in their spring freshness. It is hard to realize, as we look upon the fair landscape and apparently firm structures before us, that this is a land of earthquakes, and yet, on the night before, our house had been rocked like a ship at sea, and after the first severe shock we had a series of slighter ones which kept us uneasy for some time.

We have a little Sunday-school now, and some priests from Shi-ba come almost every day for Bible instruction. This is a new feature in our work. Their attention was directed to Christianity by reading Goodrich's *General History of the World* with a Japanese teacher. We hope that they are sincere, and will yet be brought to believe in the Lord Jesus.

CHAPTER VII.

RO-KU-BAN.

THE NEW MISSION-HOUSE—THE TYPHOON—A CLASS OF BOYS—YOUNG SAMURAI—THE BIBLE CLASS—THE YA-CU-NINS—OUR NEW YEAR.

THE new mission-house, on lot No. 6—*Ro-ku-ban*—of the Foreign Concession, is opposite the island *Sku-da-ji-ma*, just below the place where the river Sumida empties into the bay. It is made of wood, with tiled roof and walls, and boasts of veritable doors, windows and a chimney.

The house was built by Japanese workmen, under the superintendence of one of the missionaries. The location is pleasant and healthful. Directly in front is the bay. From the upper veranda we can almost look down into the junks and sail-boats as they pass. The north windows command a view of the river, and to the south-west we can see Shi-ba's magnificent trees.

The distant mountains, on pleasant days, are beautiful, standing out clear and distinct against the sky. Far above the others rises old Fu-ji, in summer of a soft, deep purple hue, and in winter all glittering and resplendent as his snow-crowned head catches the sunbeams.

One Sunday, soon after coming over here to live, we had a fearful storm of wind and rain. In the fall the north and south winds have terrible battles, which last until the north wind prevails and brings cold, clear weather, occasionally with snow. In the spring the conflict again begins, and the south wind gains the victory: then we have heat, dampness and frequent rains.

In August and September we expect these typhoons (Chinese *tai-fu*, "great wind"), but they are not so severe here as in China.

Typhoon of September.—This was a wild storm, and lasted nearly all day. The bay was a grand sight; the waves dashed over the breakwater as though they would like to sweep us all away. Rain and wind, with the sound of the angry waves and the noise of the falling tiles and timbers of the yet-unfinished house, made that Sabbath-day one of terror. Some Japanese were killed not far from us by a falling house.

But the storm ceased suddenly, and there was a "great calm." The bay was as quiet as if nothing had ever occurred to disturb it. The sunset was magnificent. Bands of crimson and gold stretched across the western horizon, and eastern sea and sky were brightened by a golden light slightly tinged with pink. Directly overhead, in an ocean of deep blue, floated clouds of a rich salmon-color. It is not often that we have a sunset scene like this.

A large boy whom we call Ma-ki has been reading for some months with us. He is a plain and delicate-looking person, but exceedingly kind. A week seldom passes without some little token of gratitude from him. The gifts are sometimes rather peculiar. Once he brought a live cricket in an exquisitely-made bamboo cage. The Japanese are very fond of hearing these insects sing, so they cage them and feed them on cucumbers. Mine was carefully fed, but it did not sing very long.

I have had two classes of boys this winter, one rather plebeian in its nature, consisting of Ru-so, the barber's boy, Chiu-taro, a merchant's son, the son of the hotel-clerk, and others. All of these boys were diligent. The other class was quite aristocratic, consisting of nine or ten little Samurai from Sat-su-ma's country. They all wore two swords, even those who were so small that their eyes just came above the table when they stood around it to read. They were nice little fellows, and the afternoon was pleasantly spent in teaching them. It is a grief to me to think of them all as scattered now, I know not where.

On the first Sabbath of December one of the missionaries began a Bible class—the first ever attempted in the Tokio mission. It was held in the parlor of the new house. A fire was kindled in the large stove, benches were brought, and the dark-skinned, black-haired natives gathered in to hear the teaching of the word. Outside, the sun was shining brightly, the bay sparkling in the glorious light, and sail-boats were gliding noiselessly by. Some of the young men had English, and some Chinese, Bibles. The verses were carefully explained in Japanese, and at the close the pupils heard a prayer to the true God for the first time. Friends at home would have been much gratified could they have seen the earnest attention paid by the pupils. These meetings were kept up, with increasing interest, for several weeks, and we hoped and prayed that great good might result from them.

Christmas came on Sunday. On the day before, we went to *U-ye-no*. This is a charming place. From some of the tea-houses there are fine views of the great city and the river. It is said that the government intends to establish a hospital there. In former days there were temples and mi-yas here as beautiful as those at Shi-ba, we are told, but during the revolution of 1868 a battle was fought at U-ye-no, and, with the exception of a few small temples, we saw nothing but ruins.

In one temple we found some women with heads shaven like those of the priests. They were beating drums, ringing bells and reciting prayers in a loud tone, making more noise than we could endure. They diversified their worship by drinking tea and smoking. While wandering about the really beautiful grounds we discovered an immense idol. We sat down to look at him, and felt ourselves very small in comparison, for he was thirty feet high. He wore a very complacent look. The winter day was warm and bright, after the sun had dissipated the morning mist. The rich sunlight poured through the trees, and the quiet retirement and beautiful scenery made the day a pleasant one.

On Christmas-day the class assembled as usual; but a few days after, we heard that some one had informed the ya-cu-nins at the customhouse of their meeting, and that these officers were going to report to the government, so that the pupils were in danger of losing their liberty, if not their lives. The missionaries felt it to be their duty to warn the pupils of the threatened danger, and it has resulted in breaking up the class. Even the interesting school of little ones has dwindled down to four scholars.

A few young men are coming to read the Bible privately. They creep cautiously, by night, over the fields, or singly in the daytime, to elude the vigilance of the ya-cu-nins. Our new year (1871) has thus dawned rather sadly upon us.

"Oh," said one of the missionaries as we discussed these things, "if O-ga-wa should be cast into prison, I would stop all work here, and do nothing for a while but write home, begging God's people to pray for us. Only prayer can be of any use now."

We are forcibly reminded that the death-penalty still exists, and that the cross of Christ is a shame and a dishonor here. "I fear not imprisonment or beheading," said a young Japanese. "I want to study the Bible." We stood by one of the front windows of the mission-house. The day was dark, the waves dashed sullenly against the breakwater, and the way seemed dark to us.

Thus it often is in the morning. The sun comes up clear and bright, and we imagine that all the day will be fair. Then clouds arise, hide the blue sky from view, and it grows dark, but when they roll away we find not only that the sun has still been shining behind them, but that he has really been mounting higher and higher, and growing each moment brighter and stronger.

CHAPTER VIII.

PICTURES AND BOOKS.

ANCIENT WARRIORS—COURT-LADIES—DAIMIOS—HA-RA-KI-RI—JO-RO-REI—JAPANESE BOOKS—RELIGIOUS—HISTORICAL—ENCYCLOPÆDIAS—ALLEGORY—MORAL TEACHINGS—POETRY—NOVELS.

WHEN we go to call on our Japanese friends in the city, they usually entertain us with pictures. These look to us like strange caricatures, but no doubt appear to them perfectly natural, and even to our eyes, as we become more familiar with the land, they lose much of their grotesqueness.

True, the Japanese have no proper idea of perspective, and they put into the picture whatever they consider would look well there, without regard to true size or relative position; but these objects, viewed singly, are all delineated with a great degree of perfection. Thus, trees, birds, flowers, fish and human beings are accurately described as looked at individually, but when grouped together there is a most grotesque disregard of all proportion and proper position. There are but few animals in Japan, and this accounts for the invariably absurd, and sometimes hideous, delineations found on their vases and in the carvings of the temples. It would seem as if they had heard of such things, and their vivid imaginations had attempted to depict them, but in this respect there is an utter failure.

These pictures are, however, interesting as giving us an insight into national life and society which could not be otherwise obtained. We see ancient warriors ready for battle or fighting with brave, composed faces. The dress is very peculiar, and looks to us exceedingly cumbersome. There are pieces of armor for the protection of head, breast and limbs, and we see them bearing all the ancient weapons of war—swords, spears, bows and arrows, and battle-axes—and over all are gorgeous robes with wide, full skirts, and pennons streaming from head and shoulders—a marked contrast to the simple dress and accoutrements of the modern soldier.

We also look at pictures of court-ladies in white robes and with hair streaming down their backs. Their eyelashes and eyebrows are plucked out, but a tinge of dark paint higher up on the forehead supplies the loss. They are represented as playing on the samisen, the ko-to or the bi-wa, and embroidering rich robes, and painting beautiful flowers or butterflies on silk.

Then we have views of the interior of ya-shi-kis, and see the daimios at their great feasts, where the saki is drunk and songs sung, and where geishas and dancing-girls entertain the guests. Or we see these great lords walking in the fields, complacently viewing their broad possessions; and some of the pictures show us farmers kneeling at their feet, begging relief from their oppressive taxation.

We then look into the private reception-room, where sometimes the daimio, in the presence of his retainers, performs the solemn act of *Ha-ra-Ki-ri* (disembowelment). This is done under the sense of a real or imaginary insult; and when a high officer is subjected to the death-penalty he has the privilege of inflicting it upon himself, and thus escaping all disgrace.

Many of these pictures represent the *jo-ro-reis*, which are large establishments where the women live who sell themselves or are sold, when children, by their parents. This is esteemed no particular disgrace in Japan; for a girl to sell herself to relieve the poverty of her parents is considered the highest proof of filial virtue. The names of the most celebrated of these *jo-ros* are on every child's tongue, and their pictures are painted in most brilliant colors.

Books.—In printing books, blocks of wood, with the letters cut on them, are used. These are thickly blacked with India-ink and sheets of paper put on, and the impressions are then taken by a simple and rapid process. In course of time the letters on the block are worn down, and this accounts for the faintness of some of the words in their books. They have no binderies, but all their books have paper covers, stitched in their own peculiar style.

As is usual with all Oriental books, they begin at the last page (as it appears to us), in the back of the book, and read down in columns from right to left—precisely the reverse from what it is with us.

The best literature of the Japanese is borrowed from their neighbors, the Chinese. Their religious books are written in this language, but sometimes their own characters are intermixed. These are stories of the gods and Buddhas. Some of their illustrations represent mild, placid Buddhas sitting calmly on lotus-leaves, and others fierce, ugly little devils and frightful scenes of the Buddhist places of torment.

In their historical books, in which Chinese characters are also largely used, there is so much of the fabulous history of the gods, set forth in fantastic allegory, combined with the stories of their heroes, that there is little satisfaction in reading them.

The encyclopædias, which are embellished with pictures, are more interesting to us. There is one queer old book of this sort in which the impressions of the people in regard to different countries are described. In one picture the men of a certain country are represented as having long ears which serve as a covering in the night. These encyclopædias are very copious, embracing all varieties of subjects and giving the Japanese ideas upon things foreign as well as home-born. They sometimes run up to nearly one hundred large volumes, are profusely illustrated, and are the most handsomely printed of all books published in Japan. The illustrations given are very interesting as portraying the ideas held by that people in regard to many things in Nature. Thus, in one we have their conception of thunder—a terrific-looking god in a dense cloud striking with a drumstick the dark surface. Their island is also set forth as resting upon a turtle, the uneasy movements of which cause the earthquakes so frequent there.

The Japanese are very fond of allegorical literature, and many books of that kind may be found in their libraries. The most famous of them is the *Mu-so-bi*. This is the name of a man who traveled through the air, visiting many different kingdoms—as they are called—such as Childhood, Avarice, Lying, and others. He tells what he saw in them all. In the kingdom of Childhood he found funny little people who could neither walk nor talk, and had no teeth and no hair. In the kingdom of Lying he came across a notice upon a schoolroom-door stating that the teacher would begin a class there on a certain day. He went at the appointed time, but no teacher was there. This was repeated several times, until he went after the teacher and asked him the reason of such strange conduct. He replied that to teach lying was his special object, and this he did by action rather than by word.

In his descent into the kingdom of Avarice he became entangled in the branches of a tree. The people of the country were so afraid that they would not receive a proper equivalent for their services that he could hardly persuade them to bring ropes and ladders to rescue him from his perilous position.

None of these books are very intelligible to Japanese women, except to those who resolutely break over the barriers of restraint and are ambitious to acquire more learning than is usually allowed them. They are kept back from learning the Chinese characters, and of course find it impossible to get the full sense of what they read. For them, however, books of a special kind on topics of morality are prepared. The most celebrated of these is the *On-na-Dai Ga-ku* ("*Woman's Great Learning*"). Every girl is expected to read this book and be well acquainted with its contents. It is written in large, straggling Chinese characters, with the Japanese *ka-na* (alphabet) in the margin of each column. It consists mainly in the enumeration of many petty duties, with frequent injunctions to women to be quiet and not talk too much. It says: "Until children are six years of age boys and girls may sit on the same mats at school, but after that they must be separated. . . . Girls must learn to read well, and afterward to sew. . . . When they are seventeen or eighteen they must remember that in a short time they will leave father and mother and go to a new home. . . . They must remember, also, that the father-in-law and the mother-in-law are the husband's parents, and try to love them." Of the seven reasons for divorce, the first is disobedience to the mother-in-law. A woman may also be divorced if she has no child.

This book also says: "Children must be obedient to their parents, attend diligently to their business, get up in the morning in a good-humor, and eat what is set before them without looking around, complaining or asking questions."

There is also a particular book on obedience to parents. They have some stories of Confucius and Mencius, the great Chinese sages; among these will be found many good and useful maxims, worthy of a place in the literature of any land, but the greater part is a compilation of ethics exceedingly dry and of little profit.

"Japanese poetry," says one of their own people, "is like a tree with its roots, trunk and branches." It is very difficult for us to understand the precise meaning of this, but their poetical history seems to be the root, the short poems the trunk, and the various renderings and meanings the branches. Even to the natives the poems are so difficult, and the words used differ so materially from both the ordinary book-language and the vernacular, that unless they attend a regular poetry-school they are never able to comprehend their meaning.

The great book of Japanese poetry is the *H'-ya-ku-nin-shi* ("*The One Hundred Poems*"). These were written by one hundred persons, among whom were a number of women. The first poem in the book was written by Ten-ji Ten-no, a great man of ancient times, and is about the "full, round harvest-moon." The fifteenth day of the eighth month is the moon's festival, and this poem is written in honor of that. To us its brevity is worthy of notice, for it consists of only twenty-six characters, occupying the space of not more than a single stanza of a hymn. And yet so hidden is its meaning, demanding in its interpretation the unfolding of symbols, the bringing forth of historic and ethical lore—in fact, so deeply mysterious is it—as to require the efforts of the most learned men (*ga-ku-shas*) to expound it before a wondering audience. It is said that it would take a long lifetime to learn the meaning of these hundred poems, and yet they are contained in a book in length three inches and a half, in width two inches and a half, and just half an inch in thickness, and then fully two-thirds of each page are taken up with an engraved illustration and deep margin. It seems to be the essence of all the learning, history and poetry of all the ages reduced to an almost infinitesimal point.

It may be interesting to consider several of the poems said to have been written by women. *Ji-to-ten-o* sings about "white" things. "Although spring is past" (the cherry-blossoms faded), "there are still white things—white cloths spread out to bleach, and snow on Fu-ji." The idea here is expressive of purity. Ko-ma-chi was a beautiful woman. In reply to the praises of her admirers she spoke of fading flowers: "My body will likewise fade." I-se and U-kon tell us of love: "No matter how short the time may be, we think it long when separated from our loved one." I-dzu-mi-shi-ki's strain is familiar: "In this world we love: shall we love again? I am far away from the one I love: shall I meet him again in this world? But if not, shall we love in the next? Even then I would see him again here." In Sei-so-nan-gon's poem we have something of the root. The daimios were obliged to spend six months of each year in Tokio. During the time of the To-ku-ga-wa dynasty there were apprehensions of trouble at the capital from the provinces, and the daimios were compelled to leave their wives in Tokio as hostages when they returned to their separate homes. Most of these princes were obliged to cross the *Ha-ko-ne* Mountains. There was a gate at the one pass over these mountains. Ya-cu-nins were stationed to search carefully every woman who approached the gate, lest she might prove to be the wife of a daimio returning with her husband to their home. The women of the ya-shi-kis had their hair dressed in a peculiar way, and so were easily recognized. Sei-so-nan-non said,

"I lie awake at night to listen for the voice of the bird. But there are many obstacles in our path in getting to those we love." (The word translated "obstacle" is applied to the gate above mentioned.) The swan, in his capacity as letter-carrier (for which in China he is sometimes used), is the bird for whose voice she listens. We can perceive in these few instances something of the meaning of the one who represents the poem as a tree. Its roots are set in symbols and hidden facts; its trunk is the poem as it appears to sight; and its branches are the renderings and explanations which a skillful expounder can give to such terse effusions. In no other way do we see how this expression can be interpreted.

There are also a great number of novels in the language, written in the easy colloquial. They are to us insipid stories, all about lovers and tyrants. They commonly exhibit a marvelous facility of extension, the same novel being carried through hundreds of volumes. One of them has been translated into English, and is the usual tale of a girl who sold herself in order to save the family from poverty and ruin, but is rescued by her lover, Sa-ki-shi. It ends in a familiar, and even home-like, style: "Of course all their sorrow was now turned into joy; nor had they suffered in vain, since the trials they had undergone had thoroughly tested the strength and constancy of their affection. . . . Being distinguished for filial duty and affection, they were blessed with a numerous offspring, and led henceforward peaceful and happy lives."

The women have no books to read except dry books of ethics and these novels. Some books on the distant provinces, on the productions of their own country or its history, might be made quite interesting for the women if written in characters and language intelligible to them.

We must take another chapter to consider a very important class of books—those designed for the use of the children of Japan.

CHAPTER IX.

GAMES AND TOYS.

JAPANESE NEW YEAR—DIVISION OF TIME—MO-CHI—ORNAMENTS—O-MI-SO-KA—MONEY—DRIVING AWAY EVIL SPIRITS—NEW YEAR'S FESTIVITIES—THE DOLLS' FEAST—GAMES—TOY-SHOPS—JAPANESE CHILDREN.

THE year just closed has been a long one with the Japanese. It was leap-year, and the tenth month was doubled, making the year to consist of thirteen months. And now New Year's day has come late in February. It is very difficult to understand the Japanese division of time. They reckon by cycles and dynasties in numbering their years.

They divide the year into twelve months, naming them respectively first, second, third, etc. These months consist of thirty days each, and thus, after certain intervals, to make the solar and lunar year agree, they put on the additional month.

The people are busy for many days in preparing for their New Year's festival. We saw them making *mo-chi* in the streets all through the city. This is rice beaten in a mortar with a little water until it becomes a thick, hard paste, bearing little resemblance to the original ko-me. It is dried in cakes, and baked over the hi-ba-chi. This is very much liked by the people, but rather distasteful to our palates.

The houses are all ornamented with branches of the pine, *dai-dai* (a kind of orange), bamboo and plum-blossoms. These are placed over or near the entrance. The pine tree is an emblem of perpetual joy; *dai-dai* means "from generation to generation," and expresses perpetuity of family. The bamboo never changes its color, and is a symbol of constancy. It is straight, and thus teaches man to be upright. The plum tree blossoms in cold weather, and shows us that man should rejoice in time of trouble.

The houses are also ornamented with deep fringes of straw, which look very handsome as they wave in the wind. Cooked rice in a pyramid represents the island of eternal happiness, which they imagine to be somewhere. A crab shows their desire for longevity, and fish-skin is a sign of politeness and a desire to have their gifts graciously received.

The day before New Year's is the *O-mi-so-ka*, the great day of casting accounts. Then the merchants close up their business transactions and collect their debts. Every one is busy settling up affairs, to be ready to begin afresh the new year. The little girls of Tokio have a song about the O-mi-so-ka, which they sing when bounding their balls.

Japanese money is very curious to us. They have in circulation gold, silver, copper and scrip. Iron cash—coins of very small value—were formerly used. The largest gold coins are the *o-ban* and the *ko-ban*, the great and small *ban*. These are of an elliptical shape, and are not often seen at the present day. There are also small gold coins of various values; but having been extensively counterfeited, they are not in general use. Our principal coins in use now are the silver *boos*, *ni-shius* and *i-shius*, of the respective values of twenty-five, twelve and a half, and six and a quarter cents. These are oblong in shape, with Chinese characters stamped upon them.

There is also a variety of copper coins; the largest is the elliptical *tempo* (one cent). The smaller coins are worth one-fifth, one-sixth and one-tenth of a tempo. Then there are the paper *satz* (or scrip), the *rio* (one dollar) and the *ni-bu*, *ichi-bu*, *ni-shiu* and *i-shiu*, or two boos, one boo, half boo and quarter boo. This scrip is the principal money in circulation, but is easily counterfeited.

O Tot san is away at Ha-ko-da-di, and O Ka

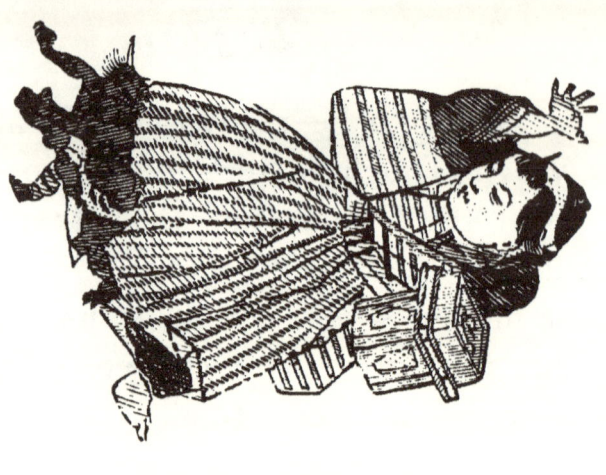

CASTING OUT EVIL SPIRITS.

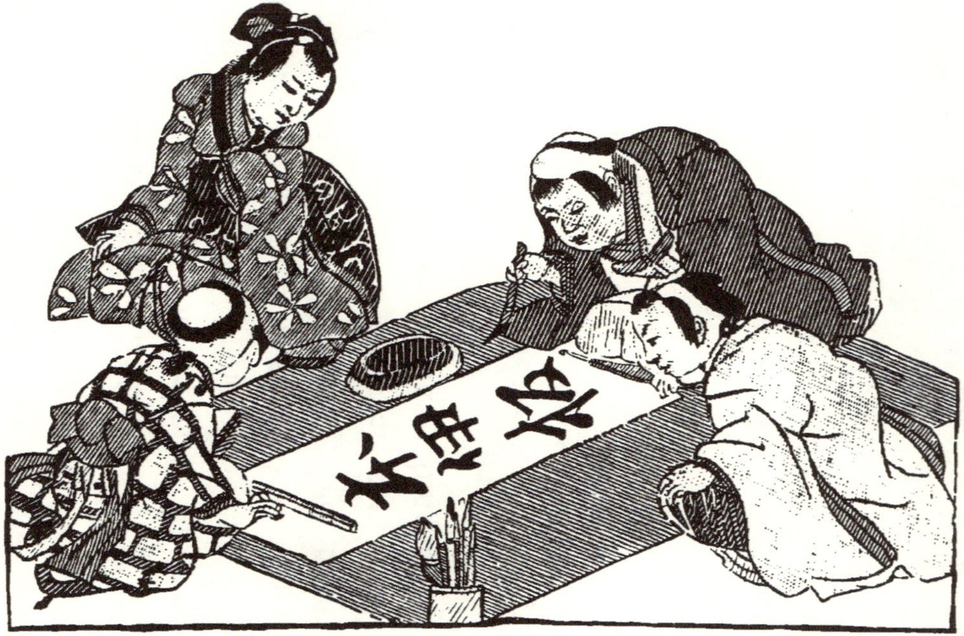

WRITING THE NEW YEAR'S COPY

Page 113.

san and O I-ne san are at O-ji, spending the holidays with the grandmother. On the O-mi-so-ka the house was carefully swept, the few vases and other ornaments arranged neatly, the former filled with camellias and other flowers. Pine branches, bamboo, oranges and plum-blossoms were put over the doorway. The children watched all the preparations with great interest.

At night they did something which would seem very curious to American children. The servants brought parched beans, and O I-ne san and Sen-ki-chi put them in boxes, and then sprinkled them all over the floors. This was to drive out the evil spirits. It is a strange custom, but at the same time suggestive. It is a good thing to commence the new year with banishing evil spirits, though what connection beans had with it we could not see.

O I-ne san was up long before the sun rose this morning. She slipped quietly out of the house, got some water from the well, poured it on her ink-stone, rubbed it with ink and wrote a copy. She did this very quickly, before Sen-ki-chi joined her. Why was this? When there are two or more children in a Japanese family, they see which one can get up the earliest on the first morning of the year, wet their ink-stone, and write the first Chinese character. The fortunate one will be the best writer of the family. Often the pine ornaments are burned before a temple, and with them the children put their "copies." The higher the wind blows the paper, the more famous will the child be as a writer—so say the children.

When Japanese meet on New Year's morning, they say, "*O-me-di-to*" ("Great happiness" or "Many congratulations"). The women smile and say, "The spring has come," although the weather may still be quite cold. As in our country, the gentlemen go out to call, and the ladies, dressed in silks and crapes, and with hair ornamented with amber hairpins, remain at home to receive their guests. It has been remarked that either this custom was introduced by the Hollanders into Japan, or that the Hollanders derived it from the Japanese; it is uncertain where it originated. The sweetmeats are arranged on little tables in pyramids, and beautifully ornamented with sprigs of pine and flowers. These sweetmeats, with tea, are offered to the guests, who usually bring a present. A picture represents a gentleman starting out on these calls as attended by a boy with a boxful of presents, which consist generally of pieces of silk, crape, hairpins and dried fruits.

All little girls in Tokio have battledores and

shuttlecocks, and look very happy as they toss up the pretty feathers, counting all the time. O I-ne san's new battledore is very large and handsome, and the under side is covered with beautiful crape. All the little boys in Tokio are playing with kites to-day; these are made in various shapes and painted in bright colors. Some of them represent men with arms extended, and some birds, and others, which they seem particularly to like, represent dragons, devils and evil spirits.

There are singing kites, which in the air emit sounds like those produced by the passing of wind over wires. And whilst flying them the boys chant,

> "Blow, wind, blow!
> The god of the wind is weak;
> The god of the sun is strong;
> Blow, wind, blow!"

Fathers and mothers are playing with their children, and the whole city is filled with pleasant sights and sounds. The New Year's feast continues for seven days. The schools are all closed, and there is nothing but play and rejoicing.

On the third day of the third month, O I-ne san will have a happy time. It is the little girls' holiday, the feast of dolls. The dolls are arranged on shelves sloping one above and a little back of another, the emperor and his wife occupying the topmost shelf. Then a feast is prepared of white sweet saki and two cakes of mo-chi, placed one above another on a dish. The under cake is green, and the other white. Whether there is any special significance in this I cannot say. This feast is first offered to the dolls, who, not being troubled with sensations of hunger and thirst, do not partake heartily; so the children have the benefit of it all, and drink the saki and eat the mo-chi with great satisfaction.

Japanese dolls (*nin-gi-yo*, "resembling men") are very worthy of consideration. They are as much like real babies as anything can possibly be, and we are frequently deceived by them as we see the women carrying large dolls in their arms. The best dolls are made in Ki-o-to. They are of wood, with real hair. The others are made of a kind of composition and are very frail, being in constant danger of losing heads and limbs. A-sa-ku-sa is the principal mart for dolls in Tokio. Some of the dolls there are beautifully dressed like grown ladies, with several changes of headgear. The women in the ya-shi-kis play with these large dolls, dressing them in fine clothes, and taking them out with them when they go to call. The little girls have tiny futons and pillows for their dolls, and little dishes, but they are just as fond as American children of playing with broken plates and cups and all sorts of make-believe things.

Playing ball is the favorite amusement of girls. Some of their balls are very pretty, being covered with bright silk threads. They bound them on the ground with their hands, counting the beats in a sing-song style, and often keep them going an almost incredible number of times. Boys seldom play ball, but are contented with stilts, tops and kites.

The little girls also play, with small bean-bags, a game similar to our childish one of jack-stones. These bags they call *te-da-na*, and they are very dextrous in managing them. They have also games with little cards, matching them and playing "grab." Checkers, which they play in various ways, among which " go-bang " is prominent, are used by the men. The word *go-bang* means "five checkers."

One of the most singular amusements for children is called *h'ya-ku mo-no ga-ta-ri* ("the one hundred things"). A hundred tapers are put into a large saucer of oil and lighted. The children sit quietly down in a dark corner of the room, at some distance from the lights, and begin to tell ghost-stories, with which Japanese literature abounds. Then one child is sent to extinguish a light. When this is done, the story-telling again begins, when another child is sent to put out another light. The stories become more and more frightful in their character; the room becomes darker and darker as light after light is extinguished; the imagination of the children becomes more excited, until the room seems to them filled with hobgoblins and demons; and at last the screaming little ones rush from the house, and the game is over.

Japanese children have a great deal done for their amusement. We often pass large toy-shops filled with pretty things for them, such as windmills, kites, tops, balls, dolls, toy cats, dogs and other animals, all highly colored. The children who play about the streets are merry little people; they have sparkling eyes and bright, intelligent faces, and seem to enjoy their sport as much as little ones at home. Many of the girls have babies strapped on their backs. These babies' heads roll from side to side, and the poor little unprotected eyes blink in the sunshine. Some of these children are covered with loathsome sores. Skin-diseases are very common here.

It is said that Japanese children do not cry or quarrel as do those in our land. Several causes have been assigned for this. Though parents are very strict in exacting obedience, they do

1 and 2. Beginning and end of H'ya-ku-mono-gatari.   3. Street-children.

not subject their little ones to so many orders or restraints. Then their clothing is much lighter than in this country, giving more freedom to their limbs, and they are more the children of nature than of artificial life. And another cause may be found in the fact that they have less vitality and nervous energy than European or American children have, and hence are more indifferent to both pleasure and pain. These little Asiatics are quiet and patient generally, content to go on in the same routine day after day. They do not give us so much to write and talk about as the children of our land, with their pretty sayings and doings. They do cry sometimes, and their screams are long and loud.

The mission of the little street-children has been very sweet to us. When we first came here, the people seemed like inhabitants of another planet. The only way we could gain any feeling of kinship was by shutting our eyes to their strange customs and letting the sound of the children's voices in their happy laughter or grieved crying enter our ears. It was then that we heard familiar sounds, and realized that these strangers are indeed our flesh and blood. And so we pray God to bless the little children of Japan.

CHAPTER X.

WHAT LITTLE CHILDREN READ.

THE NAMES OF THEIR BOOKS: "THE APE AND THE CRAB" —"THE RAT'S WEDDING"—"MO-MO-TARO"—"KIN-TA-RO" —"THE TAIL-CUT SWALLOW"—"STORY OF SHO-SET-SU"— "THE TREASURE."

WHAT has our little O I-ne san to read? Hundreds of small books with bright pictures, the chief peculiarity of which is that the story is written, not under the pictures, but on their face. We have some before us—gay little specimens of infant literature, and filled with intensely glaring illustrations of men and animals in every grotesque form and dress. In each picture are scattered columns of curious characters, to us incomprehensible, but containing to them the story designed to be illustrated. Let us now glance, by the aid of an interpreter, at what a few of these stories will tell us.

The Ape and the Crab.—A hungry Ape met a Crab with a piece of mo-chi in its claws, and to his begging for it the Crab promised he would give it if he would go home with him and gather some persimmons from the tree.

The Ape agreed, ate the mo-chi, and went home with the Crab, who sat on the veranda with his pipe, while the Ape climbed the tree. But instead of handing them down to the Crab, he pelted the Crab with them, until he succeeded in killing him.

But the Egg, a friend of the Crab, suddenly appeared, and the Ape ran away. Then the Egg went and consulted with his friends, the Rice-Mortar and the Bee. The three friends invited the Ape to a feast, and gave him a seat upon what appeared a box, but in reality it was an "infernal machine," which they had secretly prepared. This blew up; and while lying prostrate on the ground, he was thrust through with spears and quickly despatched. In this ludicrous way the moral is given that those who treat others unjustly shall be themselves served in like manner.

The Rat's Wedding.—A young-lady Rat was out walking one morning, followed by her servant. She met a young Mr. Rat, who was much pleased with her. He went to a friend to ask him to act as a go-between and consult with the young lady's father. The friend sat on the floor with his pipe, and the hiba-chi was beside him; and his wife listened with interest to all that was said. The go-between then went to the father, who received him graciously, and preparations were made for the wedding. The happy day came, the guests assembled at the house of the bride's father in two large parlors, the Rat-men in one room and the Rat-women in the other. The go-between, the bride and groom, with two maids, retired into a separate apartment.

In Japanese houses the place of honor is a dais, or raised platform, at one end of the room. The bride, arrayed in white, sat before this platform; opposite her sat the bridegroom, and the go-between sat between, a little way off; the maids sat opposite the go-between, the parties occupying the four angles of a square.

A little table with three lacquered cups was placed in the centre of the square. The cups were of different sizes, the smallest one being on top. The maid nearest the bride had the pot of saki, which she took, poured a portion into the little cup, and gave it to the bride, who drank and then handed it to the bridegroom, who also drank. The cup was then handed back and put away under the table, when the second cup was likewise filled, and bride, bridegroom and go-between partook, and the same process was gone through with the third and largest cup, and the ceremony was ended.

The design of this book is evidently to

illustrate to children the simple form of marriage adopted and in use.

Mo-mo-ta-ro.—An old woman found on the bank of a river a large beautiful peach. She took it home to her husband; and while they were admiring it, it burst open, disclosing a baby. Greatly surprised, to the childless old couple its appearance was yet one of great joy. They put the child in water, and he upset the tub. *Mo-mo* is the Japanese word for peach, and they named the child *Mo-mo-ta-ro*, or "Peach-boy."

As he grew older he became very strong. One day he begged a cake from his adopted parents, and they hastened to give it to him. Then he started off to fight the devils in a distant island and take their treasures. On the way an ape, a dog and a beautiful white bird met him, and begged the cake. He gave it to them, and they became his followers. They went with him to the island, where they fought the devils, and Mo-mo gained the treasures and then returned home. The moral is obvious: Generosity meets with its reward.

Kintaro.—A great many tales are told of Kintaro, a child born in the mountains, whose friends were rabbits, apes and birds, who subdued terrible dragons and monsters, and at last became a daimio. He is represented in the pictures as being very red. In the autumn, at the great display of chrysanthemums, among other human figures we easily recognize the ruddy Kintaro.

The Tail-cut Swallow.—Once upon a time an old woman made some paste. A pet swallow got out of the cage and ate the paste. The old woman was very angry, cut the bird's tail, and sent it away. The old man, her husband, O Ji san, was sorry when he heard of this, and went out to make inquiries about the tailless bird. On the way he met Mrs. and Miss Swallow, and after making his kind inquiries was invited to their house. He went, and Mrs. S. made a feast, at which there were music and dancing.

She then showed him two boxes, and asked if he would take home with him the light or the heavy one. He said, as he was old, he would take the lighter one. So he went off with the box on his back, and was accompanied a part of the way by Mrs. Swallow, as is the usual courtesy shown to an honored guest.

When O Ji san reached home he opened the box, and treasures fell out, at the sight of which he started back astonished, while the old woman looked on amazed. She, hearing of the other box, hastened to call upon Mrs. Swallow, and begged her to give it to her. She readily gave it, but when it was opened out flew *ba-ke-mo-no* (ghosts), which frightened her dreadfully.

The pictures of this little book would tell the story to one of us without the interpreter's aid. You can read it readily and learn the moral—that cruelty and avarice will surely be overtaken with dreadful vengeance, while a tender heart and modest unselfishness are to be approved.

Story of Sho-set-su.—In the province of Shinshiu lived a man named Sho-set-su. He was once walking upon the seashore, when an old man, riding upon a large fish, appeared, from whom he learned many of the things of the spirit-world such as are not usual for men to know. In a mountain he learned the art of fencing; and coming across a man one day, he made such dextrous use of his sword as soon to kill him. While sitting alone after this, a frightful ba-ke-mo-no appeared: it was the spirit of the murdered man. But he was not frightened, and ever after he was distinguished for his great courage, fearing nothing in this or the other world.

The Treasure.—O Ji san petted his dog, and the dog was very grateful, and told the old master to go and dig under a certain tree, where he would find treasure. He did so, and found *ko-ban* (gold coins). But while both he and the dog looked on this new-found treasure with happy look, an old woman living in the neighborhood stealthily came up, and saw it with covetous desires. She told her husband about it, and they borrowed the dog, to have him point out to them where another treasure was hid. He did so; but instead of digging up ko-ban, most offensive things came out of the earth. The old man was so angry that he killed the dog and buried the body under a tree. That night the good O Ji san was visited in a dream by the spirit of the dog, which told him to make a mortar for mo-chi out of the wood of the tree under which the dog was buried. He did so, and every time he pounded the rice ko-ban came out in profusion. The wicked old man, hearing this, went and borrowed the mortar; but when he pounded rice, the same horrible offensive things came out, which vexed him so much that he burned the mortar.

The good O Ji san gathered the ashes of the mortar in a vessel, with which he climbed a tree under which daimios were sitting, and scattering some of the ashes over the branches, they all burst into the most beautiful bloom, at which the daimios were astonished. But the wicked old man, trying to do the same, only succeeded in throwing the ashes into a daimio's eyes, who was so irritated that he ordered a servant to give him a terrible beating.

The moral: With the good all things are good and beautiful; while with the bad all things are offensive, and in the end turn out badly.

Such are some of the best of the stories which O I-ne san and Sen-ki-chi read. Most of the children's story-books are filled with tales of ghosts and hobgoblins and embellished with most frightful pictures, so that their imaginations are constantly tortured with the horrible visions thus called up.

Dear little Christian children, with your sweet, pure stories, told in such beautiful language, and with enough to meet every need of your souls, remember these little ones in Japan, and be thankful for your own happier lot. Their minds are starved and stunted in their growth, while yours are fed with nourishing, strengthening food.

CHAPTER XI.

A JOURNEY FROM TOKIO TO O-DA-WA-RA.

A LETTER—POLITICAL DIVISIONS—POSTMEN—SETTING OUT ON A JOURNEY—THE TO-KAI-DO—TEA-HOUSES—KA-GOS—NO-RI-MO-NO—THE ROAD TO FU-JI-SA-WA—THE HOTEL—A DAY'S JOURNEY—NIGHT AT O-DA-WA-RA.

THE postman called, "*O' ta-no-mo-shi-ma-su!*" O Cho ran and got a letter, which she carried on a waiter to O Tot san. It was written on much coarser paper than the one which O Ka san sent to O-ji. The address was in large characters, and the outside bore the writer's name, his town and the date. There were no postmarks except the government's stamps. The words too differed from those of O Ka san's letter, for men and women use different forms of expression in their letters. The divisions of Japan correspond to our States and counties, so that letters are directed to such a town in such a *ken* of such a province. The ken answers to our county. The large cities are called *mi-a-ko* or *o-ma-chi;* towns are *ma-chi*, and the *mu-ra* is a village or hamlet.

Postmen travel continually between the cities, carrying letters in a bag, which is tied on the end of a pole. With this on his shoulder, the postman goes at running speed. He is clad in tight clothing, as the robes generally used would be in the way of a runner. There being constant relays, letters are carried rapidly through the empire.

This letter was from a friend in the province of *Su-ru-ga*, which is on the other side of the Ha-ko-ne Mountains. The friend wished O Tot san to meet him at Ha-ko-ne in the sixth month (July). There is always a great deal of talking to be done before anything can be decided in Japan. So a family council was called, and even O Cho and O Kin were invited to give their opinion. At last the decision was made: the whole family would go.

An answer was sent to the friend in Su-ru-ga, telling him what time to expect them. Then preparations were made for the journey. Gon-ji-ro, the old man whom we saw drawing water from the well, was delighted to have the privilege of carrying the baggage. This was not heavy, for the clothing was all packed in two paper boxes, each one about three feet long, one and a half wide and two in depth. These were carried suspended at the ends of a pole on his shoulders.

The whole party started from the house on foot. O Ka san and O I-ne san had each a blue-and-white cotton kerchief tied over her head. Their dresses were partly fastened up in their belts. They had each a blue towel in one sleeve, and their purses hung down from their belts. Each of the travelers carried a staff, an umbrella and a fan; and Gon-ji-ro followed them with the baggage. O Cho and O Kin accompanied them a short distance, then said their good-byes with many a bow and went back to the house.

So our little O I-ne san became a traveler, and trudged on by O Ka san's side under the shade of an umbrella. She did so with gay anticipations. They went down the To-ri to Shi-na-ga-wa, one of the suburban towns of Tokio.

They were walking, but could often stop to rest at the tea-houses on each side of the To-kai-do (the prolongation of the To-ri), as their journey lay altogether along this road. As traveling is done almost entirely on foot, these tea-houses are indispensable for rest and refreshment. They are little open houses where a cup of tea, sweetmeats and a melon may be had, and also the pipe can be lighted at the hi-ba-chi. We find them often built over the water, on the mountain-sides, by the waterfalls

—wherever the view is pretty or wild or grand; showing that the Japanese appreciate the beautiful in nature.

Once during the day our travelers came to a long avenue of beautiful trees, where they saw one sad thing. This was a man confined in a box on wheels, in which he was carried around from place to place to be exhibited as a criminal: this was his punishment. Sometimes travelers in Japan see the heads of criminals stuck on poles by the highways.

On they walked all day, stopping to rest at the tea-houses, and at noon having dinner at a large hotel, until late in the afternoon, when they reached Ka-na-ga-wa. Looking across the water from here, they could see the foreign buildings along the Bund at Yokohama, on the other side of the bay.

O Tot san now got a *ka-go* (sedan-chair), and O Ka san and her little girl jumped in and were carried the rest of the day. There are two kinds of these chairs—the *ka-go* and the *no-ri-mo-no*. The first is open, with a little roof on top, while the latter can be entirely closed. Both are borne by means of a pole fastened along the length of the roof, and carried on the shoulders of two men. These men wear pads to prevent their shoulders being rubbed; but notwithstanding this, they often become sore and bleeding. The large no-ri-mo-nos of the gods and nobles require two poles, carried by four men. The motion is easy, although the cramped position in sitting would be uncomfortable to us.

As the little company—O Ka san and O I-ne san in the ka-go, O Tot san walking by their side, and Gon-ji-ro trudging along with his boxes—went along the great highway between Ka-na-ga-wa and Fu-ji-sa-wa, the women in the tea-houses called out, "Come and rest!" "Come and rest!" The people at work in the rice-fields looked up to see who was going by. Occasionally trains of packhorses passed along, or a solitary pedestrian, or laborers, in groups of twos and threes, returning from their work.

They had many little hills to climb, but the ka-go-men trotted easily over them, stopping every few minutes to change the pole from one shoulder to the other. The daylight was almost gone when they reached the large town of Fu-ji-sa-wa, having traveled about twenty-five miles. In the gathering darkness they went down the main street and found a hotel. The landlord came out to meet them, and O Tot san and the landlord bowed low. "Have you room?" said O Tot san.—"Yes" (using the most polite form of expression), answered the landlord. "How far have you come to-day?"

was the next question.—"Thanks! From Tokio." Then O Ka san and O I-ne san got out of the ka-go, and all were escorted to the best room, in the back of the building. The hotel is simply a large dwelling-house, the entrance often appearing very uninviting, as the kitchen is in front and numbers of coolies gather there; but we pass on, at first in disgust, to find large, airy apartments, and often beautiful gardens, in the rear. It is a noisy place, from the coming and going of guests at all hours of the night, the loud talking of coolies, the clapping of hands to call the servants, who all respond with a loud "*Hai!*" the frequent opening and shutting of the slides, and the constant splashing of the water in the bath-room, which occupies the most conspicuous position in the centre of the house. After the guests have gone through with their ablutions, the servants are all accustomed to do the same.

O I-ne san was tired, and felt a little homesick as she thought of O Cho and O Kin, but she ate her supper, and was soon asleep on the hotel futon.

At Fu-ji-sa-wa is a famous temple, to which they all went up to worship before starting on their journey the next morning. After the devotions were concluded, while a priest talked pleasantly with O Tot san and O Ka san about the journey, O I-ne san watched a group of pilgrims from Fu-ji, who came into the temple-enclosure. She thought they must be very good, because they had made this pilgrimage, and had worshiped on Fu-ji's top. She liked to see them in their white dresses, and listened with pleasure to their jingling bells. They washed their hands in the stone basin, and then went up to the temple.

In the summer, for two months, Fu-ji is "open," and pilgrims from all parts of the country flock thither, to worship at the top. Fu-ji is covered with snow more or less throughout the whole year, and its summit is only accessible during the months of July and August. Hence the natives then say that it is "open," the bars of the gateway being taken down. Pilgrims also visit the mountains of O-i and Nik-ko and the island E-no-shi-ma, and other sacred shrines, quite numerous in Japan, so that when we travel in the summer we are meeting them on every road. Most of them are men from the lowest classes of society. Their songs and jests are of the coarsest character; but among them may be found men and women of rather superior intelligence, who are sincere in their pious purposes, and go to seek relief from a burdened conscience.

O Tot san said that they must reach *O-da-*

wa-ra by night—a distance of thirty miles. So the coolies lifted the ka-go, Gon-ji-ro shouldered his burden, and on they went again. The way for a time led through a beautiful country, and the travelers had glimpses of lovely valleys, with hills stretching far into the distance. The fields were green and fair; the flowers bloomed along the roadside. They saw groves of the bamboo, with its bright foliage, and the dark rich green of the pines, and the still different tints of the maples. The variety of shades of green in a Japanese landscape is very noticeable. Our little girl also saw the ferns and ivy that grew on the hillside, and the beautiful rice-paddies, and the picturesque thatched farmhouses. Not so pleasant to look upon were the beggars, who crouched by the roadside asking alms, and to whom O I-ne san threw cash as they passed.

The sun grew warm and the road was sandy and hilly—a weary, toilsome way for our pedestrians. At noon they came to the *Ban-yu-ga-wa*, one of the broad, quiet rivers of Japan. Toiling through the sand to the river's brink was hard work for that warm summer day, but by the water the breeze was pleasant and refreshing. O I-ne san dipped her bare little feet in the stream to cool them while waiting for the ferry-boat. She watched two boats coming from the other side; the boatmen were poling them across, as the water was quite shallow. In one was a packhorse with a load upon his back; in the other was a woman with her head tied up to protect it from the sun; also a man with a pipe in his mouth and wearing a large scoop hat of straw that answered the purposes of an umbrella in sunshine or in rain. Close by this man, in the same boat, were two men with burdens on their backs and wearing comical straw hats like bushel-baskets inverted, and wholly hiding the face. The Japanese are remarkable in the care they take to protect themselves from the rays of the sun or the effects of heavy showers. Their headgear and high wooden shoes are far from being neat or handsome, but are exceedingly useful in times of rain and mud, or when the sun pours down his heating rays.

Besides these objects, O I-ne san saw the fields and houses on the other side of the river, and looked up at the mountains of O-i, lying like a bank of clouds, soft and dark, against the western sky. Their own ferry-boat now came, and they were quickly poled across. They climbed up a steep bank and reached a little town, where they took dinner. The afternoon journey was warm, but occasionally a breeze from the sea relieved the sultriness.

Sometimes high hills were in sight, and frequently little paths leading into pleasant meadows tempted them to leave the dusty highway.

Through the open slides of the houses they could see the inmates, most of them stretched on the floor asleep. Occasionally they saw a woman spinning or a man sitting up and amusing a baby. There seem to be many idle people in Japan, and apparently much of this idleness is fostered by their mode of sitting on the floor and on the *ta-ta-mis*, or soft straw mats.

Late in the afternoon the travelers had grand views of the ocean. Once they saw a surf-beach, where some boys were fishing, and in the distance a great promontory stretching far out into the sea. They heard the thunder of the waves as they broke against the shore. Just before reaching O-da-wa-ra they crossed another river by a long bridge built on trestle-work. Formerly the current of this river was so rapid that no bridge could be constructed of sufficient strength to withstand the rush of water. From what cause we cannot say, but the rivers of Japan are losing their volume, and now wastes of sand and rock are seen where once broad, deep waters flowed. We have a picture showing how passengers were taken across when the river was so rapid. They are seated each on a platform nailed across two poles, the ends of which rest upon the shoulders of four stout coolies, who wade or swim as necessity may demand.

O-da-wa-ra, where the night was spent, is a large town at the foot of the Ha-ko-ne Mountains. It is a great place of rendezvous for all the ka-go-men, packhorse-drivers, pilgrims and traders. The high mountains shut off the western breeze from the city, and the sea-breeze from the east died away, making the night excessively warm, while the coolies in the street kept up an incessant talking, and the drivers ceased not their cries, giving our weary travelers but little opportunity to gain the refreshment of much-needed sleep. They were glad, when the morning came, to renew their journey and set their faces toward the mountains.

CHAPTER XII.

ON THE HA-KO-NES.

Sai-o-na-ra—Mountain-scene—Ha-ta-ji-ku—Up to Ha-ko-ne—The Lake—The Temple—Ji-go-ku—A-shi-no-yu—Mi-ya-no-shi-ta—Yu-mo-to.

THE ka-gos were brought to the hotel-entrance. O Ka san and O I-ne san crept into theirs, and O Tot san also had one for this day's journey. The landlord and his wife, with all the servants, assembled to say "Good-bye" to the travelers and wish them a pleasant journey.

"*O Ki-no-do-ku sa-ma,*" said the landlord. ("Your stay has been poison to your soul.")—"*O Ya-ki-ma-shi-ku,*" said O Tot san. ("We have been very noisy.")—"*O ki ni ar-i-ga-to,*" said O Ka san to the landlady. ("A great thank you.")—"*Do-i-ta-shi mas-ta ka,*" answered the landlady and the servants. ("What have we done?") Then the low bows were made, the *Sai-o-na-ras* ("Good-byes") said, the ka-gos lifted on the strong shoulders of the men, and the journey up to Ha-ko-ne was begun.

From O-da-wa-ra the ascent begins. In some places the road was densely shaded, but through many openings they had grand views of the surrounding mountains and looked down into deep valleys. They passed many little shops, where tiny cups and boxes, very neatly and beautifully made of the mountain-wood, were temptingly arranged. The shop-people begged the travelers to buy as they passed. That day's journey was not very long. About noon our travelers reached *Ha-ta-ji-ku*, a little village on the mountain, and concluded to remain there all night. *Ha-ta no mi-yo-ji sama* is the name of the old hotel at which they stopped.

The traveler in Japan is constantly surprised at finding in the smallest hamlet large, pleasant hotels. These were built originally for the accommodation of the daimios as they traveled through the country with their retainers. The emperor once took dinner at this very hotel on his way to his summer-resort in the mountains. O Ka san examined the dark carved wood of the building, while O I-ne san was delighted with the pretty garden made on the hillside, with the three waterfalls. The water came down from the mountain, which towered above them, gushed out of some rocks, and fell to the second terrace, then made its way quietly through the grass, had another tumble, then was again almost lost to sight, until it made a third leap, into a fish-pond over which was a tiny arched bridge. The gold and silver fish in the pond were very large. Some were from twelve to fifteen inches in length. A woman threw in some food—a wafer-like substance prepared expressly for gold fish; and while the fish came out from under a rock to get it she talked to O I-ne san about them, and told her they had been there for a hundred years.

In one corner of the garden was a shrine for I-na-ri sa-ma (rice-god), and azaleas grew on the hillside. The evening at *Ha-ta* was lovely. O Tot san and O Ka san walked through the village at night by the light of the new moon and a single lantern. It was all quiet—nothing to be heard except the sound of the wind among the cedar trees and the hum of insects, until bedtime, when the women clapped their hands over the fish-pond—"to send the fish to rest," they said.

O I-ne san was sorry to leave the waterfalls and the fish and the kind people of the hotel when the ka-gos were brought the next morning, but it was time to continue the ascent of the mountain. The road was very steep and rocky. No horse can travel over it without great difficulty. The ka-go men said that even they could not walk were the boulders with which the road was paved taken away.

Tall cedar trees shaded the travelers, and the sound of falling water, which they never saw, constantly excited their curiosity. The ka-go men went up, up, up, carrying the party into the mists of the mountain and into the pleasant October-like weather, singing as they went. Their song was weird and strange, but not at all unmusical. There were six men to the three ka-gos. They had a ka-go for the baggage this morning, so that old Gon-ji-ro was relieved of his burden; and when they stopped to change the poles, one would begin a song and the others take up the chorus. Then another solo was begun, and at the second chorus all would march off again. The minor strains sounded very sweetly in the mountain. When will it re-echo to the music of Christian hymns?

On they went, almost into the cloud-land, meeting pilgrims and country-people, and occasionally a packhorse led carefully down. Just before reaching Ha-ko-ne they had a charming view of the lake. Two little promontories jutted out into it, and between them was Fu-ji, looking even grander and higher than he does in Tokio. Then they went down an avenue of cedar trees into the village, and there, waiting for them at one of the hotels, were the friends from Su-ru-ga, and the bows were many and low and the rejoicings great.

Ha-ko-ne is a town of hotels—the Saratoga of Japan. Its chief attraction is a lovely lake, which lies between two and three thousand feet above the level of the sea, and is supposed by some to be the crater of an extinct volcano. It is surrounded by mountain-peaks, and its clear water reflects each peak and cloud. At one end is a tunnel, two and a half miles long, made for purposes of irrigation. This is a great work, but who did it and when it was done no one knows.

The little company of friends much enjoyed their excursions on the lake and trips from Ha-ko-ne to the neighboring villages. One day they went in a sail-boat to the other end of the lake, and visited an old temple. They had to climb one hundred and five steps to get to it. The entrance was very grand, with rows of tall cedars and lanterns. on each side, but the temple was old and dilapidated. A Buddhist temple is much like the religion itself at the present day. The entrance is so imposing that you wonder what the temple itself may be, and enter the gateway to find nothing but an old building tumbling into decay.

The most wonderful place about Ha-ko-ne

is what the people call *Ji-go-ku*, their name for the infernal region. To reach this our travelers took a sail-boat and went to the extreme end of the lake, where they moored the boat, and all got out and climbed the mountain. The ascent was very steep and difficult, but O I-ne san toiled along bravely by her mother's side. The guide led the way along a deeply-shaded road to the springs. Clear water, boiling hot, bubbled up out of the ground, and crowds of miserable people were bathing in the water, some covered with sores and almost naked. Men, women and children throng to these springs in the summer to obtain, if possible, relief from their diseases.

Our friends did not stop here long, but went still higher up. From some points on the road they had grand views of Fu-ji (the "matchless mountain"), rising high above the clouds. As they toiled upward the way became barren and desolate, and the fumes of the sulphur almost intolerable. At one place they dared not step to the right or left of a narrow foot-path, as the ground on either side was full of deep holes. The water which issued from the ground was boiling hot.

At two little huts by the way men were preparing the sulphur for use, and at a little distance from these places of shelter arose dense volumes of smoke. Onward still the guides led to where boiling sulphur hissed, and where clouds of steam prevented them from seeing anything distinctly. "Keep away from the edge of the chasm," called the guide to one of the party who ventured too near. "The earth will give way." Ji-go-ku was a fearful place, and O I-ne san was glad to get away.

Near Ha-ko-ne is *Ashi-no-yu*. The "Twin Mountains," two peaks just alike, are distinctly seen from here. Down the mountain from Ashi-no-yu is *Mi-ya-no-shi-ta*, the emperor's summer resting-place. From Mi-ya-no-shi-ta to *Yu-mo-to* the scenery is most romantic and interesting. High mountains shut in the narrow path, and a river rushes and foams over great rocks. These mountains are noted for their springs. Water, hot and cold, gushes out of the rocks in every direction. The hotels are crowded with invalids in the summer.

Oh how we long for the time to come when the missionary can go and preach to these suffering souls, to tell them of the "living water" which can quench their thirst and give them everlasting life!

CHAPTER XIII.

PILGRIMS ON FU-JI.

PILGRIMS COME TO HA-KO-NE—DESCENT OF THE MOUNTAIN —MI-SHI-MA—YO-SHI-WA-RA—THE BASE OF FU-JI—THE CINDER CONE—THE HUTS—GOING UP TO THE CRATER— THE STORM.

A MOTLEY crowd had assembled at the entrance of the hotel when our travelers left Ha-ko-ne to return to Tokio. Ka-go men, pilgrims, travelers, drivers with their packhorses, —all were congregated there. Those bound for Tokio went down the mountain on its eastern slope, while the pilgrims turned their faces westward toward Fu-ji. Let us follow them.

They went up the one steep street of Ha-ko-ne, out of the gate through which the old daimios passed, and just outside of which some old idols stood, as if keeping guard in the place of sentinels.

Under grand old trees, between mossy banks from which hung tangled masses of vines and ivy, and where ferns grew in rank profusion and fair white lilies bloomed, went the pilgrims, stepping from rock to rock and stopping to

PILGRIMS.

Page 147.

quench their thirst at some cooling spring. At noon they halted for dinner at *Mi-shi-ma*, a large town at the foot of the western side of Ha-ko-ne.

Just opposite the hotel was a large temple, and back of the temple a beautiful grove. Pretty winding walks under the shady trees, with thatched cottages and people walking to and fro, made the place very charming. But the most attractive object at Mi-shi-ma was the stream which the pilgrims passed as they went out of town. Down from the mountain it came, pure and fresh, and in such volume that it was sufficient to quench the thirst of all the people of Mi-shi-ma through all time. Truly, Japan is a well-watered country—" a land of brooks of water, of fountains and depths, that spring out of valleys and hills;" and these bright waters flow over a green, sunny land. It is strange how earth's most lovely regions are the ones most defiled by sin. Even Sodom and Gomorrah stood in that plain of Jordan which was like "the garden of the Lord."

At *Yo-shi-wa-ra*, a large town near the base of Fu-ji, the pilgrims passed the night. Everywhere they performed their devotions, going for this purpose into all the large temples. And now they came to the mountain.

Fu-ji (Fuji-yama) is an extinct volcano, which

stands by itself in the centre of a large plain. It rises (taking the average of several estimates) thirteen thousand feet above the level of the sea, being the highest point of elevation in Japan. Perpetual snow lies upon the summit. Its cone is made of cinders, and is one of the most symmetrical in the world. It is the steepest of all volcanoes, the angle being forty-five degrees. Its ashes cause at a distance the peculiar purple hue which distinguishes the mountain. A hundred years have elapsed since the last eruption.

As the pilgrims started on their journey in the early morning their way lay for a time over a plain whereon beautiful flowers grew. Beginning the ascent, they passed through a grove of cedars, then through fields of flowers, where the vegetation was rank, and then reached hut No. 1.

At nearly regular intervals on the mountain are these places of refuge for the pilgrims. They are built far into the side of the mountain, boarded inside, with immense blocks of *scoriæ* on top to hold down the little of the hut which projects outside. One would scarcely imagine them to be huts from seeing the outside only, but within they are quite spacious. There are eight or nine of these huts, numbered respectively No. 1, No. 2, No. 3, etc., and without their shelter travel on the mountain would be almost impossible.

No. 1 looked very pleasant that summer morning as the pilgrims stopped to rest. It bore quite a resemblance to a regular house, and in this respect was superior to the other huts, farther up. Near this place was an old hermit, living all alone in a little hut.

Then they went on until they reached No. 2, a wild, desolate spot. Below were the clouds, and only through the rifts could the pilgrims catch glimpses of hills and valleys far beneath them. Above was the top, like a great ash-pile, black and barren. An old woman had charge of No. 2. She had a fire of wood built on the floor; there was no chimney, and smoke filled the room. Guides, ka-gomen and pilgrims made up the company within. Here the pilgrims ate their midday meal. Water, very cold, came down from the summit; it was the melting snow. Everywhere the pilgrims found rice and dai-kon, but not much else.

Then began the real ascent of the cinder-cone. It all looked black and desolate. Vegetation suddenly ceased, with the exception of a few patches of a sickly green shrub, and the feet of the pilgrims sank deep into the ashes at every step. The way was strewn with cast-off sandals—the *waraji*, a very cheap style of shoe worn by coolies. They wear out quickly on Fu-ji. Ka-gos can be carried no farther than the third resting-place.

After reaching No. 6 the way up to the crater became yet more steep and difficult, and the scenery of the mountain the very extreme of desolateness. On went the pilgrims, toiling slowly upward, purposing to sleep at the crater. Large stones impeded their progress, and their feet sank deeper and deeper into the cinders. The air became so rarefied that it failed to satisfy their lungs, and breathing became difficult. Patches of snow lay along their way. It was a blessing indeed that the running water was so cold and plentiful, for the ashes, flying up at every step, made the throats of the pilgrims very dry, so that they constantly wanted to drink.

At last they stood on the summit. A priest sat by the side of a deep well, constructed no one knows how long ago, and a most remarkable feature in such a scene—a well of water at the very crater's mouth. He pulled the buckets up and down by a rope on a windlass, and as the cold, sparkling water came, he gave it to the weary, thirsty pilgrims. How interesting and deeply suggestive this incident, though happening in a heathen land and in a false pagan worship! There is the counterfeit, and there is the true. Can we doubt where the true well is, and the real water of life?

The pilgrims, refreshed, went on to worship at the crater. Around the deep, yawning pit were the idols of wood and stone, similar to those in their temples and homes. All was quiet—no smoke or smell of sulphur, or anything else but the crater itself and its cold black ash-piles, to indicate the presence of a volcano. It was by no means so fearful a place as Ji-go-ku, with its boiling, hissing sulphur. Near the crater was quite a village, in which were men and boys, but no women. This is their home for the two months of summer when the pilgrims come, to whose wants they minister.

The air was sharp and cold. All night the tinkling of the pilgrims' bells was heard as other parties made their way up the mountain. The morning sun rose upon a scene of wondrous beauty to the pilgrims. Far, far below them rolled a sea of clouds; and when the sun emerged, it was like a perfect sea of glory, which turned into deep crimson and gold as the sun shone over it.

The pilgrims started early down the mountain. It is necessary only to worship at the crater and spend one night on the mountain. As they descended the glory of the early morning faded away, and a terrible storm of rain and wind overtook them. The mist entirely concealed the path from view. Often they fell down in the ashes, but the bed was soft, and no one was hurt. Occasionally the scene brightened for a moment, and the clouds parted. But the wind again swept down from the mountain, driving before it a dense fog, and everything became obscured. The pilgrims were drenched to the skin; they stopped at each hut to rest and get a cup of tea, and then went out again into the wild storm, and in this way they reached the foot of the mountain. But the prayers had been said, their worship paid at Fu-ji's top, and they were satisfied.

"Why do the pilgrims ascend Fu-ji?" This question was asked of a Christian Japanese. "They wish to be holy," was the reply. "As long as they are on the mountain their conduct is good, but when they come down they drink saki, gamble and cheat, and do many wicked things. But the Christian religion is like being *always* on the mount. People need never come down. They can always be holy."

BOOK II.

CHAPTER I.

AN OPEN DOOR.

"And I said, What shall I do, Lord?

"A great door and effectual is open unto me, and there are many adversaries."

AFTER the dispersion of the scholars in the winter of 1870–71 we waited patiently for brighter days to come, and waited not in vain, for this year (1872) we seem to breathe a new atmosphere of religious freedom. In March some converts were baptized, a native church was organized in Yokohama, and in one of the mission-houses On-ga-wa conducts daily family worship. Even in the capital Bibles are sold and Bible classes taught without interference from the ya-cu-nins.

The Tokio of to-day is very different from the city to which we came nearly three years ago. Few two-sworded men are now seen in the streets, and we go among the people with much freedom. The foreign population has greatly increased, and the house at Ro-ku-ban is no longer the only foreign building in this part of the Concession. Soon a railroad will connect Tokio with Yokohama, and a church for foreigners will be erected. It seems as though the mere sight of a Christian church here will have its effect on the Japanese. And yet even this spring we heard rumors of rebellion and of the possible expulsion of foreigners from Japan, and stories of a general massacre, to take place some time in April, reached our ears, but the bright spring days passed away, bringing no signs of intended violence.

And now the thing for which we have longed and prayed these many months has been granted. A door of access to the women of Japan has been opened, and, strange to say, in the providence of God, by the Japanese themselves. So has it been in all our intercourse with this people. They have always *come to us* to beg instruction. We know not to what the path in which we have begun to tread may lead. One thing we do know: it is the only way open now, and there is no question as to duty. The desire to study English has been aroused in the hearts of some of the girls, or in the hearts of their parents for them, and in this way they have been brought under Christian influence. It seems but a little thing, the daily teaching of English to a few girls, but the results none can foretell.

Early in March, while the weather was still cold, Hama Konda, the first pupil, came to Ro-ku-ban. She was not very young, and was plain in her personal appearance, but wore dark, rich clothing. Her regular lesson-book was a *First Reader*, but after that had been learned we had a book of simple religious truths, in which she seemed much interested. She was learning English in view of teaching little children herself some day. She (O Hama san) did not remain in Tokio very long, but went to Yokohama, where she is still under Christian instruction.

One evening, after the lamps were lighted, Chimura Goro, a man who was going to America with a daimio, brought two girls to be taught English. They were quite different from O Hama san, being gayly dressed, with bright sashes and hairpins and powder and paint. They have been coming to school quite regularly ever since. The little girls are named Mishi and Kiyo. One room in the second story at Ro-ku-ban was fitted up for school-purposes. From every window we could look out upon the water. It was April when O Mishi san and O Kiyo san came, and the fort near Sku-da-ji-ma was just turning green.

Soon after the little girls came we had one of those terrible conflagrations which so often sweep over Tokio. We saw it, early in the afternoon, in the direction of the castle, never dreaming that it would come near us, but the wind blew in the direction of Ts'kiji, and it soon became evident that the greater part of the Concession was doomed.

From the veranda of the mission-house we kept watch as one by one the old landmarks were swept away. Toward evening the scene grew wild. Men, women and children, with what they could carry in their arms and on their backs, fled to the open common near us. Terrified horses and frightened, screaming birds sought the same place of refuge. The fire seemed to be forming a circle around us. There was no way of escape except by the bay, so a boatman was engaged, and waited for hours, ready to take us off at any moment. But the mission-house was spared that time, and became a place of refuge for some of the homeless ones, who crowded on the lower veranda and protected themselves by screens.

Such fires are not the same calamity to the Japanese that they would be to us. They expect them, and can easily save all of their houses except the framework, which consists of poles and sticks of timber that can readily be replaced at very little cost. Their fire-engines are mere pumps, throwing a small jet of water, and are scarcely more efficacious than are the poles with long strips of paper attached which they bring out to appease the gods. It is strange to see them running around with lighted lanterns, even in the full blaze of burning houses. It is the law of the land, and they must obey whether it be necessary or not.

One day after this the little girls came from their home near Shi-ba to find nothing of the pleasant house at Ro-ku-ban but the chimney and a heap of smouldering ashes. The house had burned that morning, taking fire from the kitchen stove-pipe. Books, dictionaries, manuscripts and translations, the work of many months, perished in the flames. Homeless, we found a temporary shelter in the third story of *Shin-yama da ya* ("New Mountain House"), a large boarding-establishment on the corner of one of the busiest streets of Tokio. We had the whole of the upper story. There were a number of families below us. The landlady occupied part of the lower story, and near her room was a family consisting of the mother, a grown son, a little daughter and an old grandmother eighty years of age. The head of the latter was perfectly bald and she was bent almost double, but she was the brightest, cheeriest old lady imaginable. On the second story was a music-teacher, a large, fine-looking Japanese woman, and opposite her an old man and a young girl. They were all exceedingly kind, but had a great many inquiries to make. "Where are you going?" was a question which had to be answered many times when we went through the building to go out.

I went one evening to call on the family in the first story, and sat on the floor to have a cup of tea with them. The tea was very hot, but the mother took a large fan to cool it. I told them how old I was, and the ages of father, mother, grandfather and grandmother, and they told their ages. All this is etiquette. The old women especially esteem it a great compliment to be asked their age. They had many questions to ask about the journey to America. I told them about our Sabbath and the God whom we worship, and then the man took a picture of his god out of his pocket. It was an exceedingly small affair, but he said that he prayed to it every morning, and that it would keep the house from burning down.

The music-teacher entertained me pleasantly in her room on the second story. She was giving a lesson on the samisen to a little girl sitting on the floor. The music is very simple, consisting of one part only, and is learned entirely by imitation. The woman had many inquiries to make about our little cabinet-organ, which was up stairs. It was an object of great curiosity to all, and a real missionary in itself. I could not touch a chord without bringing people up from all parts of the house. Sometimes I would stop working the pedals, and then they were puzzled, and would get down to see where the sound came from.

For about a week after we went to Shin-yama a storm raged, and the Japanese house was very gloomy. But after that the sun came out, the days were bright and warm, and we could throw open all the slides.

It was interesting to watch the people on the street and to listen to the street-cries, which, like those in our own cities, sometimes bear little resemblance to the words supposed to be uttered. At night the noises were very annoying. Samisens, drums and other musical instruments, with singing, the cries of the peddlers and the shrill whistles of the a-mas, rendered sleep almost impossible until long after midnight, and then there were only a few hours of quiet, for other noises began very early in the morning.

Our pupils soon found us again after the fire, and went on with their lessons. Then Tama, a large girl, and Rio, a grave young woman of twenty-two or twenty-three, with To-yo, a bright, active child of six, were added to our number.

Soon O Ka san (Japanese term for "mother") heard of the school, and one bright June day brought her little I-ne, then a little more than eight years old. Her hair had all been cut short and fell over her forehead, and she wore a short coat; and when O Ka san asked permission to send her to school, I said, "Why, this is a little boy, and I have only girls in the afternoon." But O Ka san laughed and said, "Oh no! This is a girl—my little daughter." And now the young and tender rice has been brought under cultivation: may it develop into beautiful refined grain!

Soon after I-ne came a little girl about the same age, named I-no, the daughter of an officer. The children brought beautiful wisteria-blossoms and pink roses to ornament the room. The rose is not a Japanese flower, and its cultivation is somewhat difficult. The people call it the "thorn-flower."

When the lessons were over in the third story of Shin-yama, the little girls gathered around the organ to learn some English hymns. The very first one was "In the Light," and they learned the meaning of "light," "God" and "walk" in their own language. They sang out the chorus loud and strong, and it sounded pleasantly in Shin-yama. Oh that the little feet may soon find their way into the kingdom! Then indeed shall they "walk in the light."

The warm summer days had come when we went back to Ro-ku-ban. We had only two small rooms, one above the other. The lower apartment served for dining-room, parlor and schoolroom. A board put upon some bricks and covered with a carpet made a bench for some of the scholars, and as the house-building progressed we were moved from room to room, all assisting merrily in carrying chairs.

We had no dictionaries, no translations of any kind, and progress was necessarily slow, but the little school increased in numbers. The children learned many hymns—"Little drops of water," "There is a happy land," "Jesus loves me," and others—and partly committed and learned to chant the twenty-third Psalm. The words of all these were taught them orally by constant repetition.

Little I-ne always had an English sentence ready to say when she came into the schoolroom, and she would repeat it with the utmost precision. O Ka san came with her every day, and sat near while the lessons were being read and explained. One day I overheard her saying something about the creation of the world and Adam and Eve; and referring to some Japanese tradition, she said: "That" (the tradition) "is a lie."

It was always pleasant to go into the school and see the bright, happy girls around the table. The first thing in the afternoon was Mishi and Tama's lesson. They read in the New Testament, as they had learned some English before they came to Ro-ku-ban. After this, I-ne, I-no and Kiyo read their lesson in the *Reader* and had their writing examined and copies set; and last of all came the large class of beginners. Then the books were carefully wrapped in pretty fu-ru-shi-kis; and after the general exercises of spelling, catechism and singing, the "Good-byes" were said, and the girls went to their homes in the great city. Now they are "resting:" the time for the summer holidays has come. They all promised to come back punctually at the end of a month.

We think that by this time the children have learned to regard our Bible as a very sacred book and to reverence the Sabbath. They have also learned of the true God and the precious name of Christ. Is not this a beginning? May we not hope? Truly, God has opened the door: let us enter in with true faith and holy boldness.

CHAPTER II.

MIDSUMMER HOLIDAYS.

"Be not afraid; for I am with thee."
"For I have much people in this city."

NOW that the girls are "resting" we have time to go about the city and into the suburbs. The introduction of the *jin-ri-ki-sha* ("man-power wheel")—a little two-wheeled carriage drawn by a man—adds greatly to the ease and enjoyment of travel.

One Saturday morning O Ka san came with a jin-ri-ki-sha to take me out to the beautiful home at O-ji. It was well that when first the door was opened for me to approach the women of Tokio I found this one waiting to take me by the hand; she has done so much to make me feel less of a stranger in the land and to introduce me to her countrywomen. She always brings to me beautiful flowers and choice fruits arranged in the most tempting way, as expressions of her gratitude and esteem, and is ever helpful and kind.

O Ka san's invitation was accepted with pleasure. We seize eagerly every opportunity of getting nearer to the people and being with them in their homes. She had two jin-ri-ki-shas at the door—one for herself, and the other for her guest. We got into them, the coolies lifted the shafts, and we were rolled rapidly along through the streets of the city. It was a great festival-day, and poles were erected in front of houses and temples, with gayly-colored papers flying from their tops. Crowds of people in holiday attire thronged the streets. It takes a long time to get into the country, as Tokio is a very large city. Through street after street lined with low wooden houses the coolies pulled the jin-ri-ki-shas before we reached the suburbs. The road to O-ji lies through the great shrub-district of Tokio. We saw tea-plantations and rice-paddies and wheatfields with patches of yellow mustard-flowers. On this road are many nurseries, where flowers and trees are sold. Farmhouses, cedar trees, bamboo-groves and hedges make the road very pretty and attractive. After we had passed the entrance of the village of O-ji, we turned off into a lane, went through a gateway at the end, and were met and welcomed warmly by the kind people of the house. In the same enclosure with the house is a cotton-mill, in the operation of which the proprietors receive valuable aid from a skillful Englishman. Part

A JINRIKISHA.

Page 164.

of the house is built in foreign style and nicely furnished.

The Japanese rooms were beautifully neat and clean. The large parlor (*o-za-shi-ki*) was open on all sides, and the view of the terraced garden was lovely. There were the usual artificial lake with gold-fish, a fountain, and small hills made so that many shrubs and flowers could be planted in a limited space without any appearance of crowding.

The dinner consisted of fish, small potatoes cooked very nicely, rice, sweetmeats and fruit, and all served in Japanese style.

The afternoon was the pleasantest part of the whole day, when jin-ri-ki-shas were brought for a ride. Down the narrow lane, over the arched bridge which crosses O-ji creek, up the one long street of O-ji, with its streams of running water on both sides, past hotels and temples, the coolies drew the jin-ri-ki-shas, and at each turn there was something new to admire.

The object of the ride was to visit the fountains of O-ji, and very beautiful they were. A little river almost hidden from sight by the dense shrubbery was near the first fountain, whose waters gushed clear and bright out of the living rock. A strange group of people were gathered there. On some faces marks of intense suffering were indelibly traced.

Those tortured with brain-diseases stood under the rock and let the cool water pour over their heads. Country-people from all the region round about O-ji seemed to be gathered there that day. At another fountain a similar group could be seen. From a high hill back of the one large temple at O-ji (there are several smaller ones there) we had grand views of the surrounding country. The old women who were with us went to the temple and worshiped most devoutly, but O Ka san says she does not pray to idols. The rest of the afternoon was spent on *Sa-ku-ra-ya-ma.* It was pleasant under the trees; we had tea and fruit and a little melon which the people call *ma-ka-wa-u-ri.* At O-ji are many bi-wa trees, which bear in the early summer a yellow fruit about the size of an ordinary plum.

Sa-ku-ra-ya-ma has a gentle, easy ascent on one side, but the other is a high precipice. Little flat stones like small earthen plates were sold us, that we might throw them down and tell in that way how far it is to the bottom. Through a green valley flowed the Sumida, looking like a silver thread in the distance.

In the coolness of the evening the jin-ri-ki-shas were pulled rapidly home. The long summer day was over, but the recollections of sunny skies and fields of "living green," of fountains and clear, running streams, of sweet flowers and kind friends—even those of another land and speaking a strange language—linger in the memory. Yet with these memories come the words of the prophet: "In that day shall a fountain be opened for sin and uncleanness," and our hearts ask, "When will the eyes of this people be opened to see it?"

Another day we went in a house-boat a short distance up the Sumida, and then turned off into a canal to a distant part of the city to visit a temple where are the images of the deified five hundred disciples of Buddha. It was another festival-day, and the crowd in the temple prevented us from examining the statues, as we wished to do. Some of the figures were very striking in their appearance, being in the form of venerable old men, but most of them were badly mutilated. In the principal temple, which was old and dilapidated, priests were chanting a service. One, who appeared to be a high priest, with a mitre on his head and clothed in rich robes, sat on an elevated chair. Above the heads of all towered an immense idol. The people who thronged the temple seemed to have no idea of worship, but were rude and noisy, and many of them drunk.

That night was the end of *O Bon*, a great

festival which continues three days. During this period the people imagine that they are entertaining the spirits of the dead. It is a long, solemn festival, and the houses are swept and feasts prepared before it begins. It is during these three days that the "fan-dances" are performed. In these the men, who are mostly common coolies, or jin-ri-ki-sha men, move in a circle, waving their fans and keeping time gracefully to a weird melody which they chant in unison. As we came down the river that evening we saw lanterns floating down with the tide, and lights in various places near the shore. The spirits were supposed to go back to their abodes in the fire.

But the greatest festival we have seen this summer was the *Ka-wa bi-ra-ki*, the "river-opening." It took place at night, and the display of fireworks attracted thousands of people to Ri-yo-go-ku and Ad-zu-ma Bashi. The space between these two bridges was filled with boats ornamented with gay Chinese lanterns; while in the boats people were dancing, singing and playing on samisens, fifes and drums. There was nothing remarkable in the fireworks, but the whole scene was most animated.

Exactly what the meaning of this feast is we cannot ascertain. Some of the people say that it has something to do with a strange superstition concerning a fabulous water-monster, the *Kappa*, who requires to be periodically aroused or awakened.

Another of our pleasant little excursions this summer was to *O So so sama*, a temple in the south-western suburbs. We were there in the evening, and the gathering darkness rendered the great temple in the solemn grove yet more impressive. A priest showed us a number of native offerings which from time to time have been made. There was a quantity of human hair hung up, and very singular figures painted or carved on wood. On one side of the temple was a garden. Trees had been trained to resemble a line of hills, and the effect in the uncertain light in which we saw them was most peculiar and beautiful. The talkative priest also showed us the "holy water," which he said would cure diseases of the eye.

Just at dusk one day we stood in an old cemetery. The cemeteries in Japan, which are always near the temples, are very different from those we see in our country. The stones are crowded closely together, the inscriptions are in Chinese character, and in some stones a place for water is hollowed out, and flowers, with the ever-green leaves of the camellia, are kept in them.

At death the body is carefully washed and

the head shaved. The dead person becomes a priest, they say. The relatives gather together, and there is much noise and drinking. The coffin is like the no-ri-mo-no, and the dead are buried in a sitting posture. Money and shoes are often placed in the coffin for the use of the deceased on his journey to Hades. Then the corpse is carried to the temple, and from thence to the grave. A new name is written on the tombstone, and the old one is sometimes forgotten.

One joyful event has marked this summer: the foreign church has been dedicated. It stands near the mission-house. A church dedicated to the worship of the true God stands in the midst of this heathen city. Praised be God for this fact!

O Ka san brought beautiful white flowers with which to decorate the church, and said that she wanted to learn about our way of worship, for she did not believe in idols and had none in her house.

It has been pleasant thus to go about the city and mingle with the people; but often, seeing the multitudes who thronged the temple-gates or mingled in the festivals, or even the ordinary crowds in the streets, a feeling of responsibility, and almost of despair, which was wellnigh unendurable, would steal over us, and we would cry out in our hearts, "What *can* we do among so many?" No missionary is a stranger to this feeling. Viewing mankind in the mass is always discouraging, but there is one thing of which we are sure, and on that we lean: "The Lord knoweth them that are his."

Like Paul at Corinth, we can hear him saying unto us, "I have much people in this city." For there are here in this very city, where now heathenism and superstition prevail, many who will hear of the Lord Jesus, believe in his name, confess him before men, and proclaim him to their countrymen. Some of them may have already passed middle age, some may be strong men and women, some merry toddling children, and some little feeble babes. The Lord knows them all. Their names are written in his book. We do not know them, but he does. May we not pray, "Lead them to us—lead us to them"?

CHAPTER III.

THE GOSPEL IN JAPANESE.

"And I saw another angel fly in the midst of heaven, having the everlasting gospel, to preach . . . to every nation and kindred and tongue and people."

EARLY in October, when the oranges were turning from green to gold and purple grapes and figs hung from vines and trees, when persimmons, red and yellow, bent the boughs and chrysanthemums made all the city gay with their bright colors, there came a book which was brighter and more beautiful than all else to us in Tokio—the Gospel of Mark in the Japanese language.

Who of the early missionaries in Japan will ever forget that volume, with its yellow paper covers stitched in real native style, and Chinese characters on the title-page? Who will forget with what joy we opened the book, turning the leaves from left to right, and read in Japanese the first words: "The beginning of the gospel of Jesus Christ, the Son of God." Quickly following Mark, that Gospel which so concisely sets forth the power of Christ, came John's beautiful Gospel of love.

Those who know something of the Japanese language can appreciate some of the difficulties in making a translation of the Scriptures acceptable to the people. Let us look at some of the questions which have to be considered by translators.

In what form shall the Scripture first be given to the people? Will it not be best to put it in colloquial, so that all can read it? That is something easily decided: it will not; for that would lower the character of the translation. That being settled, what form of book-language will it be best to use? Shall it be written with many Chinese characters and in high literary style, that it may please the scholars of the land? In that case the merchants, artisans and coolies, women and little children, will not be able to understand it at all. Shall it be written in very simple language, without the Chinese? Then all the great scholars will think it unworthy of notice. And while we believe that God "chooseth the foolish things of the world to confound the wise," and while our hearts yearn toward the poor and lowly, we cannot, in the present state of the country, let a translation go out which will be utterly despised. Will it, then, be necessary to make two translations, one for the upper and one for the lower classes? This would involve great labor and expense, and it is not deemed expedient just now.

The best course to be pursued is to endeavor to give a translation that would so *combine* the various forms of book-language as to be generally intelligible and free from the charge, on the one hand, of being too vulgar, and, on the other hand, of being beyond the comprehension of the masses. The first translations will necessarily be imperfect, but they must be sent out and used until, in the years to come, the final accepted version shall be made.

One of the great difficulties is in the selection of the characters to be used. Japanese books are invariably made up of a mixture of *Hira-kana* and *Kata-kana*, with Chinese characters. The Hira-kana is subject to many changes, as it is simply the reproduction in print of the chirography of the author, and of course is as varied as is the handwriting of different authors. The Kata-kana is fixed and is more like our capitals, and yet is not easily read by the people. The translation of Mark and John came out in the Hira-kana, with a few Chinese characters.

Another difficulty arose in regard to the word to be used for "Deity"—whether it would be better to originate a new name for that purpose, or to take their own word, *Kami* ("Sintoo god"), and have them gradually learn to attach a new meaning to it. The latter was considered the better way. The heathen will soon learn that our God is not as their god.

We must remember that the beautiful words of Scripture, which have been familiar to us from childhood, mean to the heathen at first, even when translated into their own language, simply nothing. Take, for instance, the expressions, "Behold the Lamb of God, which taketh away the sin of the world," and "The good Shepherd giveth his life for the sheep." What meaning would these words convey to this people, who know nothing of pastoral life, and to whom the very existence of such animals as sheep or lambs has been unknown until very lately? They who come into the kingdom have a new, heavenly language to learn, but the Holy Spirit is a great teacher, and they who permit themselves to be drawn under the power of the gospel will readily acquire its language, while little children who come into the mission-school will become familiar with it in their early years. Thus in prayer and faith the gospel is given to the people.

Wonderful changes are taking place in the empire. We realize the importance of the events of the day and the record they will make in this nation's history. We can see the hand of God in all, though they do not.

The imperial railway between Tokio and Yokohama was formally opened in October, and the Mikado—the once secluded "Son of Heaven"—was present, attended by his nobles, and with the crowds of Japanese we all looked into his face as he sat upon the throne which had been erected at one end of a platform. Pillars beautifully decorated with chrysanthemums (the emblem of royalty) lined the way on either side to the throne. Flags of all nations waved in the breeze, and a band of native musicians, led by an Englishman, played national airs.

The ceremony was very impressive. The young emperor sat upon his throne with much dignity, and his lords arranged themselves in rows on each side. All were clad in the courtdress of ancient times. Papers unintelligible to us were read, and then the lords and the emperor, in solemn, slow procession, retired.

Shi-ba, the ancient sacred spot, which no one might enter save the tycoon and the high officers, has been thrown open to the public. A great festival was held there, and thousands of people thronged the temple-grounds, eager to gain a view of the holy shrines. The priests, ever ready to seize on such occasions, had beg-

ROKUBAN.

Page 177.

ged that this festival might be held in order to raise money for the temple.

Another great change has been in regard to the reckoning of time. Henceforth the Japanese year will commence with ours, and the seventh-day rest—our Sabbath—will be observed instead of the *Ichi rokus* ("one-six days"). This is decidedly the most hopeful change that has taken place. It will seem almost like an actual recognition of Christianity when the next step is taken and they begin to reckon their years from the Christian era. Of course the people know nothing of the sacredness of our Sabbath, but it is much gained that they now are obliged in some measure to regard it.

But we must go back to the little school at Ro-ku-ban. The schoolhouse, designed also as a chapel, was finished in November; it stands at one side of the new mission-house. The walls are tiled on the outside and penciled with white plaster. The room inside is about twenty-four feet in length and sixteen in breadth. The ceiling is high, and the floor covered with a neat matting. From all of its six windows we can see the bay. A small stove heats the room, and on a platform are the blackboard and a little organ, while pictures, maps and mottoes adorn the walls.

Over the blackboard is the motto, "Little children, love one another." At the front door are shelves for shoes: they are apt to be greatly in the way when no such arrangement is made. This room is a great comfort to us all, and the girls seem to enjoy it much.

One of the ya-cu-nins at the custom-house (Kidera) brought his daughter Chiye ("Wisdom") to school this fall. She is a bright, rosy-cheeked girl, and a most diligent scholar.

December was a cold month, and the snow, which usually does not fall in Tokio until February, found its way to us then. Our little schoolroom looked pleasant and cheery on one of those snowy days in December. The wind came from the north and the snow fell all day, but the fire was kindled early and the door opened.

Ko-ba-ya-shi san, a studious girl, who is always called by her family-name; and I-no, a faithful little scholar, arrived first, stamping their feet and shaking the snow from umbrellas and cloaks before they came in. Then came our funny little Toyo, on the back of a man-servant. Her head was wrapped in a purple cloth (*dzukin*). Almost all of these dzukins are purple, and when the girls come with their heads wrapped up in them it is impossible to distinguish one from the other. This little damsel took off dzukin, *mino* ("raincoat") and shoes (*geta*), and ran across the floor in her bare feet. It always seemed strange to have these little ladies, with their rich robes, running about barefooted. Next came a jin-ri-ki-sha man, toiling through the snow with O I-ne san and her mother.

The afternoon passed away quickly, while lessons were read in the schoolroom and the fire blazed in the stove and the snow fell over the city and into the dark water. Then the girls had a merry time getting ready to go home.

They all learn well. Besides their reading-lessons, they have oral exercises on the map of the world, learning about different countries, and also spelling-lessons. *The Catechism for Young Children* is faithfully studied, and every day they sing. Their Bible verses are written in large letters upon the blackboard, and translated for them word by word. Each word is precious seed sown in their hearts, and the ya-cu-nins cannot steal it away. O Ka san has bought a copy of the Gospel of Mark.

The year ended happily for us, because great progress had been made in the work. Old Fu-ji looked out from behind the clouds when the sun set for the last time that year, but the gospel Sun has arisen upon Japan. Light is so penetrating! Even those who try to shut up their hearts to prevent its entrance must know that the Sun is shining.

CHAPTER IV.

LOAVES AND FISHES.

"And Jesus took the loaves; and when he had given thanks, he distributed to the disciples, and the disciples to them that were set down; and likewise of the fishes, as many as they would."

ONE Friday we had for our lesson in school the story of that scene on the Lake of Tiberias when Jesus lifted up his eyes to see the hungry multitudes who had followed him so many hours and listened to his words, and having compassion on them asked Philip, saying, "Where shall we buy bread, that these may eat?" We talked together of the lad who had the "five barley-loaves and the two small fishes," and of how he had given them to Jesus, and how in his hands they multiplied and multiplied until all that great multitude had enough and to spare. What if the disciples had rejected the few small loaves and fishes as being indeed nothing among so many? Then the people would have gone away faint and starving. What if they had tried to go about the villages to buy bread? They would never have obtained enough.

Oh, well it was that they took the little they had and gave it to Jesus!

The simple gospel narrative has ever been in my thoughts since I read it with the girls, and mingles with them now as I write the story of the last few months, the record of daily routine—always pleasant, never monotonous—in the schoolroom; the record of little everyday duties, nothing calling forth any great amount of courage or fortitude, all being the same old story which every missionary can tell of "loaves and fishes" given in faith to the Lord Jesus, believing that he can multiply them until thousands of hungry souls are fed.

Bright dawned the new year, 1873. The house was ornamented with nan-ten and flowers, and the little girls came in the morning, dressed in their best, with belts of heavy silk, and new hairpins in their hair. They had all learned our form of salutation, "I wish you a happy New Year;" so we exchanged greetings in English. When O Ka san came, she presented, in the name of the scholars and in a most graceful manner, New Year's gifts to their teacher—ducks, oranges and dried persimmons. After they had all sung some hymns they went away to enjoy the day at their own homes with battledores and shuttlecocks.

The first Sabbath of the year was a bright, pleasant day. O Ka san brought some camellias and plum-blossoms. The girls read the first ten verses of the eleventh chapter of Matthew in English, and Ko-ba-ya-shi san read in *Line upon Line* after the others had gone. We talked of the blood upon the door-posts and of the precious blood of Christ. The girls have little hymn-books of their own now, and enjoy them much.

The school, through the winter, was not quite so prosperous as it had been. The Japanese are not a strong people, and are liable to consumption, insufficient food and clothing being the principal causes, so that cold weather does not seem to increase their energy.

A man, by name Takahashi, came in January to inquire about the school for his sister-in-law, O Yasu san, a gentle, pleasant girl, who entered soon after. We have heard that this man has been to missionaries of each different faith, Roman Catholic, Greek and Protestant, to make inquiries concerning religion.

One day we read in a Yokohama paper that toleration in religious matters had been proclaimed. It was joyful news to us, but the report proved to be without foundation, for in June there began to be whispered again apprehensions of the dreaded ya-cu-nins. Some of the girls were afraid to come to the little Sabbath-school, which had been so faithfully attended during the winter and spring.

Ko-ba-ya-shi san, who was afraid of the officers, sent a note in which she said, "I know it (Christianity) is an important thing, but it is not permitted."

I asked O Ka san if she was afraid to come to the Sunday-school, and she said, "No; I think I will come," but added, "I do not care for myself, but I-ne is so little yet." Poor people! it is hard that they cannot worship as they please.

We found in the school-yard one day a little amulet, and on opening it discovered a cross made of two pieces of twisted paper, with the name "Jesus" written on another paper. It was I-ne's. I said, "Why, O Ka san, what does this mean?" and she said, "I-ne wanted the name of Jesus in her amulet." She tells me that I-ne and Sen ki-chi pray to Jesus, never minding the ridicule of the rest of the family. The story of the first prayer that I have heard of among the scholars is touching. O Ka san says that I-ne formerly sang lies, but now she has good, true songs to sing—the hymns she has learned at school.

We hear rumors of the probable dismissal of all Christian teachers from the government schools. It is trying to have to encounter all these things, after the bright hopes of the winter, but no one is discouraged.

The castle was burned one cold night in March, and the emperor has taken refuge in the house of his mother. Some of the people saw the occupants of the palace as they were forced thus suddenly from their seclusion, and told how the court-ladies in their white robes ran affrighted through the streets of the city in the early morning.

Some young men called, not long ago, to consult about revising some of the Chinese Christian literature, translating it into a style of Japanese writing which will be intelligible to the people. Whether they will carry out their purpose time alone will prove. Many things are begun in Japan which are never finished; but we stop to talk with all who come, and listen to their plans.

The new house is completed, and the third story has been made into a dormitory for the Japanese girls who may want to come and live in the house. The large windows at each end of the room give light and air.

Japanese slides divide it into little compartments. The ceiling is papered, and there is a pretty blue-and-gold paper around the windows. The veranda makes a nice place for the girls to play.

The first girl who came to live with us was O Toki san. She was a very studious girl, and a Chinese scholar. She would sometimes tell of her wish, in early childhood, for an education beyond what was deemed sufficient for girls, and of the sneers and jeers she endured in endeavoring to accomplish her desires, being obliged to attend a boys' school. She read with me the Gospel of John, but it seemed to make no impression on her heart. Only last month three sisters—I-so, Kuma and Nori—and a little cousin of theirs entered our family. The father of these girls, Mr. Koga, came with them, accompanied by a daimio, and they brought flowers and cake and crape. It is pleasant to see the fathers so interested in the education of their daughters.

Life in the mission-house now is very different from the loneliness of days gone by. The house is filled with the sounds of children's laughter, and echoes to the patter of children's feet. They seem very busy and happy. The little hymn, "Jesus loves me," has been translated into Japanese, and we have now *The Catechism for Young Children—The Happy Book*, which is its name in their language. Matthew's Gospel, with a map of Palestine, has come to us, and we have the *Jujika no mo-no gatari* ("*The Themes of the Cross*"), written in simple language, the first tract put forth in Japanese. For all these things we are truly thankful.

Last Friday we read the hymn "Beautiful Zion" and had it explained. The day was excessively warm, and the text written on the blackboard was, "Neither shall the sun light upon them, nor any heat." The lesson was on heaven, and the girls seemed much interested.

It is hard to have the little flock dispersed, for it is scarcely probable that they can all be gathered together again. They have learned a great deal this session. Their faces show that their minds are developed, and they understand a few great truths. Every day they have a verse written on the blackboard, and they copy it on their slates. To-day the verse was, "I am the good Shepherd."

The girls have become very dear to their teacher. To tell the message of salvation to these precious souls is worth any sacrifice. Since January only three have left the school, and the number on the roll has increased to seventeen, while the attendance has been more regular. Nor is this all. Through the girls we have gained access to their homes, and now we can talk to them about father and mother and brothers and sisters.

A pleasant day was recently spent with Ko-ba-ya-shi san. She came with jin-ri-ki-shas, and we went to her home, in the direction of Shi-ba. The mother met us at the gate and gave a pleasant welcome to her daughter's teacher, and all day they entertained their foreign guest with the greatest ease and grace. They showed me pictures and books and took me to *Atago yama*, a high place back of the city, to point out the view. The aunt, who is quite a musician, played on the ko-to and sang. The old father is very fond of flowers and has a pretty garden, and there is an uncle who is a flower-painter. They had works on botany and paintings of flowers.

And I have been in O Toki san's house, near the castle, and to I-no's pleasant home, in the suburbs, and to see O Rin san and O Chiye san, in the neighborhood of Ts'kiji, and also to visit I-so and Kuma and Nori's home in the old ya-shi-ki where the poor dear little blind baby is.

Who will not say that the "loaves and fishes"

are multiplying? Sometimes we long to do some great thing, to go and preach to the multitudes, endure great hardships, and then the story of the "loaves and fishes" comes with comfort to our hearts. Better give a little to Jesus than to try to do a great deal of ourselves.

CHAPTER V.

THE HOLY SPIRIT ALONE.

"Except a man be born of water and of the Spirit, he cannot enter into the kingdom of God."

WE stood, one day, at Sakura-yama and looked down on the village of O-ji, lying far below us. The houses looked pleasant in the summer sunlight, and the simple-hearted people were quietly pursuing their customary easy tasks. From one place and another smoke curled lazily upward. In the distance gleamed the Sumida, and O-ji creek ran swiftly over rocks at the foot of the hill. We could not see the sunny fountains, but knew that only a short distance away they were leaping and sparkling just as when we saw them last year.

Gazing on that peaceful scene, the thought arose, "Is it wise or best to disturb this people in their present state of content?" The gospel often brings, not peace, but a sword. "The brother shall betray the brother to death, the father the son, and children shall rise up against their parents." "He that knew not, and did commit things worthy of stripes, shall be beaten with few stripes." Is it well thus to make the irresponsible responsible? We long so earnestly that the seed which is sown in the girls' hearts may spring up and bear fruit; yet when it does, there will surely be a time of trouble for them—perhaps even of persecution.

Let not any one wonder that such thoughts arise in the heart of a missionary. It is well to stop sometimes and consider carefully what we are doing, and it is well not only for us, but for those who are helping us; for letters from across the sea tell us of societies organized and mission-bands formed, that women and children at home may work better with us among "the women and children in heathen lands." Let us see if even children who give their pennies for the heathen cannot understand the reasons why we send the gospel to them.

Every Christian is a soldier. We have all entered into the army of the great King, and are bound to obey his commands, whether we fully understand them or not; and when he says, "Go, win those lands for me," must we look over into the enemy's country and say, "O Lord, they are all content with what they have. Their fields are very fair, their homes look peaceful and pleasant; we would not disturb them in their quietness, and bring trouble and fire and sword"? No; we must obey his command. It will not do, in religion, in science, or in anything else, to keep back the truth from the people because they may be happier or less responsible in a state of ignorance. The King's army bears aloft the banners of truth, and with them we must push on until all the world be won.

But let us look at Japan and the Japanese more closely. Under all this lovely landscape are hidden elements of destruction; at almost any moment the earth may open and swallow us up. And the longer we dwell among this people, the more sensibly do we realize that there is also deep degradation and misery underlying all their fair and pleasant exterior.

We have seen how goodly is this land, how bright its skies and how sweet its flowers, and have seen, too, how fond the people are of all these things, and yet how far their hearts are from purity and holiness. We have heard something of their gods, and know that most revolting tales are told concerning them; we have looked upon the temples, to find that under their very shadow the grossest sins are committed and the vilest language used. We have found in their books some good moral maxims, and even some which bear resemblance to the teachings of Christ; and their laws and injunctions concerning obedience to parents and other virtues show us that the commandments involving man's duty to his fellow-man are written in their hearts. They know what is right and wrong as well as we do, but all this, while we see the degradation of the people, only proves to us that man cannot make himself good.

The Japanese are a cultivated people. Their books, to be sure, do not teach them much that is useful, but their minds are disciplined by the study to which they are obliged to apply themselves. In Japan religion and science have literally gone "hand in hand." In some countries missionaries make both the schools and the literature, but here we have to strain every nerve to make our schools as good as those of the natives.

We have seen this people in the early dawn of their new life, almost in the darkness, and yet struggling for something—they scarcely know what. We have seen them running eagerly after Western science and civilization, and have marked their rapid progress. Even before we came to Tokio the great government-school for boys (*Kai-sei yak-ko*) had been established. German, French and English teachers are employed there, and thousands of boys and young men may now receive a complete education in the science and literature of these different nations. A government-school for girls was opened just about the time that the mission-school was begun, and a foreign lady employed as teacher. Railroads have been built, and the telegraph is in active operation. We have seen the emperor come out from his seclusion and many walls of superstition broken down, but we believe that Japan can never be holy and happy without the Bible.

The simple creed of the missionary is this: "I believe that *all men* have wandered away from God; I believe that the one way back to God is through Christ; I believe that only by the breath of the Holy Spirit upon the word, as it is sown in the hearts of men, can they be purified and made fit to enter heaven." And so with earnestness and faith we sow the seed, and we are glad to have those at home working with us. For them too a "door" is "open." They too can give in faith "loaves and fishes" to the Saviour. They too can pray for the blessing of the Spirit.

What says the children's *Happy Book?* "Can any one go to heaven, with this sinful nature? No; our hearts must be changed before we can be fit for heaven."—"What power can change a sinner's heart? The Holy Spirit alone." And with the sound of the summer wind ever mingle the words of the text, "The wind bloweth where it listeth, and thou hearest the sound thereof, but canst not tell whence it cometh and whither it goeth: so is every one that is born of the Spirit.

The days pass quickly at Ro-ku-ban. It seems but a little while since, in the spring and early summer, we looked for wild strawberries and vines and flowers on the common, and twined them around the vases and picture-frames, and opened all the windows to let in the air. Now there are fires in the grates, and the windows are closed; the children gather beautiful fall grasses and autumn leaves.

Since September we have all been busy in school. We have a catechism class entirely in Japanese on Wednesdays, which all the older girls attend regularly; we also close with prayer in the native tongue. It was hard at first to use this language in prayer to God, for a new form of expression had to be acquired in addressing the Deity; but after the form of petition had been learned the rest became easy, and we found how true it is:

"Prayer is the simplest form of speech
That infant lips can try."

One of the girls bought an extra *Happy Book* to leave at home for her parents.

One day the girls had a good native elder from Yokohama (O-ku-no) to talk and pray with them. And now O-ku-no and another elder, Ongawa, have gone on a journey together, the first missionary-tour. They knelt down and prayed before they started. We have not heard from them yet, but we follow them with our prayers.

Our children are studying the map of Palestine. Even the little ones have learned the mountains, lakes, rivers and cities of Palestine, and they know it is called "The Holy Land."

The work is all-absorbing. There are cares and anxieties in it, and it is hard to know just what is right sometimes, but we trust that God is guiding us.

Our lesson last Sabbath was on the indwelling of the Holy Spirit, our bodies being the temples of the Holy Ghost. It was a new doctrine to the girls, and they listened attentively, finding their proof-texts with interest. Next Sabbath their lesson will be on FAITH.

CHAPTER VI.

CHRISTMAS AT RO-KU-BAN.

" We love to sing around our King,
And hail him blessed Jesus,
For there's no word ear ever heard
So dear, so sweet, as ' Jesus.' "

WHAT a New Year's day for Tokio! The wind is from the north; the water is cold and dark. All day snow has been falling, and the trees and roofs of the houses are covered with it. The girls could not come to give their usual greetings and little presents to their teacher. In the afternoon we took a walk in the storm. The streets were almost deserted, but within-doors the families seemed to be enjoying the day. Sounds of laughter and singing, with the familiar twang of the samisens, reached our ears.

Our house is quiet without the girls, who are at home spending their New Year's holidays. We have had a great deal of earnest work during the last fall. There have been four classes to be taught. The older girls, who have been longest in the school, have been reading in an elementary book on physiology and universal history. There has been a *Second Reader* class, and one in a little book called *First Footsteps in the Way of Knowledge*, which the little ones enjoy, and there is always a class of beginners, for new scholars are constantly coming in. The last hour in school is occupied in general exercises—spelling, geography, Bible verses and singing.

These girls have very retentive memories. It is wonderful to hear them, even the little ones, repeat their English lessons, but they are too apt to repeat without trying to understand, and we find that great care has to be taken in training their minds. Constant review is necessary. Their delicacy of constitution and weakness of eyes in many cases are serious drawbacks to their education. Especially in the winter long intervals of rest are necessary to some of the most delicate ones. In the school of twenty-five girls some have already been marked by their teacher as scholars of peculiar ability and promise.

The Japanese seemed to us at first all alike, but as we become better acquainted with them we can see the diversity of character. To speak of the scholars generally, we can say with truth that they learn well and are diligent in attendance, gentle, and respectful in their manners. Some are full of fun and a little noisy at times, but a word or a look is sufficient to restrain them. The class of little ones is very interesting. It is amusing sometimes to see how earnestly they study, never pretending to play. Their little grave faces are bent over their slates as if some great result depended on the work being done well.

Japanese music is very different from ours, but the girls seem to enjoy much our style of singing. Most of them can now sing by note, and their voices sometimes sound very sweetly.

The Sabbath-school, which has been carried on without molestation from the ya-cu-nins, has usually been a little smaller than the day-school. Some of the girls even now seem to have serious thoughts about God and the world to come. O Chiye san, the daughter of the custom-house officer, appears at times very thoughtful. I talk with her, but it is hard to win our way to the hearts of this people. Their politeness forms a smooth surface which it is hard to penetrate. We feel sometimes as if we were getting in, but soon find ourselves slipping off again.

Christmas in Japan.—We were busy for some days in preparing for Christmas, our first celebration of the day as a school. It was like Christmas in the home-land to have to keep the children away from the parlor while the tree was being prepared.

The servants helped with the outside decorations. Over the gate was an arch of evergreens; around the front door was another arch, of green leaves and yellow chrysanthemums. In the veranda, just at the entrance, was a large Chinese lantern, with "Merry Christmas!" painted on it. In the hall, just over the parlor-door, was the word "Welcome!" in gilt letters, with a wreath around it. The top of the chandelier was ornamented with flowers, and the words "God Bless our Home" were wreathed with evergreens. In the niche on the stairs was a vase of beautiful flowers, and the framed motto "God is Love" was also ornamented. A wreath of vines and evergreens, with the bright nan-ten, hung in festoons from the ceiling, and at different points around the room were large bouquets. At each end of the bay-window was a beautiful gilt star.

Near the bay-window stood our beautiful tree, with straight branches and reaching to the ceiling. We had Japanese candies made in all sorts of shapes for ornament. At the top of the tree was a large fish, which looked very much as if it were out of its element.

There was a candy man and woman dangling from the limbs, and horses, melons, gourds and cucumbers, all of which looked very bright and pretty. For the girls there were small bags filled with foreign candy and apples and Chinese oranges. There were three lanterns back of the tree, and we had all the lamps lighted.

Japanese girls do not go out much at night, but all the scholars were present on this eve of Christmas. They assembled in the schoolroom and entered the parlor together, arranging themselves, according to direction, on each side of the organ. They looked very nice in their dresses of silk and crape and heavy silk sashes, with their bright hairpins. They first sang "There is no name," etc., then "Autumn," and after that chanted the twenty-third Psalm. Then reward-cards marked with the number of times they had been present during the session were distributed. Two Christmas hymns were then sung: "We three kings of Orient are," and "Who is He in yonder stall?" after which, one of the missionaries made a little address in Japanese. When the things on the tree had been distributed, the girls sang the hymn, "When he cometh," and chanted the Lord's Prayer both in Japanese and English. Each scholar was then presented with a little book. Then "I am Jesus' little lamb" was sung in Japanese, and "The Pilgrims' Song" for the end of the year.

Several of the mothers and female friends of the scholars were present in holiday attire. The dress of Japanese women is very becoming, the want of proper fastenings being the greatest objection observable. When in full dress they wear pieces of crape at the throat. The black teeth of the married women and of elderly unmarried women spoil their appearance. Little girls, until they are six or eight years old, have their hair "banged" or cut in a variety of ways, leaving bald places on their heads. They have various styles of hairpins for different ages—those for little children, and those for girls of fourteen and fifteen, and those for women; amber is preferred by the wealthy. They also wear very handsome tortoise-shell combs.

But to return. The children doubtless have a pleasant impression of Christmas, and their singing and behavior were highly complimented by the foreigners who favored them with their presence that night.

Christmas day was bright and warm. In the morning I went to call on the father and mother of O Chiye san, and to see the children. The father is very proud of them all, and takes great pains with their education. They are nice children, with an amount of spirit and life uncommon to Japanese. The father gave many thanks for the entertainment of the previous evening. When anything is done for one member of a family, all the others will repeatedly thank you for it, until the "*Do i-ta-shi-mas-tu ku?*" ("*What have I done?*") becomes irksome.

The father said that the children had never seen a foreign apple before, and Riujiro, the little brother, had the empty candy-bag in his hand. Our Japanese friends have brought us many little gifts for Christmas, and we have had a pleasant time giving and receiving presents, and are happy in feeling that we are gaining our way into the hearts of the people.

A normal school has been established in Tokio, where children are taught geography, history, etc., and have graded Japanese *Readers*. Teachers from all parts of the country visit it.

The Union native church was organized this fall. Christians have not yet been troubled by the ya-cu-nins. And now we have another year of work before us.

CHAPTER VII.

THE "PEEP OF DAY."

"Through the tender mercy of our God; whereby the Dayspring from on high hath visited us."

THE little book *Peep of Day* has been translated into colloquial Japanese, and has already found its way to the homes of some of the people. It has been the young children's Sunday-book in English for a long time, and now they have it in their own language. They call it *Yo Ake* ("*The very Beginning of the Morning*").

Last summer a girl who had been baptized while a member of the Yokohama missionschool came to live with her old father in Shiba. She attended our Sabbath-school occasionally, and the girls all knew that she was a Christian and had been baptized. One day O Ya-su san came to me and said in a whisper so soft and low that I could scarcely understand her, "I wish to be baptized like O Kwai san." After that we studied the *Little Catechism* together, and she attended regularly the Bible classes, and in January was baptized.

Soon after, she married her brother-in-law, who has become settled in his faith at last, and is now a Protestant Christian. She is a young wife and stepmother, being only sixteen now. She had no opposition to fear in her own home in regard to her baptism. Indeed, the other members of her family desired it.

It was during that same month that Deguchi Taka came to live with us. We call her Deguchi san. She is a middle-aged Japanese widow, well educated in the Chinese language. She has been a pilgrim, going from shrine to shrine, vainly trying to obtain relief for her burdened heart, and has tried various sects of Buddhism and Sintooism, of which there are many, but as yet has failed to attain satisfaction. She succeeds very well in teaching the boarders Chinese and Japanese.

Kato san, who has a writing-class in our school, has been a teacher of the Japanese language in the mission-house for some time, and has studied the translation of the gospel most diligently. Some believe that he is one of those "not far from the kingdom of God," but still he lives under bondage and will not break the fetters. He has two wives, one here and one in Osaca.

The wife here seems, from some hidden

cause, to have great influence over him. She is much opposed to his coming here and reading the Scriptures, as she sees that it arouses in him a sense of his sin. One Saturday morning she came here after him. Her eyes, swollen with weeping, and her long hair, streaming down her back, made her look almost like an insane person. It was impossible not to pity her, for she seemed in great distress; but she is not really his wife. She has two children of a former husband, and this man (our teacher) has two by his first wife. He was anxious that his daughter, Michi, should come into our family, and we took her, he engaging to pay for her tuition by teaching. He is an editor, and talks of starting a religious newspaper. A friend of his called to talk to us about the paper, but they will be obliged to get permission from the government before they can begin it.

Some are beginning to inquire more closely about the Christian faith. A man from Aidzu (a province in the North) often comes to converse upon the subject of our religion. He is a strange, wild-looking man. We hear that Aidzu is a very rough country, almost buried in snow during the winter.

Our new servant, Ume ki-chi, reads the Bible and attends the classes regularly. He has a wife, mother and baby to support. The old woman, O Ba san, comes in every morning to read the gospel with Deguchi san. Frequently they interrupt the reading with "*O arigatai koto*" ("A thing to be grateful for").

We have rumors of serious troubles in the South. Tales of war and bloodshed reach our ears, and there is some doubt as to the result. But the rebels do not appear to be especially hostile toward foreigners. The prime minister does not give satisfaction; taxes are very oppressive, and the subject of the Corean war is being agitated.

There is always more or less trouble among the Satsuma clan. The papers give a sad account of the state of things in Nagasaki, but nothing has yet been authenticated. It will be some time before these things are finally settled and peace and order restored, but the government will take care to protect life and property.

Everything as yet is quiet in our city; the government troops are gaining victories, and we pray here every day for protection. Many believe that all these things are the beginning of better times and of more liberty to both native and foreign inhabitants. But we often feel cramped and fettered. Our boundaries are fixed. The Foreign Concessions are pleasant, but we feel as though we should like to be free to live where we choose.

Harder to bear than tidings of war in remote provinces and restrictions by the government, because it comes more closely to us, is the fact that some "little foxes" have crept unawares into our school. There are petty jealousies and disputings and murmurings, and some of these have grown to considerable size. We have talked about it, and have knelt to ask God's forgiveness and blessing, and since then have had less trouble. The girls have their faults—deeper, perhaps, though less apparent, than those of children at home. It is hard to know just what is going on in their hearts.

Every Sabbath evening now a few people gather in the schoolroom to read the Bible. The carpenter, Ju ki-chi, comes sometimes, and the blacksmith, who has a blind daughter, and some of the neighbors and servants. They listen to the explanations given, and sing in Japanese. When the service is over they light their lanterns, and we hear the sound of their heavy clogs on the gravel as they turn away from the door toward their homes.

A mission-school for boys has been commenced, and is prospering. The old Shin-yama O Ba san is ill. She is growing very old and feeble, and our women will visit and read to her.

I took a copy of *Peep of Day* to O Ka san the other day, and had an interesting talk with her. She seems to wish to know more of our religion. We go quietly along in the same routine day after day. There is little to record, but life seems very full, and not at all monotonous. The light is growing brighter around us.

> "Christ, whose glory fills the skies,
>   Christ, the true, the only Light,
> Sun of righteousness, arise!
>   Triumph o'er the shades of night.
> Dayspring from on high, be near;
> Dayspring from on high, appear."

CHAPTER VIII.

THE WOMAN AT THE WELL.

"Then cometh a woman of Samaria to draw water. . . . Jesus answered and said unto her, Whosoever drinketh of this water shall thirst again. But whosoever drinketh of the water that I shall give him shall never thirst."

APRIL came in with a glad burst of sunshine after all the storms of March. It is always a delightful month of the year here, as the flowers are then abundant and lovely. The girls bring great branches of peach and plum trees all bright with blossoms, and of camellias in bloom. We have vases in every corner of the house, and still are at a loss to know sometimes what to do with the frail treasures.

The girls are developing very rapidly into womanhood. They have all changed much since first they began to study, and are improved in every way. Many of those who started with us have left us, but some have been faithful from the beginning. It is a fault of the Japanese character that they run eagerly after any new thing, but do not always persevere.

We hear from the teacher in the girls' department of the government school that some of the pupils are very anxious to study the Bible. They have read something of Scripture narrative in the *Universal History*, and want to learn more. How we do long for religious liberty in Japan! It seems almost cruel to let them only just peep in at a door which they may not enter.

Our girls are more fortunate. Here we have greater freedom. O Chiye san first desired more Bible instruction than she could gain in school-hours. In a little note handed to her teacher she had written, "I want to pray to God and receive help from him, and to walk in the same way in which you are walking." So, after school-hours, she remained to read the Bible. We selected the Epistles of Peter, and read of the "inheritance of the saints," of the Saviour, "whom, not having seen, we love," and of what a Christian should be—like unto Jesus in all things and ever "looking for and hastening unto the coming of the day of God;" and she drank it all in like water to her thirsty soul. She is a girl of very superior mind, grasping an idea quickly and holding it firmly. I asked her one day if she thought she loved the Lord enough to confess him before men, and she said she did; but a few days afterward she came and told me that her father was not willing that she should be baptized, as it was contrary to the law of the land.

Soon afterward O Rin san remained to read, and one after another of the girls bought Bibles and came into the class. Every afternoon, when the regular exercises of school were over and the little ones had gone, we read and talked together for an hour.

The books of Ruth and Esther interested the girls. Many scenes in Oriental life they can understand better than children at home. The story of Esther's petition to the king was one to which they listened eagerly, and after this lesson O Chiye san led our devotions in prayer for the first time. It is unspeakably pleasant to hear the voices of these people in prayer.

In the New Testament we read the Acts. We very much want a translation of that book, which seems especially appropriate to this country. We still have only the three Gospels, and the rest of the Bible must be read in English and carefully translated.

Our principal text-book is the Bible. To translate it into intelligible Japanese for the class is part of my daily work. When the sun sinks behind Fu-ji and the evening has come, the children come down to sing, and then we go up into the "study-room" to have worship. The girls have been reading *Line upon Line*, and have finished the story of Joseph. It is almost like hearing it for the first time myself to read it in a new language to those who have never heard it before.

Our Sabbath lessons have all been interesting. One Sabbath we had for our lesson the healing of the paralytic at the pool of Bethesda. How like the crowd who gathered there must be the people who congregate at O-ji's fountains and Ha-ko-ne's springs! Again, the girls listened attentively to the story of the blind man who received his sight and who said, "Whether he be a sinner or not, I know not. This one thing I know: whereas I was blind, now I see." And one Sabbath-day our lesson was in the fourth chapter of John's Gospel—the story of the Samaritan woman at the well. We talked about it, and I said, "You are like that woman. All you who have tasted these living waters, came here thinking to draw water from earthly cisterns, and, lo! you have found heavenly fountains, pure and sweet and fresh. 'Drink and never thirst again,' and then go quickly—

quickly go—and tell of it, that many in your city may also come and drink."

A short time ago the clouds which had hung for many days over us during the rainy season broke away and sailed off into the blue depths, and were seen no more. In like manner have our little troubles disappeared, floating away somewhere, and the girls are happy again.

The older girls have finished their lessons in the *Happy Book*. They read twice a week in a little abridged copy of Wayland's *Moral Science*, and like it very much; it does them good. We have interesting talks in the class.

Now the summer "resting-time" has come again. When we closed our Bible class for the summer, I asked the girls to remember the hour between four and five P. M. as a time for the study of the Scriptures, and they promised to do so.

I was glad to accept the invitation to spend a few days in *Yokosuka*, a pretty village down the coast. The invitation came from Hiyodo san, O Chiye san's aunt. O Chiye san's father insisted upon its being accepted, so she and I went in the cars to Yokohama, about an hour's ride, and then took a little steamer for Yokosuka.

We left Yokohama about four P. M., and it

was a little after six P. M. when the steamer landed at the wharf. It seemed quite home-like to find boys waiting for us at the landing, ready to carry baskets and bundles to the house, which we reached after a short walk down a shady lane.

Yokosuka is a pretty village with a beautiful harbor, shut in by hills. It is the great navy-yard of this part of the country. There are extensive machine-shops and large docks. Considerable activity was visible both in building new vessels and repairing old ones. The French are in charge of all this work, and there are pretty dwelling-houses and a little Roman Catholic church. On a compound goats were feeding, for wherever you find French people you will also find goats.

Hiyodo's house is the very neatest of all the neat houses in Japan. The servants are kept busy dusting, sweeping and scrubbing. The parlor, or guest-chamber, is on one side of the entrance, and back of this there are pretty rooms opening into a court. Each evening the man-servant went through the courts with a pail and dipper and threw water over the trees and bushes. Back of the house rises abruptly a high hill, and where the view of the ocean and surrounding country is finest there is a tea-house belonging to the family, which we enjoyed very much. The children kept climbing up and down the steep ascent, bringing sweetmeats, fruit and tea. In the front of the house we could see higher hills in the distance, and we watched the moon rising over them each evening of our stay. Down by the public road was a little summer-house with a lattice, so that we could, if we wished, watch the passers-by. The Japanese have a number of such contrivances to aid them in enjoying life.

The family, consisting of the parents, three children and servants, with their guests, made quite a large party. The children were well governed and everything in the house was nicely arranged, and nothing could exceed the ease and grace with which the mistress of the house entertained her foreign guest.

When the father went to his business in the morning, the children all bowed down to the floor and said, "*Saionara*," and when he returned all went to the door to salute him. A child never left the house without saying to the mother, "*Mo mairi masu*" ("I am going"), and on returning would say: "*Ta-da-i ma*" ("Just now I have come").

We all ate together in the best room, parents and children sitting around the little tables, while they had a high stand for their visitor. Breakfast usually consisted of eggs, rice and fish, lunch the same, while at the evening dinner there was more variety. Fruits and sweetmeats were partaken of between meals.

One evening some visitors came—a young married sister with her baby, and some other relatives. The lights were put out that the moonlight might have its full effect. The mother plays well on the ko-to, and she brought out her instrument and sang for us. A young man performed one of the slow, weird dances of his country, moving his whole body gracefully. Then we sang "Shall we gather at the river?" in English. How I wished they could all understand the words!

When night came the maids brought the futons and great green mosquito-nets, putting the former down on the floor and fastening the latter to the walls by means of strings. Then the lamps—for they had foreign oil-lamps—were put out, and we were left to sleep. The lady frequently said, "*O ki no do ku sama*" ("Poison to your soul"), meaning that I was suffering from the lack of things to which foreigners are accustomed; but she always received an answer to the contrary. The greatest difficulty was how to dress in the morning, as the mosquito-nets were taken down and all the slides opened. We are not accustomed to make our toilets in such a public manner.

We met the little child of the family on entering the lane, in front of the house, just fresh from his bath, with his hair all wet and plastered down to the sides of his head. The mother takes great care of the children, and no one would dream that she is not their own mother, nor that they each one have a different mother. It is not always pleasant to look below the surface: many disagreeable things appear to us which we hardly expected.

One pleasant Sabbath afternoon in vacation a few of the girls came to read the Bible, and our lesson was on the "new song," the song beginning in feeble strains on earth and ending in the full harmonies of heaven. Deguchi san said they wanted to learn the song. I could not but ask with joy, "What have these girls already found in the kingdom of God?" A new language to speak, a new song to sing, fountains to cleanse their sinful hearts, wells of water to quench their thirst, and, above all, the Sun of righteousness to shine for evermore on their benighted souls.

"And the Spirit and the Bride say, Come; and let him that heareth say, Come; and let him that is athirst, come; and whosoever will, let him take the water of life freely."

BOOK III.

CHAPTER I.

"THE CHURCHES OF ASIA SALUTE YOU."

"Behold, I have graven thee on the palms of my hands: thy walls are continually before me."

OUR school began brightly and pleasantly in September. But few of the old scholars were missing on the very first day, and others soon joined our ranks. O Ka san brought three new pupils to school—I chi, Sudzu and an aunt of the last named. Four sisters named Sa-ku-mo, Mashi, Yasu and Mitsu were also brought by a relative of theirs. These are boarders, the other three day-scholars. A little girl named Aida Kame came into our family before the last session closed.

We miss O Rin san from our classes. We are sorry, for she wants to come to school, but her grandmother will not allow it. Sometimes these ignorant, prejudiced grandmothers can have a great deal of influence in keeping a girl away from school. More than one missionary has had the same thing to contend with. In spite of the servitude of women, the O Ba sans contrive in some way to keep girls at home, even though the fathers have no objection to their attendance at school. But we still pray for O Rin san, and hope some time to see her.

The state of things with us just now is intensely interesting, calling forth every energy of soul and body. In July the man who brought our first little pupils, and who afterward went to America, was examined as to his faith and knowledge, previous to baptism. Deguchi san, Kato san and our girls, with Ju ki-chi, the carpenter, and U-me-ki-chi, were all present. Chimura is an elderly man and a scholar, and his examination was very strict. His answers displayed a wonderful knowledge of the Bible. He has been thinking about being a Christian for years. He was baptized soon after in our little schoolroom, all of the girls being present.

The Bible class was begun again with the new school-session. Some of the girls wish to be baptized, but their fathers will not permit it, and they cannot see clearly their duty in the matter.

O Chiye san begins to realize that God's claims are above her father's, and is sorely perplexed and troubled. More than two years have passed since she came into the mission-school. Then she was a round-faced, rosy-cheeked girl, with nothing to mark her except apparent good-nature. Now she has a thoughtful, earnest expression, and often seems sad and depressed.

Shige, a girl of fourteen, is an earnest lover of God's word. She is very bright and earnest, and anxious to do right. "I am not good," she said one day, "but I will try to be better." She told with sobs of her father's angry refusal to permit her to be baptized, and of how he threatened to take her from school. Others seem inclined to walk in the same good way, but are deterred from making a profession of religion by fear of their fathers' anger.

We knew long ago that such a time of trouble would come, and we paused and thought about it, and then went on, knowing that we were doing right. We cannot do much to help the girls, and can only commend them to the care of the Shepherd who is calling his flock from out of all the nations. We never advise the girls to go contrary to their fathers' wishes. They all need instruction, and are here receiving it. They attend the services, are thoughtful and attentive, conduct their own little prayer-meetings, and lead in prayer. Their petitions are simple and touching.

Many interesting meetings were held in the schoolroom. One evening all listened with marked seriousness to the sermon. After a hymn had been sung, those who desired baptism were requested to come forward, and seven responded. Toda san, who lives on the To-ri, was the first one, then three young men in the school, and then Deguchi san, *our* O Ba san, and U-me-ki-chi, all of whom were soon after baptized, with three others.

It was November when the church was regularly organized and elders and deacons ordained. The scene was an impressive one, and all seemed very thoughtful. An address was made to the elders, deacons, church members and outsiders. The girls chanted the Lord's Prayer in Japanese. Then a hymn was sung, the benediction was pronounced, and the little company dispersed. Thus did another "church in Asia" (Japan) salute their brethren of like faith throughout the world.

Our first little hymn-book in Japanese came to us last summer. It has eighteen hymns, besides the Doxology. The first one, which we sing to "Old Hundred," is "Ye people who on earth do dwell." We have "Rock of ages," "There is a happy land," "Joyfully,

joyfully," "To-day the Saviour calls," and others. But the great favorite is "Jesus loves me." No one who has been associated in any way with the early Japanese church can ever forget that hymn. It has been sung at church, inquiry-meetings, prayer-meetings and Sunday-school. The children love it, and we often hear them singing it as they play about the room. How many first things we have seen in Japan, the beginnings of various changes! How we have welcomed each help as it came! How we have hailed with joy each indication of progress in anything!

Events are pressing rapidly upon us now. Toda was anxious, as soon as he received baptism himself, that friends and neighbors should hear the gospel. So we went one night to his house on the Tori—*Ginza* we call it now, with its foreign-built houses. Chimura Goro held a lantern to light us through the back streets of the city, but on the Ginza no such aid was required. The lights in the houses and the lanterns of the jin-ri-ki-sha men made the scene very animated.

In the upper room of Toda san's house quite a little company had gathered, and among them five women. The men were all in one room, and the women in an adjoining apartment, with the door between opened that they might listen. They did listen, and with some degree of interest, but occasionally would all go away—perhaps to have a smoke.

Toda san's wife is a young, pretty woman, and can read a little English. These women grow old very fast. There were two or three who were only twenty-three or -four years of age, they said, but they looked as though they might be thirty. Their habits of smoking, tea-drinking, and others equally pernicious, cause them to look older than they really are.

Meetings are held in different parts of the city. Chimura san's house is near Shi-ba, and one bitterly cold night we all went over there. The girls begged to go. The way was long and the night dark, but we enjoyed it as we walked along the quiet streets by the light of the lanterns.

The large rooms were thrown together, and candles and lamps gave light, while in the hi-ba-chis the charcoal glowed brightly. A number of the neighbors gathered in to listen to the preaching and join in the singing. All these things are encouraging to us, and we gladly go as we are called from place to place.

But the little schoolhouse grew too small to accommodate the numbers who gathered there on Sunday afternoons; some had to go away. So a large wooden building was erected, and dedicated to the service of God. It is near Ts'kiji, but out of the Concession, and we bought it in the name of a Japanese. The building is low and plain, but neat and cheerful. The platform is covered with a carpet, and has a desk and a little table. The seats are wooden benches, but comfortable. On the broad aisle is matting. There are some mats for old and feeble persons to sit upon if they prefer the Japanese way of sitting.

The dedication of this building to the service of God was an interesting occasion. The house was well filled. An invocation was offered, the Lord's Prayer chanted in Japanese, a missionary made an earnest prayer, and Chimura san read the Scripture lesson. Then one of the oldest missionaries preached a sermon on the text: "They shall be one." The subject was the oneness of believers. All listened, and even children understood how they who believe in Jesus are *one*. Chimura san's servant, Sawa, was baptized. His wife, O Kiyo san, had been baptized some weeks before. Now the whole family are in the church.

We sang "Old Hundred," "America," "Joyfully, joyfully," and our sweet little hymn "Jesus loves me." Soon afterward our Sabbath-school was organized with seventy members.

Who remembers the time when Takejiro, Toichi and his mother stumbled over a few English words and sang "There is a happy land" in the little Japanese house on the corner? And now we have a church-building filled with worshipers and those who come to hear the word. We have also the Gospels and a hymn-book, with some tracts and the *Happy Book*, and also a Sabbath-school.

Oh, Christians at home, it is so little compared to what you have, and yet it seems so much to us! And now indeed "the churches of Asia salute you." They say unto you, "Rejoice and be glad with us; for the Sun which has so long shone over you is rising upon us—not to leave you in darkness, for it shineth night and day, but to be our Sun also."

Christians at home, our little church in Asia salutes you, saying, "*Ohayo!*"—a glad "Good-morning!"

CHAPTER II.

ENO-SHIMA.

"He hath made everything beautiful."

"A LOVELY, happy day." This is an extract from a diary, and the day was the 31st of October, 1874, when O Chiye san and I started on a little trip to Eno-Shima, an island down the coast.

It is one of the "compensations" of missionary-life, if we need any, that our homes are often in beautiful, pleasant lands. There are few missionaries with whom I have been brought into contact who do not find relief from loneliness in the natural beauties around them. The flowers are dear companions in our exile; the sea tells of the power of the Creator in its deep thunderings, and in its soft murmurings whispers stories of love and peace; while the mountains are our grand old friends, symbols of constancy and fidelity. There are many "lovely, happy days" to record.

This one was an autumn day. The maple-leaves were red and glorious in the rich October sunshine, and the familiar road to Fu-ji-sa-wa was even more beautiful than in midsummer. At Fu-ji-sa-wa we turned off the main road to reach the seacoast. The road was narrow, and we had difficulty in passing the frequent trains of packhorses. All around rose little hills still green and fair.

It was only a short journey across the fields in the jin-ri-ki-shas; then a hard pull over the sand brought us within sight and hearing of the glorious Pacific, and before us rose E-no-Shi-ma, a mountain-island clothed in richest green, with the sea thundering at its base, and just enough mist gathering over it to heighten its beauty. At one time, probably, it was entirely separated from the mainland, but gradually a sandy isthmus has been formed, over which people can walk to the island. Its lofty sides are almost perpendicular, with overhanging cliffs. Trees grow over it, affording in places beautiful bowers and shady retreats. It is covered with an almost tropical verdure.

On the island are numerous tea-houses and little open shops where shell-work is kept for sale. The island is dedicated to the goddess *Benten*, who is one of the "happy gods." She ought, at least, to be content with her island, for it is a rarely lovely spot, and a week there passed rapidly away. The hotel was comfortable and quiet, as there are no pilgrims—or very few—at this season of the year.

We had a delightful walk over the island. Up and down stone steps we climbed, often stopping to enjoy the magnificent views of sea and coast and distant mountains. At one point on the road we peeped into a yawning chasm. Numbers of divers passed us, going easily down the steep path, which was so difficult to us.

We climbed carefully over the rocks, gradually making our way to a deep cavern. The roar of the ocean at its entrance was almost deafening. This entrance was a narrow, slippery path along the rocks, which widened by degrees until the road became less dangerous. Within the cave, dimly lighted by tapers, sat an old man, and two little boys acted as our guides. We had to stop often, had once to crawl through a hole, and at the end of this dark, dangerous way we found an idol with tapers burning before it—doubtless one of the representations of Benten, for she is said to have appeared in many forms.

We were glad to get out into the bright daylight once more, and stopped to watch the divers go down in the water and bring up shellfish. We, too, gathered shells on the sandy isthmus, and looked at the shell-work and marine curiosities in the shops. Little screens with figures of men and women, birds and flowers, were pretty, but the natural curiosities were more attractive. Here is found the beautiful glass coral, resembling in texture and appearance finely-spun glass. We are told that it is only to be found here and on the coast of Spain. The calls of the old women at the shops to come and buy were frequent and importunate; we would stop to chat with them, and occasionally buy some of their little things.

We took a kago one day, and went over to see *Dai Butsu*. The road lay along the seashore. The natives were busily engaged in gathering seaweeds. They had long wooden hooks, with which they secured the seaweed as it was washed on the shore. Between the breakers they would run out into the water, sometimes up to their knees. Occasionally a wave would be too quick for them, and they would be well soaked; but as their clothing was very scant, it made little difference to them.

From a little hamlet on the shore we turned off into the country, and went through rice-paddies to Dai Butsu, "the Great Buddha."

DAI BUTSU.

This is a bronze image fifty feet high and well proportioned. It is in a sitting posture, with hands clasped and head bent forward. The features are regular and the forehead bears the round drop in the centre—the peculiar mark of Buddha.

No temple is near the Great Buddha now, and there he sits all alone, looking down with mild, placid countenance on those who go to see him. We went inside of him, walked around him, asked questions about him, bought his picture, and did not go away without turning back to see him, high above everything else in the vicinity, looking down upon us, but with manifest indifference. Near Dai Butsu is *Kamakura*, the ancient capital of Japan, where the great hero Yoritomo lived, and where in a temple his armor, shoes and no-ri-mo-nos are still preserved. The tide was very high, almost covering the isthmus, as we returned to E-no-Shi-ma. The waves came rolling in splendidly, and the walk was exciting.

The next day the rain came down in torrents. It knows how to rain in Japan. But the scenes, even on rainy days, never lose the charm of novelty to me. The straw rain-coats, and the hats which serve some of the people instead of umbrellas, are very peculiar. The rain pours off the roofs of the houses and runs in streams down the gutters, while dogs, ducks and chickens crowd close to the house, looking wet and miserable. We sat in the hotel-entrance and watched the travelers as they passed, until too many sought refuge in the hotel, and we went to our own room. But there was only one cold, rainy day, and E-no-Shi-ma was lovely that first week in November, so that we came back with pleasant remembrances of the island.

Associated with these remembrances is also the memory of another pleasant day the same autumn, spent in some gardens where there was a brilliant display of chrysanthemums. These flower-shows are usual with the Japanese when the chrysanthemums are brightest and most abundant. There were figures dressed in the leaves and flowers, which were very pretty and evinced much taste and skill. Some of them were ancient historic characters, others figures of men, women and children; but the prettiest thing of all was a white bird.

The display of chrysanthemums was magnificent: all colors and all sizes were on exhibition. The beautiful trees, with their rich varied foliage, red, yellow and different shades of green, in some places grouped together and looking like enormous bouquets, formed a scene beautiful beyond description, and one never to be forgotten. One scene was especially gorgeous. We were riding in jin-ri-ki-shas through a long avenue of trees with dark-green leaves, when we passed some red maples. The bright sun shone through the red leaves, producing a most brilliant effect.

These are some of the pleasures that come to us in our mission-homes.

20 *

CHAPTER III.

THE STRAIT GATE AND THE NARROW WAY.

"Because strait is the gate and narrow is the way which leadeth unto life."

AT last the girls came up to the strait gate: they could not walk any longer in the heavenly way without going through it. The time came when they had to choose between obeying the commands of God and yielding to the fear of man. Some of them turned away and went back; for some, the entrance did not seem so difficult; while others waited long without, fearing and trembling and shedding many tears. And all the while the gentle Saviour stood near and said, "Come unto me." "Be not afraid of them that kill the body, and after that have no more that they can do." "Whosoever shall confess me before men, him shall the Son of man also confess before the angels of God." Angels beheld the conflict and rejoiced over each victory, and teachers and Christian friends watched with eager solicitude and constant prayer.

We sent once in the fall for O Chiye san's

father to come and talk about his daughter's baptism. He said that he had no objection himself, but in his department the ya-cu-nins were obliged to send the names of any who received baptism to the general government, and his own daughter's name might cost him his office and means of support; but he promised to give his consent within three months.

At the close of the year I had an earnest talk with O Chiye san about life and its work. She and her father were pleased with the proposition made that she should teach the younger girls their translations, and she took classes after the school began in January. The manuscript copy of the Epistle to the Romans was sent me the first of the year, and Deguchi san copied it carefully.

The first Sabbath of this year (1875) was a beautiful one. Some of the girls offered prayers in the little meeting before church, which at least showed their earnestness in wishing for a blessing. Deguchi san brought several people to church. Two young men were baptized. The services were long, but no one seemed wearied. Every morning of the "week of prayer" found a number of native Christians and those who were interested in religion at the church, and the meetings were all pleasant.

That week Deguchi san went to see our little O Kame san, and found her in trouble. Her brother was sick, and could no longer pay for her tuition and support her in school. Deguchi san found her hard at work. She is such a bright child that we could not bear to give her up, and so we took her back, hoping that some means would be provided for her support. So the winter days passed on with their busy cares.

The first communion-season of the year was on the 18th of January. O Chiye san seemed to feel much her separation from Christian people, and went home sad and crying. She said she feared nothing but the trouble which her baptism might bring upon the family.

Our girls were all troubled. Deguchi san says that woman in Japan has her head down and man has his foot upon her neck. It does seem so. Often in those days, when I saw the young men of the mission-school coming out one after another and being baptized, and yet not one of our girls ready, it seemed as if work for woman here was a hopeless task. Kato san's Michi was one who desired baptism, but she "waited" for her friends.

At last, however, *three* of the girls decided to be baptized. O Shige san, after a long struggle, thought it best to come out boldly as a Christian without her father's permission, which had been angrily refused. It is exceedingly difficult to decide the right in these cases, yet here the responsibility seemed to be lifted away from every one. She was fully persuaded that she was right, and promised bravely to confess the truth if called upon to do so. She and her little sister Nui are faithful, diligent pupils, and have ever been comforts to their teachers. We dreaded losing them from our school, should the father in his anger take them away.

Michi had nothing to fear from her father. The third was our little orphan girl Kame. She is thirteen years old and not advanced in her studies, although learning very fast. There was some hesitancy about admitting her into the church, as she was so young and had been so short a time in school. But she was so anxious, and answered every question so well, that she was baptized with the others. It was touching to see her carrying her *Little Catechism* about with her, that she might study every spare moment.

When O Chiye san heard of the intention of these girls to be baptized, especially of O Shige san's determination to brave her father's displeasure, she seemed very thoughtful and sad. Over and over she said that she feared nothing that her father might do to her personally, but only the trouble she might bring on the family. Yet there was a sore conflict going on in her mind. One day she came to Ro-ku-ban to say that a new baby-girl had come into their family, when a messenger arrived from her house saying that she must go home immediately. She did not return, and Deguchi san went over to see what the trouble was. It seems that she had spoken to her mother about her strong desire to be baptized, and her mother had told her father of it. He was exceedingly angry, and sent for her and forbade her coming to the mission-house any more.

Deguchi san, after reporting these things at home, went again to beg that she might be allowed to see her sick teacher once more. Her father very reluctantly gave his consent, and she came with Deguchi san, crying and sobbing most pitifully. She promised not to give up her faith and trust in God. She was soon sent for. All these things were very trying, and we knew not how it would end. The next day she came running in, panting and almost breathless. Her father was out of the house, and her mother had given her permission to come for a while.

Michi, Shige and Kame were baptized on

the next Sunday. Chiye was here all day, and was very sad. Her mother told her she might come, and she managed to elude her father's vigilance in some way.

The next Sunday another of the pupils, Mashi, and Hara san's wife, with four others, were baptized. In the morning a note came from O Chiye san. She had fully made up her mind to be baptized, but that day she could not get out of the house, as her father was at home. She said that she would rather do the hardest work than to be so bound. "I am bound by an iron chain, which is the will of the father," is an expression she has used.

She came in on Monday, after her final decision was made. Oh what a change! On Friday she was here, her face swollen with weeping and her whole expression one of such sadness that it was painful to see her; on Monday she came into the room, her face beaming with joy, and there has not been a tear in her eye since, I think. She said, "The rain has all gone. The clouds have broken away, and it is light." In the afternoon she came again to be examined previous to baptism. A wild storm of wind and rain was raging. We gathered around the fire in the bedroom. Only four were present, and we listened to her confession of faith. The fifth commandment was particularly dwelt upon. When asked why she would go contrary to her father's wishes in this respect, she said that she felt God's command was higher. She came several times that week, and always seemed strong and happy.

The Sabbath that she was baptized was a cold, stormy Easter day. She stood up alone, and received the water of baptism on her head. For her many a prayer had ascended, to her many an anxious thought had been given, but that day the burden of the joyful song was—

> " 'Tis done! the great transaction's done!
> I am the Lord's, and he is mine;
> He drew me, and I followed on,
> Charmed to obey the voice divine."

There are now fourteen women in the church, and thirty-eight members in all.

No one in her home has said anything to O Chiye san about her baptism. We cannot but think that her father is aware of it. The other children know it, but they are quiet, discreet little things, and say nothing.

O Tama san, little Sudzu's aunt, came one day, and knelt by my bedside and whispered her wish to be baptized. "While you were sick," she said, "I first learned to pray. I knew not whom to ask to make you well, and I turned to the true God." This woman had no opposition to fear from friends at home, and was soon after received into the church. We miss some of the girls who have long been with us. The past few months have been stormy, troubled ones, but now the sun is shining out brightly again, and all are at peace.

What of our little O Ine san? She is growing tall and developing rapidly. She has once or twice expressed to one of her friends in school, or to her mother, her desire to be baptized, but she does not yet seem to have come to the time when she feels that she must decide one way or the other. I tell her mother that I often fear she is too ambitious for Ine, and is crowding her mind. She is anxious that she shall excel in all Japanese accomplishments as well as go on in her foreign studies.

I went with her one day to the "tea-school." Presenting tea to guests and making all the necessary bows and complimentary phrases are such important things for Japanese women that they are taught them as a regular science. The teacher has his pupils to come one by one. There were a number of Japanese present, and we all sat on the floor and watched the little girl as she took the tea from its canister and put it into the tiny tea-pot. The other things were all in a little drawer, and she got them out, then folded the napkin, fanned the charcoal, poured boiling water on the tea, and then presented it in a little cup gracefully to the spectators, who were supposed to be guests. All this was very daintily and nicely done, and we thought the tea-school quite interesting.

Ko-ba-ya-shi san is one who causes me much anxiety. She is out of the more immediate sphere of our influence now, as the family have moved into the country, and she does not attend school. The whole family are exceedingly kind. The father and mother are nice old people, but do not seem favorably inclined toward Christianity. "I imagine," says a missionary friend, "they think the gate is very 'strait' and the way very 'narrow.'" They seem to enjoy much of the pleasures of this life, and care not for any others.

Doubtless those who have just entered the "strait gate," and begun to walk in the "narrow way," will stumble and fall sometimes, but their faces are turned heavenward; and when they rise, it will be to walk on in the same direction. They will wander sometimes, there will be many temptations to turn them aside, and there are many false teachers who will try to lead them astray.

Our girls are learning the tenth chapter of John's Gospel. In their own soft, musical language they repeat the words, "He calleth his own sheep by name and leadeth them out; and the sheep follow him, for they know his voice. And a stranger they will not follow, for they know not the voice of a stranger."

Yes, the sheep know the true Shepherd's voice. False teachers are all around, but we fear not the voice of strangers for our flock, for they know them not. They will not wander long nor far from the shining road along which the Shepherd is leading them, nor go back into the dark mazes of Buddhism, Sintooism or Confucianism, for they have heard the Lord's voice and are following him.

"And I give unto them eternal life, and they shall never perish, neither shall any one pluck them out of my hand." It is in this word that we rest without fear or doubt.

O Chiye san has had more to contend with than the others, so far. Soon after her baptism, she was taken away to Yikosuka, much against her desire. But her aunt came back with her, brought her to our house, and persuaded her father to let her come to school again. This aunt has great influence over her brother, O Chiye san's father, and is a woman of bright intellect. Soon after, without any difficulty, we gained the father's consent to have her come into the house as a teacher-pupil, supporting herself in this way.

And now indeed the clouds have all gone, and our school closed very happily for the summer vacation. Most of the older girls are members of the church, and the little ones believe with childish faith.

On these summer Sabbaths the house is open all day and filled with Japanese, who come to attend service or to talk about our religion. Friends of the girls come, dressed neatly and prettily, to go to the church and Sabbath-school. The Sabbaths are happy days here, and every one is so glad to go to church. The windows and doors are all open, and the pleasant breeze comes in from the sea. Twice a day the people go from the mission-house to the church. At noon the girls have their prayer-meeting. The hymns—Japanese words set to our own familiar tunes—fill the house with music, and it is no uncommon thing to hear the low murmur of prayer.

In June our funny little Toyo of long ago came back to us; she has the same quick, nervous manner as of old, and always makes her presence felt.

Last evening the closing exercises of the school were held in the church. The house was filled. Fathers, mothers and friends came to see and hear the girls, who sang English hymns, and some of the older ones played on the organ. They had recitations and readings and dialogues, and the little ones went through with their exercises in calisthenics. All passed off very successfully, and both natives and foreigners expressed themselves as highly pleased with the appearance and efforts of the school.

So another school-year has closed brightly and hopefully. It has given us great encouragement to go forward, and "woman's work for woman" here is an established fact. We look for still more hopeful results, when many more shall seek the "strait gate" and enter upon the "narrow way."

CHAPTER IV.

A JIN-RI-KI-SHA JOURNEY.

"Every place that the sole of your foot shall tread upon, that have I given you."

WE have been traveling in jin-ri-ki-shas down the Tokaido, from Tokio, the eastern capital, to Saikiyo, or Kiyoto, the western capital. To do this we had to obtain passports from the government, as it is death to foreigners to go beyond certain bounds without permission. Through the kindness of the American resident minister, these passports were obtained without difficulty, and proved an effectual protection to us all through our journey. The road from Tokio to the foot of the Ha-ko-ne Mountains has been described in a previous chapter, and we need not go over that already familiar route.

It took us fifteen days to make the journey of three hundred miles, including all stoppages for rest and the Sabbath. Since we left Mishima, at the foot of the Ha-ko-nes, we have had the same jin-ri-ki-sha men, who have on an average traveled thirty miles a day, stopping to rest once in the morning, then at noon, and once again in the afternoon and at night. These men were exceedingly anxious to go all the way to Kiyoto, and kept up their strength very well, although we should have preferred obtaining fresh men at different stations.

Day after day we followed the road, scarcely turning to the right or the left. It has led us over hot, sandy highways, across three mountain-chains, through pleasant valleys and under grand old trees. We have crossed rivers on flat-boats. Twice have we sailed over an arm of the sea. We have walked, or been carried in ka-gos, over the mountains, enjoying the fresh mountain-air and the beautiful scenery. In these mountains, we are told, there are treasures of gold, silver, copper, lead, quicksilver and coal. We saw carnelians, agates, jasper and crystals. We passed by fields of tobacco, rice and cotton. Some parts of the country seemed to produce but few vegetables. The *sa-to-i-mo* (Japanese "sugar-potato") was abundant. Rice and eggs were usually found, but sometimes even eggs were scarce. We were generally dependent on our own supply of provisions.

The road led us through a number of large

towns. They are very similar to each other and to Tokio, and the houses in Japan are so much alike that every evening, in going into our new hotel, it seemed as if we were entering the very one we had been in the night before; the rooms and the gardens, the servants, the candlesticks, dishes and washbasins, —all seemed the very same.

Some places, however, deserve special mention, and first I must tell of the river Fu-ji. Fu-ji-ya-ma was all covered by mists and clouds when we passed him, and we went directly on to Fu-ji-ka-wa, or the river Fu-ji, which runs near the base of the mountain. Before reaching it we crossed a singular spot to find in this "garden of the world." It seemed to have been the ancient channel of Fu-ji-ka-wa, and was wild and desolate in the extreme. The river at times overflows its banks to the extent of a mile and a half with a rushing torrent, as indicated by the efforts of the natives to protect the embankments by means of huge cobble-stones enclosed in strong bamboo network. Even then, although comparatively small, the river rushed over its rocky bed with so swift a current that we almost feared to cross it. It seemed as though the rowers could scarcely stem the rapid current, but we soon found that, like the Japanese in general, the men were good boatmen, and we were rowed across in safety.

Shidzuoka.—Our noon rest one day was at Shidzuoka, the capital of the province of Suruga. There the old tycoon, Stotsu Bashi, resides. After his defeat in 1868, instead of being put to death or commanded to commit hara-kiri, as was the usual way in old times, he was allowed to go into retirement on his own estate, where he now lives in honorable exile.

In the government school at Shidzuoka a Christian gentleman is engaged in teaching. He gave an interesting account of religious matters there. Twenty-nine persons had been baptized.

Yoshida.—This was the only town where we had trouble in finding a place to sleep. With the shadows growing deeper and deeper about us, we tried one hotel after another. The jin-ri-ki-sha men were wearied with their day's travel, and were sorely in need of rest. Finally, an appeal was made at the police-station. A crowd gathered around the jin-ri-ki-shas. A courteous policeman accompanied us on the search for a lodging-place, but even his entreaties were of no avail.

At last some people offered the use of a

kura (a fire-proof house). There were no windows, and only two holes in the wall to admit the air. In these close, heated quarters the night was passed. The policeman was very polite, and came in the morning with many apologies for the people of the town. He said "'*O ki-no do ku sama*" many times ("Poison to your soul"), and bowed very low as the coolies picked up the jin-ri-ki-sha shafts and trotted off.

Nagoya.—Reaching this city on Saturday morning, we concluded to spend the Sabbath here. The entrance to the hotel was dark and forbidding, but the upper rooms, which were allotted to us, were airy and cheerful. From one room there was a view of a wide street and the entrance to a temple. Dinner was served on one of the small tables; the usual tea and rice were brought, with watermelons for dessert.

Nagoya is a large, important city. Here is one of the *Eigo-gakkos*, or "English schools." The buildings are very fine. Here, too, is a castle, where a prince once lived who just missed a chance of becoming a tycoon. The ya-shi-kis which are passed on the way to the castle were all closed, with the exception of two. The ponderous gates looked as if they had not been moved on their hinges for many a day. After passing a grove we came to a wide road; here the scene was very pretty. In the moat around the castle lotus-flowers were blooming. The castle was more like a real one than any we had hitherto seen. It had a high wall flanked with towers.

There are many temples in Nagoya; among them, the Atsuka temples, near the city, are famous. The streets of the city were wide and clean, and the articles exhibited in the shops were quite tempting. Always, when we stopped to look at anything, a crowd collected, rendering it unpleasant; and when we walked in the temple-grounds, men, women and children followed us.

The people at the hotel gave us nice white-fish for supper. The maids brought in the beds, which were comfortable enough, but the noise of some travelers in a lower room, who seemed to be having a particularly merry time, kept us from sleeping.

Early Sabbath morning we were aroused by the bell ringing and the drum beating in the temple. The worshipers, a large crowd, came pouring through the gates. The hotel-people said they had been to hear a sermon. The day passed quietly. The people talked a little with us, and the children seemed glad to see the foreign ladies, and to get some papers from them, and to be told about the pictures.

The hotel-people said they would be lonely when we left them. They gathered at the entrance as we were starting in the morning to say "*Saionara*," and the landlord waited at the street-corner and bowed low as we passed.

Kame yama.—This is a pretty little town, and as the jin-ri-ki-shas rolled rapidly through the streets the crowd following kept increasing. Children ran after us, laughing and shouting; the babies' heads rolled from side to side; and when the coolies stopped at a hotel, the group presented a singular appearance. From the upper window of our hotel that night we could see the castle and look over a beautiful wooded country.

In the morning the road led us again over mountains, the views of which were glorious. Over one mountain a man was leading some goats. The people did not know what these animals were.

A town near Lake Biwa was our resting-place for the night. Over a bridge across one end of the lake Biwa, which is the largest lake in Japan, the men drew the jin-ri-ki-shas the next morning.

The rain began to come down, and umbrellas and oiled paper had to be taken out for the first time. But it did not rain long. The road was all up hill and very bad. At many places the jin-ri-ki-shas had to be lifted over. One thing which seemed peculiar as we entered Kiyoto was the number of oxen employed as beasts of burden. A bamboo-grove made the road near the city very pleasant.

Will this land ever be thrown open to foreigners? No one can tell, but we hope that some day this may be accomplished. One thing is a source of comfort to the Christian: we can never be out of our Father's kingdom. The Japanese may set their boundaries as they please; we may wander or be in exile anywhere: our feet are in our Father's territory, and we are ever at home. And the land is ours, for the Lord has promised it to his Son, and in him we possess all things. Thus we believe that this fair "Land of the Rising Sun" will be covered with the brightness of the Saviour's glory.

CHAPTER V.

THE TWO CAPITALS IN 1875.

"Paul departed from Athens, and came to Corinth."

THE Western Capital.—August 7, *1875.—* Kiyoto, or Saikiyo, as the people here best like to have it called, is the great religious centre of Japan. It was formerly the residence of the spiritual emperor, or Mikado. It is very different from the city where we dwell. Accustomed to the breezes of open plain and sea, we feel oppressed here by the close surrounding mountains. Yet it is in many respects a far more imposing city than Tokio. Its temples are larger and grander, its pagodas more numerous, its streets wider, and its manufactures more extensive and various. There is a preponderance of dark red in the color of the houses and temples.

The great temple *Choin* is a wonderful building. Everything is on a gigantic scale. The high place (*Kiyomidzu*), from which there is a fine view of the city, is very beautiful with its dense shrubbery and pleasant tea-houses. At one temple we saw an immense bell, said to be one of the largest in the world; it is broken now. Here also was a large image of Buddha.

But the most wonderful thing we have seen in Kiyoto is the temple where Buddha is seated, with his warriors standing around him. In the centre of a long, narrow room is the large gilded image, and on either side of it are five hundred statues of life size, richly gilded, each having three heads and six hands, and all bearing the same gentle, sweet expression which generally characterizes the image of Buddha. It seems as if this were significant of the merciful feature of Buddhism in regard to animal life. We have already noticed the Japanese tenderness toward flies and insects, to kill one of which wantonly or unnecessarily would provoke the anger of their gods. It forms a part of their devotions to release insects from captivity, and in the temple-grounds are venders of insects for that purpose. We saw beetles sold for pieces of cash to such devotees, who doubtless in their prayers asked Buddha to remember their kindness and gentleness.

As a strange commentary, however, on this merciful disposition, it appeared to us as if they would not be loth to slaughter one of us, their white brethren, the hated foreigners, even though they turned aside from the crawling worm or gave glad freedom to an imprisoned insect. Their creed has been so learned that animal food never crosses their lips, because life has to be taken, and yet, with bitter ferocity, they have made their swords to drip with the hearts' blood of Christians, and might be ready to do the same now if the power of the government were only relaxed. To love insects and worms and yet hate a fellow-man is certainly remarkable inconsistency, and presents a wonderful contrast to that religion whose foundation-principle is love—even love for enemies.

Still, as we stood before that image of Buddha attended by his thousand golden-clad warriors, with the light of the declining sun reflected in their almost angelic countenances, we could not help feeling sentiments of awe and veneration; and though Buddhism has many a dark aspect, we came away deeply impressed with the benignity stamped on these beautiful statues, and with something of respect for the faith whose expression they are. A creed is not always to be judged by the life of its professed adherents. Christianity itself, the essence of divine holiness and love, has often been brought into disrepute by the inconsistent lives of its professors; and so charity would teach us that even Confucius and Buddha are grossly misrepresented by their followers, since he may profess to be the upholder of gentleness and mercy who yet would not forbear to take the life of his fellow-man. With these reflections we emerged from this temple of Buddha and his thousand warriors to visit other scenes in this interesting capital of the West.

A great temple in the suburbs of the city was attractive on account of its bamboo-groves. From a point higher than Kiyo-midzu we had a grand view of Kiyoto one evening just as the sun was setting and throwing long rays of golden light over city and mountains. We looked across the roofs of the houses, down over the temples and pagodas to where the hills on every side shut off the surrounding country from our view.

They tell us of the great mountain *Haizen*, in the neighborhood of Kiyoto, where the scenes are wondrously fair and the temples interesting from their great antiquity; also that in the suburbs of the city are many pleasant spots. But our investigations have been confined principally to the city itself. We have watched men painting porcelain and manufacturing the cups and plates which are so celebrated as "Kiyoto-ware." We have examined the fans, vases and children's toys made here in such variety and rich abundance.

Theatre.—Yesterday we went to the Japanese theatre, and were fortunate enough to see the performance of one complete play, a short tragedy. And we may properly notice just here the Japanese theatre as it appears throughout the empire. We have looked into the theatre at Tokio for a few minutes, and we saw this one play at Kiyoto, from which, and from all we have heard about it, we presume that one is the type of all. The performances commence early in the morning, continue through the day with scarcely an interruption, and close at sundown. Theatres are never open at night. The buildings are wooden, barn-like structures, without gilding or ornament save the usual lanterns, colored papers and painted Chinese characters. This theatre at Kiyoto had no galleries, but simply a sloping parquette a little higher in the rear than in the front. The audience was constantly changing, some coming in and some going out, while the performance was going on, and boys went around selling sweetmeats and fruits.

As in the Roscian period, only male actors were on the stage. The chief performers— doubtless the "stars"—came in from the front of the house, and walked on a narrow platform the whole length to the stage, spouting and stalking with majestic tread, all in such stilted style as to be irresistibly comical, although the play was a tragedy and this lofty prologue was to tell of the hero's dire wrongs and how he was to suffer till Justice had wrought her work. The dresses of these actors were more like those represented on vases and in pictures than those of ordinary every-day life, being robes of gorgeous hue, well bespangled and with ample folds.

The play was the usual one of a tyrant usurper, who prospered for a while in his cruel oppressions, but whose evil designs were finally frustrated and the proper heir was restored. The tyrant died by his own hand. He first committed hari-kari, and then cut his own head off. We saw his head falling into a basket. The Japanese are masters of jugglery.

The orchestra was peculiarly Japanese, and most distressing to our ears. It consisted of fife and drum and a kind of flute; but the chief effect was that produced by the pounding of mallets on blocks of wood without regard to melody or tune—at least, so it seemed to us—and we could well dispense with this accessory to the stage. Still, a vigorous blow may properly accompany the tale of a tyrant's acts, and doubtless, to the Japanese ear, there was more of harmony than appeared to our untutored and unappreciative taste. For the play we saw was certainly operatic, and this thumping music was evidently intended to give effect to the sentiments expressed by the actors. The natives relished it, if we did not. When anything peculiarly striking was expressed by an actor, it was accompanied by a corresponding crash from the orchestra and a hissing kind of applause from the spectators.

We saw nothing immoral, or even objectionable, in the play, the audience or any of the surroundings. And thus we may pronounce the theatre in a heathen land as immeasurably superior to that in our Christian country. The adjuncts of a theatre are generally its worst and most injurious features. The bar-room, the questionable company, the mawkish and often false representations of life on the stage itself, and all the dissipating tendencies of the surroundings in our theatres, have brought many a youth to ruin. We may have a pure and classical stage, but there will have to be great changes also in the theatre. None of these adjuncts mentioned are found in this heathen theatre.

The jin-ri-ki-shas of Kiyoto are larger and

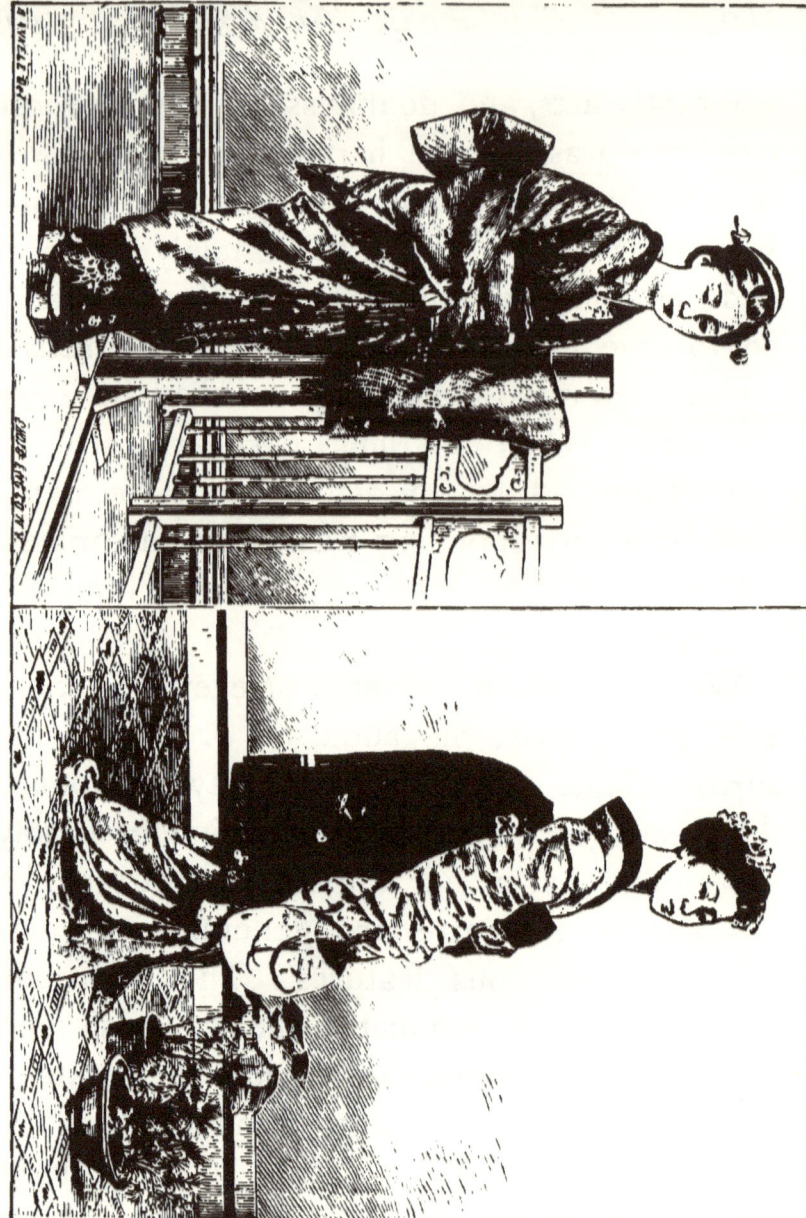

TOKIO WOMAN.

KIOTO WOMAN.

Page 261.

handsomer than those of Tokio. The people look about the same, except that the women let their sashes hang loosely behind instead of looping them up, as in Tokio. The dialect is a little different, but not enough so to trouble us much.

The Eastern Capital.—Monday, Sept. 6, 1875. —We are glad to be at home again. This has been a very lovely day, and Kadzusa's mountains, across the bay, look very tempting.

The mission-house is full of life, for school began last Wednesday. In the morning the day-scholars come over the fields, bright and happy, to begin the work of the day. There is usually a line of children waiting on the stairs, with bright faces peeping over the banisters.

The two weeks which intervened between the homecoming and the beginning of school passed away rapidly. Almost every afternoon, when the heat of the day was over, jin-ri-ki-shas were called for, and we made a little journey into the city and visited a number of the scholars at their homes.

The Tokio of to-day is very different from the Yedo of old. It is a great city, and contains much that is interesting. The State government is all divided into departments, or *shius*. There is the finance department, the naval, the military, the agricultural, the religious, the engineering, mining, etc., etc. All, or almost all, of these have their headquarters in Tokio. Although some of these departments are located in old temples, yet many of the buildings are of foreign style, and foreigners are employed largely in them. A new building for the *Kai sei gakko*, or government school, has been erected, and one for the normal school for girls is now going up.

The police-force of the city is large and effective. The post-office department is finely organized, and letters are faithfully delivered at the door. The streets are named and the houses numbered.

The Ginza differs materially from the old To-ri. The stores are built in European style and filled with foreign articles, as well as with everything that a Japanese can want. All over the city, indeed, foreign vegetables and fruits of all kinds may be found. Butchers and bakers are numerous, and bread and meat are no longer scarce, as they were a few years ago. Milk is sold at tolerably reasonable rates, and ice can be procured in any quantity on the Ginza.

Coaches and jin-ri-ki-shas roll along the streets. Many of the men wear foreign clothes. No two-sworded men are seen any longer, and the Mikado goes about among the people, not fearing to show his face. And one of the most remarkable things to be noticed is the utter absence of tramps and beggars. Beggary was once a system, but now it has been abolished, and the beggars have been put to work. Many have been sent to Yeso, and others are employed in the factories.

Missionaries of different countries and societies have their homes here. Some are allowed to live outside the Concession by accepting a position as teachers under the care of a Japanese, and these missionaries and teachers are permitted to hold meetings in their own houses.

The Japanese women are not all the painted, soulless dolls of old Japan; there are now among them some educated, intelligent women. As fathers see their daughters learning and becoming good, wise women; as the educated young men seek wives among the girls who have been taught in the schools, and intelligent women have the care and training of children, and boys no longer despise their mothers, and husbands learn to trust their wives—the family relations will all be changed, and the power of pure womanhood will be felt in the land.

It is pleasant sometimes to take a mere

surface-glance—to go to the little houses when the slides are drawn back in the late summer afternoons, and the little glass ornaments are tinkling musically, and the wind is gently stirring the flowers of the little garden, and to look at the pretty pictures of Japanese life which are unconsciously shown to us.

Thus we have been visiting the scholars in their homes, into many of which the teachers were warmly welcomed. We sat on the mats, drank tea, and talked about the school and the church, and how the little ones were learning. At one house we were treated with great ceremony. We were conducted into the best room of the large house, and all the family gathered in. They told us that the children were anxious to begin school again, and when we went away they loaded us with fruit.

All this is real, unaffected kindness on their part, but the making our visit a thing of so much ceremony prevents us from going to visit them in a friendly, social way as often as we should like. Such overwhelming attentions are irksome to us, and must be burdensome to them. And when this practice is carried to such an extent as it is in this country, it must interfere with informal neighborly visiting.

O Sen san's father is Deguchi san's brother.

He is an officer, and lives near the Ginza, in a foreign house. When we went to see the family, the room where we were entertained had doors and windows, a carpet, tables and chairs. He entertained us so well and kept us so long that the greater part of an hour was spent there in looking at books and photographs, and in talking about Japan and America.

One lovely summer day we went to see O Shige san. Her father has a beautiful home in the suburbs. We pass the high place *Kudan* to get to it. The light wooden house, with the slides all drawn back to admit the air, looked very charming, embowered in the green shrubbery. They have a fine garden, which the master of the house showed with much pride, while he told of contemplated improvements. He has five daughters, of whom Shige is the eldest. The third one, Fu-sa, is a fine-looking child. There is a little new baby, a grandmother and the young-looking, gentle mother. The children in the garden and the neat, clean house made a pretty picture, and we lingered there until warned by the gathering darkness that it was time to go home.

In brief description we have had before us the two great capitals of Japan, the Western still submerged in complete heathenism and entirely unaffected by foreign influence, while the other has already undergone great changes from the introduction of foreign science, and also, in some measure, from the influence of the gospel of our Lord. And enough is manifest to assure us of the future blessed results of that gospel, and to inspire a hope that this same glorious truth may soon rise upon Kiyoto's temples and pagodas, until one wave of light may illumine the whole land, from Tokio to the Western capital, down to Nagasaki in the southern extremity, and that the light of the knowledge of God may penetrate into every heart.

CHAPTER VI.

"THE POOR HAVE THE GOSPEL PREACHED TO THEM."

> "I love to tell the story:
> 'Tis pleasant to repeat
> What seems, each time I tell it,
> More wonderfully sweet.
> I love to tell the story,
> For some have never heard
> The message of salvation
> From God's own holy word."

WE have long waited for the time to come when we might go among the poor and lowly and speak to the *people*. A peculiar phase of missionary-life in Japan is that we began our work among the upper classes and only gradually came to the lower, while in most mission-fields labor is chiefly confined to the poor. The unoccupied Samurai, looking about for something to do or some means of support, came to us for instruction, and to the merchant class we easily gained access, but until now we have been unable to work freely among the lower classes.

The poor people are ignorant and timid, and therefore superstitious and more under the power of the priests. How often, when reading the New Testament in school, have we been struck with the frequent recurrence of the words, "The chief priests and the elders"! "Who were Christ's most bitter enemies when on earth?" I asked a Japanese girl one day. "The priests," she answered. "And who now are the most bitter opponents of Christianity in this land?" "The priests," was the quick reply. It is even so: the false teachers hate the truth. But now a door is open to the poor, and we can go to them. Blessed, happy work we find it.

Deguchi san is regularly employed as a Bible-reader. She is the first one among the women of Tokio, and is an invaluable assistant. She has a wonderful gift in speaking to children. Not long ago a jin-ri-ki-sha man was baptized with his old mother, Hisa. This old woman is also employed as an assistant in the missionary-work, and since August we have been holding meetings at her house on Thursday of every week. The house is in a narrow street (*Gen-ske-cho*) on the way to Shi-ba. She gathers in the neighboring women and children, and we read the Scriptures and sing. All enjoy "*Jesu ware no aisu*" ("Jesus loves me"), and the children like to sing it every time we meet. We have been reading the

Gospel of Matthew through, in course, at these meetings. The women listen eagerly. How I wish some at home who are interested in our work here could look in upon us at Gen-ske-cho! We all sit on the floor. Old Hisa has the charcoal in the hi-ba-chis bright and glowing these cold winter days. Those who have books open them and read, then listen while others are reading.

The people are usually very quiet and orderly, but sometimes old Hisa disturbs us a little by distributing cups of tea in the midst of the talking, or some one knocks down a screen or slide. Japanese houses are exceedingly frail structures, and it is rather dangerous for a paper screen or slide to fall into a hi-ba-chi. But old Hisa is learning not to present tea until the lesson is over, and foreigners are becoming more accustomed to the slides.

One of the most interesting features of our work this winter has been the teaching of the gospel to the blind a-mas. One or two heard the word and told the joyful news to others, and a deep interest was awakened in their hearts. Old Hisa takes her copies of the Gospels and teaches them. They repeat the words after her, and thus learn large portions of the Scriptures. There are always some of them at our meetings in Gen-ske-cho. Some of them begged one afternoon that a meeting expressly for them might be held the next Saturday, and when the petition was granted one clapped his hands for joy.

So, on Saturday, Hisa and I went. An upper room, to which we climbed by a steep, narrow stairway, was filled with blind men. The sunshine poured in, but all was darkness to them. Yet one has said, "I am glad I am blind; for if I had seen, I might not have cared for God." They wanted to sing, and all knew "Jesus loves me." We sang that and "Joyfully, joyfully," repeating each line many times, so that they would remember it. They learned also a little prayer, and all were very happy.

In earth's sweetest music there is often something that strikes painfully, a discord somewhere—not in the music itself, perhaps, but in our hearts or in the misery and suffering around us. But to those whose ears are opened to the sound of heavenly harmonies, blind men, singing even in harsh, discordant voices, make sweeter music than any which earth's grandest composer ever conceived. It is the beginning of the "new song"—the song which we can always hear as we listen to these untutored, often unpleasant, voices singing the praises of our King.

It is not at Gen-ske-cho only that the poor

have the gospel preached to them. There are preaching-places in various parts of the city, where many gather in.

But before this year closes I must go back to our home-school and take careful note of what we are doing at Ro-ku-ban. Our faithful servant, Umekichi, left our house to go into a book-store. Two girls who wanted to study, but could not afford to pay their tuition, were taken in his stead. Their names were Hana and Shidzu. They soon learned the light duties required of them, and made good progress in their studies. But they did not remain in school very long. O Shidzu san was sent for one evening: her mother was sick. She stayed away a little while, and came back, but was soon sent for a second time. At last Deguchi san said she was going to be married, and brought another girl, Iseki Mitsuye, in her place. Then O Hana san's mother came and said that her daughter's uncle was insane, and they wanted her to come and take care of him. So another one, Rin, came in her place. But O Shidzu san was not married very soon, nor did O Hana san go to take care of her crazy uncle.

Another girl, O Moto san, from the northern provinces, came to school. She was an interesting pupil, and talked about going back to her country and taking the Bible to her people. Then she stopped coming, and sent word that her grandmother was sick. But the old lady was only *yakamashi*—noisy and troublesome at home. She objected so seriously to the girl's going to the school that the family had no peace, and so O Moto san had to give up her studies.

All these things are very trying, but we meet such constantly in our dealings with this people. We can all echo the prayer of one of our missionaries, offered at a late prayer-meeting: "Cleanse this people from the great national sin of hypocrisy." Oh, if they would only speak the truth!

We have been through many scenes of suffering and distress this fall. The first sick one to whom we were called was O Kame san's brother. For days he lay on his pallet, bloated with dropsy and scarcely able to speak. Once we thought him dying. The Japanese doctor said that he could not live through the day. O Kame san was very much distressed. "He does not believe; he cannot be saved," she said. But the missionary doctor came in, and under his care the patient has been recovering.

Other cases of sickness occurred. O Chiye san's mother has suffered much and long. One day I sat down beside her and said,

"Where do you go in your sickness and trouble? You have many gods, but to which do you pray now?"—"Alas!" she said, using the expressive Japanese *dogu*, "there are many, but I know not to which to go."

Then O Shige san, who always seemed so strong and well, was prostrated by serious lung-disease, and has been ill all the winter, although remaining at Ro-ku-ban to have the care of the foreign physician. So we have had a sick one in our own home. It has taught the other girls to be quiet and tender, thoughtful and prayerful. They are very kind to each other, and want to do what is right.

We have been uneasy about O Shige san, but have spoken often of her fitness to go, should the Lord call her home. She is very patient. One day she said, "I have had such a happy dream! I thought I was in church again with all the girls." Often since she has been better I have seen her with the Bible in her hands, and have gone to her with Philip's question: "Understandest thou what thou readest?" and have stopped to explain those things which were puzzling to her. This is a time of unusually severe illness and depression. Thus it often is in our journey to our heavenly home. We walk through scenes of suffering, and, like our Saviour, become "acquainted with grief."

It is astonishing with what tenacity the Japanese cling to life. The foreign physicians say that they do not suffer in surgical operations as we do: their nervous system is not so sensitive. A wound heals more quickly in a Japanese than in a foreigner—whether owing to their more simple way of living or not, we cannot say.

Eye- and skin-diseases are the ones which physicians are mostly called upon to treat. Consumption is common. Small-pox formerly raged as a fearful scourge, but now the people are required to be vaccinated, and measures are taken to prevent its spread. One peculiar disease is the *kake*, which makes its appearance in the lower limbs generally, causing much suffering, and often death. It is not yet well understood by foreign physicians, but is supposed to be a sort of granulation of the nervous marrow.

The school has been large and well attended this session. There has not been the constant change of pupils to contend with, as before. The most advanced class in Japanese have a scientific book to read, and the younger children have the *Second Reader* of the normal school. In English the older girls are reading physical geography and first lessons in rhetoric, besides spelling, etc. The second class have studied the *Universal History*, with spelling, reading and geography. The third class have had the *Second Reader*, *Table-Book* and *Elementary Geography*, and the little children are in the *Primer*.

From morning until night the mission-house is filled with Japanese. First they meet in the school for worship, reading a few verses, singing Christian hymns and uniting in prayer. Then the lessons of the day go on until noon. After the noon rest the whole school assembles for the Bible lesson and the calling of the roll. Next come the Japanese, Chinese and translation lessons. And so the busy, happy days go on.

Christmas.—Before Christmas the Japanese ornamented the church beautifully with long wreaths of evergreen, oranges and flowers, and had a tree filled with Japanese toys. In connection with the Christmas festival was the Sunday-school anniversary, and the classes had banners and designs. Each scholar of every class had an appropriate verse. It was pleasant to see the classes coming in with their banners, singing as they took their places. We feel that the Sunday-school army is gathering here in Japan. May all these youthful soldiers fight the battle well!

Dec. 31st.—The last night of the old year

has come. It has been a year of great progress in the mission-work. To-night, as its scenes come up before us, and we remember the many missionaries who are laboring in Japan, the many churches and preaching-places in this and the other open ports, the multitudes who hear the preached word and the numbers who have received the baptismal water on their heads in the name of the Father, the Son and the Holy Ghost,—memory takes us back to a bright October Sabbath of seven years ago, when in all the region round about Tokio there were only three Christians, and those foreigners.

From more than one mission-house, in the mornings and evenings, prayers and hymns of praise now ascend. Women and girls in all parts of Tokio, Yokohama, Kobe, Osaca, and even lately in Kiyoto, are being taught not only secular knowledge, but without hindrance are being trained for the service of God.

All this, and more, we have seen, and again memory goes back to the time when O Hama san came to read the *First Reader*, and when with a few girls we read and talked of the story of the "loaves and fishes." Much has been done, and hath not God wrought it all? And that which is brightest of all is that of late it may be said, "The poor have the gospel preached unto them." The blind men (*a-mas*) are receiving spiritual sight, and the coolies are beginning to recognize in Christ the Friend of the lowliest. What a glorious thing for the poor is the gospel of Jesus!

CHAPTER VII.

COMING INTO THE KINGDOM.

> "With his blood the Lord hath bought them,
> When they knew him not he sought them,
> And from all their wanderings brought them:
> His the praise alone."

IN a meeting at Gen-ske-cho the other day our chapter was the fourth of Matthew's Gospel, and the blind men were particularly interested in the verse beginning, "And Jesus went about all Galilee, teaching in their synagogues, and preaching the gospel of the kingdom." We have thought and talked a great deal about the kingdom of heaven lately. It seems very near, and it is such joyous work to point the way thither.

Our girls are growing in knowledge and in grace. They keep up their Sabbath noon prayer-meetings, and many an earnest prayer ascends from their lips to the true God. They regularly attend the Bible classes, and find the Book ever more wonderful and interesting. We close our school-week by a prayer-meeting, to which the women of the church come. We are now reading Mark, our first Gospel.

The church services are well attended, and the Sabbath-school is large. Most of the older girls have classes. Many women are interested, and we are praying and working for them. We find the influence of the Holy Spirit among us, and all speak and pray with a power never felt before.

On the bright Sabbath which closed the month of October last year (1875) some old friends came to Ro-ku-ban. They were Takejiro, with the woman Hayashi and her two neatly-dressed, polite little boys, Toichiro and Saijiro; the latter was the baby of six years ago. His black eyes have lost none of their sparkle, and I never look into them as they meet mine with such a fearless gaze without thinking of the day when we put him in the chair and he told me to "go away quickly."

We rejoiced to see this mother coming Sunday after Sunday, sometimes with one and sometimes with both of the little boys. She listened eagerly to the preaching, and her interest seemed to increase. Deguchi san and I went to see her in her home on Ginza. We read the third chapter of John, and when Deguchi san told her that special prayer had been offered for her she seemed much gratified. Soon after, she expressed her desire to be admitted into the full communion of the church. She was the very first woman taught in Tokio. We are all glad to have her with us.

Much snow fell in Tokio the first of the year (1876). It lay upon the ground for two whole days, and weighed down the fir trees. After the storm I went to old Hisa's house to see about gathering the women together for their meeting, but we cannot do anything here for fifteen days at the New Year's holidays. Every one is busy for one week making preparations for the festival, and after that they must have a " play " or " rest " for another week. Only the jin-ri-ki-ya's boy was at home. The jin-ri-ki-ya has not been doing well lately, and the burden of the support of this little child falls on his grandmother. The old woman had gone out into the country.

Just at the door, as I was going away, I met Tomi, Hisa's daughter, a pale, sad young woman, who has been thinking seriously on the good way, but has not been able to come to any definite conclusion. She asked me to go to see a woman who has been attending the services regularly. She is the second wife of a *kutsuya*, or cobbler, and has a little stepdaughter. We made our way carefully down an alley, the melted snow dropping from the roofs of the houses.

The kutsuya, who was baptized the next Sunday, has a very small house. The little room into which we were taken was about six feet square. An almost perpendicular ladder led to one above, apparently of the same size. The kitchen in front was about three feet in width, and that was the extent of the house.

The kutsuya, his wife and child, two neighbors, Tomi and myself quite filled up the lower room. One of the women was very old. "O Ba san," she was asked, "do you find this world a very happy place?" "Alas, no!" she said; "there are many cares and troubles." "O Ba san," said the kutsuya, "you are growing old. You must attend to these things now, for it is dangerous to delay." Then we talked for a time, sang our little hymn, and came away. We talked to-night at home about the meeting. This O Ba san is a hairdresser, and usually can be taught only at night. The kutsuya's wife is like Tomi—only "almost persuaded." Old Hisa thinks she is not kind to her little girl, and that keeps her from coming out decidedly.

The old woman is in trouble. Her son, the jin-ri-ki-ya, has run away; and when she had come home from the country with a "glad heart" because the people had listened to her teachings, it was to have this unpleasant news to meet her. And just now, after the other girls had gone to bed, O Michi san came, crying and sobbing, to tell me that her father had been put in prison. This is all she has heard, and we can learn nothing more to-night.

A number of days have passed away since the meeting at the kutsuya's. The fathers of two of our girls were baptized not long ago. One of our scholars, who lives in the country, is very anxious to have some one go to her home to teach her parents.

We are much interested in three women from *Sannai Cho*, or Sannai "street," who have been coming without interruption to church and prayer-meeting. I went with Deguchi san to see them one day. They are mother and daughters. With them was a woman from a distance who "wants to believe," they said. It was a long time before we could get them quiet enough to sit down and listen to a chapter and have their lesson in the catechism. The mother and one daughter answered their questions very well. This little book, beginning, "Who made you?—God," has been invaluable to us since its translation.

The wife of old Sa-sa-ki, a Christian man,

is another woman whom we have much in our thoughts. We went to Sa-sa-ki's house one day, and found him lying on his futon coughing dreadfully. The wife came and sat beside us, and listened as we read of the coming of Christ and the happy entrance of the righteous into bliss. The woman listened and assented, but with her it was the old story of not having the time to go to church.

One day O Yasu san told of an old woman who went to Gen-ske-cho to hear the new doctrine. She had long felt the burden of her sins, and had tried to find peace by going on pilgrimage or in one doctrine after another of Buddhism or Sintooism. She spoke to one of her neighbors of her long struggles and want of success in finding peace, and the neighbor told her of our meetings at Gen-ske-cho, and she went there. O Yasu san said of her, "Such a happy O Ba san!"

"If some one were to go all through this country and proclaim pardon for sin, would not many hear with joy?" asked a missionary of a Japanese Christian one day. "Oh *yes!*" was the answer; and I believe it from my heart.

Old Hisa and I went to see this O Ba san one day. She lives in a little room back of a store. She said there was not room to turn around, and indeed we three nearly filled it as we sat around the hi-ba-chi. We read the parable of the Ten Virgins. The woman told us that she could not understand the Bible very well when she read it alone, and we explained the parable to her as we could. She manifested a deep and tender interest in what was said, and we left her trusting that she had indeed tasted of the true happiness.

Deguchi san's old mother and the wife of her brother are among those who wish to be baptized, and also two of our girls, Mitsuye and Rin. Thus the work ever grows in interest, and those who are working seem to have new strength imparted to them.

The Christian girls come, and we talk of what we have seen and heard of the progress of the gospel in this land, and of how one and another has received it into his or her heart, and thus become an "heir" of the "kingdom." Prayers go up for one who is penitent, or for another who is "halting between two opinions," or for one who is wandering just a little from the path in which she began to walk, or for those who are in affliction and distress. "Praying and working—working and praying"—this is the watchword.

April.—A number of the women for whom we have been praying this winter have been baptized. Among them are Ha-ya-shi san, Deguchi san's old mother, and her sister-in-law Honda san, Sa-sa-ki's wife, who has found time to come to church, the kutsuya's wife and Tomi, whose doubts have all disappeared, with Mitsuye and Rin, our own two girls, the three Sannai cho women and the wife of Umekichi, formerly our servant. The O Ba san did not appear.

Many sightless ones (*a-mas*) have been led by the hand to the altar and felt the baptismal water on their heads. How touching is it to see these blind ones coming forward rejoicing in the hope that the eyes of their understanding have been opened, that they might behold the glory of the Lord in the face of Jesus Christ! Who can help thinking of the story of the blind Bartimeus? and the quaint verses of the old hymn always recur to me when I see them:

> "Oh, methinks I hear him praising,
> Publishing to all around,
> Friends, is not my case amazing?
> What a Saviour I have found!
>
> Oh that all the blind but knew him,
> And would be advised by me!
> Surely they would hasten to him:
> He would cause them all to see!"

Some of the most touching prayers have been offered for Kato san in prison; for it was too true that he was put in prison. He is an editor, and used some expressions in his paper which gave offence to the government. Michi tried one day to get blankets and a Bible to him, that he might suffer less from the cold, and hoping that as he had the time, so he might have the inclination, to read the Book, but she did not succeed. Every cold day, or when the wind of winter whistles around the house at night, she is greatly distressed for her father, and they all pray that he may call to mind all that he has read and heard of Christ and his word, and be converted—yes, find the way into the kingdom, even in his prison-cell.

"Ah yes, O Ba san!" This is an answer to a question about America from an old woman at Gen-ske-cho. "My country is a pleasant country, but it is a great distance away. It would take a long time to go there, and more money than you can ever get. But there is a better country which you may reach without going from this room, and without money. The sick and the poor and the little child may enter this country. It is the kingdom of heaven. God is the King. In it the sun is ever shining. In it you will find all your wants supplied. 'Let him that is athirst come.'"

CHAPTER VIII.

"OUR FATHER WHICH ART IN HEAVEN."

"And they spake the language of Canaan."

WHO knows anything about Fridays at Ro-ku-ban? Our girls enjoy them, for they like the sewing and "declamations," as they call their recitations on that day. O Michi san helps the little ones with their patchwork, and the other girls do fancy-work. In the afternoon they all assemble in the schoolroom, and read and recite in English and Japanese. Sometimes they have dialogues, and always some have compositions. Then, when the exercises are over, the report for the week is read, and after singing the little ones go away, and the elder girls, with the women, remain to their prayer-meeting. In the evening, while the winter wind is howling around the house and the waves are dashing against the breakwater, the fire is kindled in the grate of a room not often used, where we can be undisturbed, and the lamp is placed on the table. Then the two women give their reports of work during the week. Old Hisa has taught the blind men every day. Last week she was out in the country two days; reports that the people heard joyfully.

We are reading, on Friday evenings, parts of the book of Leviticus. Only the older girls have joined the class, and the lessons are exceedingly pleasant to us all, and very profitable. The voluntary offering of the best of the flock—the "male without blemish"—gives the girls clear ideas in regard to the Lamb of God, who offered himself a sacrifice for us, and shows them how they must give up their best to God.

The man standing with his hand on the victim's head leads them better to understand the meaning of the words, "Laying our sins on Jesus." The oblations, with the incense and the sweet-smelling savor that went up to the Lord, show them how to present their bodies a sacrifice to God "without hypocrisy," and with faith, peace and love. There also do they learn of the high priest going up with clean linen robes to offer his sacrifices, and they read of the fire ever burning on the altar and of the terrible leprosy, the type of sin. (Deguchi san says there are leper-villages in Japan.)

Thus the girls are learning more and more of the heavenly language, and are being strengthened to walk in the heavenly way. It is wonderful what a rest there is in teaching the Bible. These lessons always come after a week of toil in the schoolroom. We go to them wearied almost to exhaustion, and come from them strong and triumphant as those who have been drinking from a deep well of life-giving water.

Thursday, Feb. 24, 1876.—Our lesson at Gen-ske-cho this afternoon was on the latter part of the sixth chapter of Matthew. The women listened very attentively, but at times there comes such a feeling of helplessness in the effort to teach them! So many come only once or twice, and we see them no more. What shall we say to such? They understand so little of the language of the kingdom, but this wonderful Sermon on the Mount gives us the first letter of the heavenly alphabet, the very first word of the heavenly language. Jesus spoke to multitudes such as these—weary, worn, sinful, ignorant people. He spoke to them of God, and what words did he use? "Your Father," "our Father," "the Father."

Let us look at some of these verses more carefully than ever before, and read as though we saw them for the first time:

"Take heed that ye do not your alms before men, to be seen of them: otherwise ye have no reward of your Father which is in heaven." What do these heathen women know of anything done without thought of honor from men? What do they know of the Father who seeth in secret, and who will reward openly?

"But thou, when thou prayest, enter into thy closet; and when thou hast shut thy door, pray to thy Father which is in secret." *Their* shrines are in the kitchen or in the busiest corners of the house, and while they pray busy work and idle talk are going on all around them. They pray "standing" in the temples, where the multitudes who throng them can see their devotions, prostrations and counting of beads. It is well to take just the words that the Lord Jesus uses and give them to the people, for they can understand them without note or comment.

"Lay not up for yourselves treasures upon earth, where moth and rust doth corrupt, and where thieves break through and steal. But lay up for yourselves treasures in heaven, where neither moth nor rust do corrupt, and where thieves do not break through nor steal. For where your treasure is, there will your heart be also." "Take no thought, saying, What shall we eat, or what shall we drink, or wherewithal shall we be clothed? Your heavenly Father knoweth that ye have need of all these things. But seek ye first the kingdom of God and his righteousness, and all these things shall be added unto you." "And after this manner pray ye; Our Father which art in heaven, hallowed be thy name. Thy kingdom come, thy will be done on earth as it is in heaven. Give us this day our daily bread. And forgive us our debts as we forgive our debtors. And lead us not into temptation, but deliver us from evil. For thine is the kingdom, and the power, and the glory, for ever. Amen." This is what the women at Gen-ske-cho are learning. We speak such words as these to them, and they repeat them over and over again; and this is *seed-sowing*—a different work from the care of growing, ripening grain.

Our children at home are learning for their evening Bible lesson the twelfth chapter of Luke's Gospel. They commit a few verses to memory each day, and we pray that these words may be written upon their hearts for ever. In the very first verse they learn, "Beware ye of the leaven of the Pharisees, which is hypocrisy." They *are* learning to beware of it, and to hate lying. Thus is the seed planted in their minds, and we pray that even if not now, while we are so anxiously watching, yet in the years to come, it may spring up and bear fruit.

One day, Mashi, Shi-ge, Nui, Kame, Rin and I went by invitation to spend the afternoon at Willow Island, Mr. H.'s place, on the other side of the river. The girls got into the boat on the little lake, and their merry laughter seemed to accord with the joyousness and beauty of everything around. We went to see plum-blossoms and drink plum-tea, and we had sweetmeats and enjoyed the garden. As I stood upon the mound and looked down upon the flowers, the pond, the island and the boat laden with the girls in their bright sashes and hairpins, one happy thought filled my heart: They are *Christians;* they know their Father's name, and know, too, that all enjoyment comes from him.

"In my Father's house are many mansions." We want to lead many of the women to their Father's house. It is not a hard message to deliver with which those who are "sent" are burdened—simply this: "You have a Father in heaven. He it is who has been causing his sun to shine on you. He has been feeding and clothing you. You have wandered away from his house. Now he is calling you to come back. The way is through the Son. Come to Jesus!"

Much of the preceding consists of extracts from journals kept during the last winter—records of seed-sowing. The precious seed will fall by the wayside or into stony places, and some be choked with thorns, but much will fall into good ground, and we are commanded to go on sowing without fear or doubt.

I have seen O I-ne san's mother lately. The family have lost money in various ways, and have moved from the house where we first saw them. O I-ne san does not yet decide to follow the example of her school-friends in becoming a member of the visible Church. I often wonder if the first little blade which I saw peeping out after one year of waiting is going to be all choked up by weeds. But we will hope not so, and pray that she and her mother, my first friends in Tokio, will yet become true disciples of Christ.

O I-ne san shows the result of her careful training. She is exceedingly dignified in manner, and in her studies is far ahead of most girls of her age at home. Her mother may well be proud of this her only child, and we can only pray that they will both learn to say from the heart, "Our Father," and then carry the good news to O-ji.

CHAPTER IX.

LITTLE CHILDREN.

" Little children, little children,
Who love their Redeemer,
Are the jewels, precious jewels,
His loved and his own."

JAPANESE babies always seem to me the most comical little mortals imaginable. We see hundreds of them in the streets, carried on the backs of their child nurses, some of whom do not appear much larger than the babies, so that the effect is of one child with two heads. These babies are fastened into the outer garments of their nurses in such a way as to leave only the heads exposed if they are very small, but if they are large enough to make free use of their hands desirable, the arms are left free. The poor little heads are shaved, with the exception of small patches of hair, and are often covered with loathsome sores.

The young nurses play ball or battledore and shuttlecock with apparent unconcern as to the fate of the babies. It is seldom that any accident occurs, but occasionally a child will roll off from the back of its nurse. Then we know whether a Japanese baby can cry or not. It always appears to us a fertile cause of weak eyes in after-life that the head of a little infant is left unsupported and its eyes are exposed to a strong light. It must also be injurious to the child who acts as nurse to have a heavy baby strapped on her back, thus causing habitual stooping.

Yet it seems to me that babies have very good care taken of them. They are amused by gaudy toys, rattles and bells when awake, and have little mosquito-nets to protect them from insects while they sleep. Indeed, they are a contented race, and accept as a matter of course what does not please them.

Once a young mother showed us her baby's wardrobe. Its best robes were of crape and silk, all of large figures and with wide, flowing sleeves made after the same pattern as its mother's garments. For ordinary wear the baby had short dresses made of bright red and yellow cloth. For ornaments the babies have square patches of red, green or embroidered cloth put upon their backs. They wear little colored bibs, and when the weather is cold, red crape caps with cloaks much like the dresses. Then they have their bags containing amulets on their backs. When they are old enough just to toddle around they have bells fastened to them, so that the mother may know where they are. The principal dangers by accident to which they are liable are falling into hi-ba-chis or upsetting tea-kettles.

I have heard somewhere of a difference of ceremony observed at the birth of a boy-baby and a girl: the little boy is raised and the girl lowered, in token of superior or inferior position. But I have never myself noticed any difference in their treatment, and great care is taken even of sickly or deformed infants. The Japanese are not like their neighbors, who desert their blind, deformed or diseased infants.

Some girls who were in our school had a little blind sister. The mother was most devoted to this baby, nursing it continually, and hailing gladly every symptom of increased strength, for the child was very delicate. She brought her here once, dressed in most gorgeous robes, and the little thing laughed and seemed very happy. At last it learned how to raise its little hands and say, "*Takai! takai!*" ("So high! so high!"), and all were delighted. We learned much of the care and devotion of a Japanese mother in watching this one, with her poor blind baby.

MOTHER AND CHILD.

Page 295.

The first baby I noticed specially was the child of our servants. The mother performed her daily tasks with the baby on her back. It died suddenly one night. The father carried the little body away. They cried a great deal at first, but soon seemed to forget it. I watched the mother at her work, and wondered if she missed the "little hindering thing." But we could not talk about it, for at that time we did not understand each other's language. Then another baby came. They called her Kane ("money"). Little Miss Money was plump and strong, and grew nicely. She learned to walk and to sing "Jesus loves me." But neither did her little feet press the sod of God's footstool very long, for she too died after much suffering.

Another very little child whom I have known was a brother of O Yo san, one of the younger scholars. He was a fine-looking, healthy boy until a year old. He always had a smile for the foreign lady who went to the house. But he began to droop and to suffer with his head. All that was possible was done for him, but one day the baby closed his eyes, and his sufferings were over. The mother was much distressed, for the father was in America and had never seen his boy.

Doubtless the baby-spirits are safe. But

we are glad to have these little ones, children of Christian parents, brought into the church by baptism. One of the first babies baptized was our Umekichi's little daughter. She is a nervous child, full of life and play, with a comical, screwed-up little face, yet very winning withal, and a great pet with us. She wears a little bell, and when she is awake it keeps up a constant tinkling.

She has been taught to say, "Good-bye, baby," in English, and when she wants anything says these words, so as to obtain her wishes. She imitates everything she sees, sits and plays on the parlor-organ, and sings like a foreigner. She gives the calls of peddlers and sellers of fish and vegetables, takes a basket and goes around pretending to sell things, saying that she is a Chinaman. Sometimes she gets into a passion and kicks and screams like a real home-baby, but usually she is good, and it is pleasant to listen to the tinkling of the bell and hear the "Good-bye, baby."

Another one of the baptized children of the church is Toda san's strong, hearty boy. He is an active child, and never keeps still when awake. Old Hisa's little Se-no-ski is one who is being well taught in the Scriptures. He can repeat verse after verse of Matthew's

Gospel, and he tells me that he prays every day.

Work among little children always seems to me the most hopeful and pleasant of all work. To be sure, it does not seem to yield fruit as rapidly as some other soil, and "little lambs" will stray away and act in a very naughty manner. But our little ones are ever a comfort to us, and it is delightful to witness the effects of grace in these children's hearts. They all come on Sundays, bright and happy, to go to church and Sabbath-school, and pay good attention to their lessons. Their short text is written for them on the blackboard, and then they copy it on slates. "From a child thou hast known the Scripture" was the verse one morning not long ago. The children repeated it in English; then we took the words as they come in the reversed order of Japanese sentences: "'Thou.' What is that?" and the children all said, "*Anata*" ("You"). "Child-time from," "Scripture," "hast known," and in this order they got the words into Japanese, and then repeated them all together. They all learn much of Jesus, his parables and miracles, and it is far better for them than the stories of *Mimotaro, Kintaro, The Tail-cut Swallow,* etc. But we wish we had simpler books for them. We want a book about sheep and lambs and shepherds, etc., that the children may better understand such words in the Scriptures.

They have their own prayer-meetings, all joining in prayer and singing. They carry their little hymn-books and their *Happy Books* home with them. Once when Sudzu was sick I found her with the catechism under her pillow. Her baby-brother, just learning to talk, heard some one begin the prayer, "Our Father," and he bent his head and clasped his hands as soon as he heard the first words.

Have I ever told any one about our little Kiku ("chrysanthemum")? I went out to gather flowers one day, and found this one. She is a very little child, and flies around regardless of all rule, and yet she is the affianced bride of a young man of twenty-three or -four, and already talks of her husband. I saw him with her one day—she just a baby playing with some new shoes her father had bought her, and he a full-grown young man.

And O I-no san's little sister, the prettiest Japanese child I ever saw, has been given away—affianced to the son of some friends in the country, and sent off to be brought up in their family. I wonder if the father and the mother do not miss their pretty little daughter? "It is to be hoped," says a sensible Japanese, "that these ridiculous customs will soon be done away with." And indeed we hope so too, for we love the little Japanese children, and trust they will soon be delivered from such bonds.

Our dear little children in school are learning much that is good and useful. We try to have them in the open air a great deal, and they have gymnastics in the house. They study their lessons pretty well and are learning fast, and they are little Christian children, singing sweet hymns and becoming acquainted with the stories of Adam and Eve and Joseph and Moses, and, above all, learning of Jesus. Let us pray that they may all be gathered into his fold.

CHAPTER X.

THE HEM OF THE GARMENT.

"For she said, If I may but touch his clothes, I shall be whole."

O RIN SAN'S aunt was dying. Deguchi san and I did not hear of her illness, or know, indeed, that there was such a woman, until she was almost gone. Deguchi san had a copy of Mark when we went to see her, and she seemed to listen while she read of the woman who came behind Jesus in the crowd and touched his garment. On Sunday morning a priest was at the house mumbling his senseless prayers, but the woman paid little attention to him. When we were there in the afternoon she was just at the point of death. The doors were closed. Outside, the busy multitude passed by. We sat quietly beside the dying woman in the little low room. Then came a sense of the presence of the Lord. He was there with us in the room.

The woman turned to O Rin san before she died and asked her to read again the story of the woman who touched the Lord's garment, and while O Rin san was reading the words,

"If I may touch but his clothes," she died. Was he really there? Did she touch the border of his garment?

How many there are whom we feel to be but *touching* the border of the garment! Sick and weak and ignorant ones, foolish old women and young children, are just now in that position. Many of them are baptized, and rightly so; for we are told to receive even the weak in faith, and we who are strong are to help them and "bear their infirmities."

One day at Gen-ske-cho my attention was drawn to a pale, sick young girl, almost a child, who listened eagerly to every word and seemed to drink it all in. I hoped to meet her the next Thursday, but was disappointed. Again the time for the meeting came, but O Taki san was not there. Then I asked old Hisa about her. "She is ill," she said.—"Well, I must go to see her."—"But," said O Hisa san, "it would not do to go: her mother would be angry." I insisted upon going, however, so she reluctantly led the way to a kura.

The mother of the sick child heard us at the door and came out, but gave no invitation to enter. The slides were open, and we could see into the house. On a futon lay poor little O Taki san in a heavy sleep. "She sleeps this way all day, and lies awake in pain all night," said the mother, letting us know how impossible it was for us to talk with her. So we left the child in her sleep and went home. Afterward we tried in some way to gain favor with the mother, but it was all in vain, and the child died in that condition. Still, we remembered how earnestly she listened when she heard once of the Lord, and how spiritual was the expression of her face. Our girls prayed often before she died for the child who had heard the gospel, and who slept all day and lay awake all night.

There are many who hear the gospel but once. We try to give them something to remember, and some tract or copy of the catechism to take with them, and then pray that seeds dropped in faith may spring up.

The old O Ba sans, leaning upon their staffs, weak with the infirmities of age, form one class among whom we work. When we remember their lives—how they have always been under dark clouds of ignorance and superstition, and how fixed their habits of life and thought have become—we cannot wonder that they hate the doctrines they know so little about, and which they have been taught to hate. They are gentle, cheery old bodies, always smiling and in a good humor. It is pleasant to see how kindly they are cared for by sons and daughters. We often see them led by the hand in the gardens or at Mu-ko-ji-ma, taken with the children to "see flowers." Many of them are bent almost double, even those who have not attained any extreme old age. Sometimes we stop one in her walk and say, "Well, old lady, how old are you?" Then Grandmother will laugh and thank us over and over, and tell with pleasure her many years.

Our old O Ba san of Shin-ya-ma died some time ago. She was ill for a long time. Deguchi san read the Testament to her, but she was too old to grasp it firmly. The daughter was good to her. "It will not be long that I shall have her," she said, "so I must do for her what I can now;" and the old woman received the most devoted care during her long illness.

Yet some of these old women do renounce their idols and become believers. Our O Ba san, Umekichi's mother, was very old and feeble when she was baptized, but is regular in her attendance at church. She comes to the prayer-meetings, and offers simple prayers, and sometimes talks. The poor old lady likes to sit in the sun, and I have often seen her on cold winter days, when the sun was shining brightly, sitting on a mat out of doors with her sewing. I tell her she will surely take cold, but she says not. Some of their habits seem very peculiar to us.

Deguchi san's mother is one of our old people. She went alone to the elders of the church to be examined, coming early in the morning. She says, "Alas! I forget as soon as I hear. The words enter into one ear and go out at the other." And this is certainly true. But are we not to lead these feeble ones by the hand, as it were, along the heavenly road? This is a part of our work—a very different phase from that with the little children.

We who are strong must guide them along the way, be with them when they fall, and go with them to the brink of the river when they die. Happy are we if, strong in the Lord, we can bring them ever closer to his side. And we thank God that there is life in a look and life in a touch, that even those who but touch the border of his garment shall be made whole.

An old man, a Christian, is dead. The people say, "He is asleep." Formerly, when they spoke of dead persons, they said, "They are dead and finished," or "They have become nothing." Now they say, "They are asleep."

BOOK IV.

CHAPTER I.

WOMAN'S WORK FOR WOMAN.

"I will greatly multiply thy sorrow. Thy desire shall be to thy husband, and he shall reign over thee."

"Jesus saith unto her, Mary. She turned herself, and said unto him, Rabboni; which is to say, Master."

HEATHEN women are under a curse; Christian women are restored to the favor of God through Christ. The depths of degradation in the curse and the heights of blessing in the restoration are only comprehended fully by those who live among the heathen, who can compare country with country and condition with condition. Wherever in the world one woman leads another to the Saviour or teaches some poor ignorant one to speak the heavenly language, or to sing the notes of the glad new song; wherever one woman draws another from filth and vice to cleanliness and godliness, from idleness to industry, from Satan to God; wherever one woman speaks to another words of comfort and cheer and endeavors to alleviate her suffering,—*there woman is working for woman.*

But to-day we would look up from our work in the harvest-fields, from our posts in the outskirts, especially to the great body of workers with us at home. For it seems as though a vast army were gathering behind us. Every mail brings news of societies organized to aid us in our work.

We have from home some account of how the societies were organized, and of the origin of the movement, which seems, in a number of instances, to have started almost simultaneously in different denominations of Christians. The zeal and devotion of the Roman Catholic Sisters of Charity may have been felt as a rebuke by Protestant women, and the question asked, "Will not woman's love and woman's tenderness and woman's consecration win a way for the gospel where like influences have won a way for error?" Many of us, too, are familiar with the sisterhoods of the Lutheran Church. We have read of how they go to Palestine and Africa, to the desolate regions of Hungary and other places, there to establish orphanages or to do hospital-work. There are also sisterhoods in the Episcopal Church especially for hospital-service.

It has generally been thought that these

"Sisters" must be unmarried women in order to attend to the duties of their office. Most of the Protestant missionary societies do not hamper their workers by any binding promises, and yet it seems but right that, having been sent by a society into a distant field at great expense, they should remain faithful at their posts for at least some years, and not take upon themselves any duty or relation which would prevent them from fulfilling those for which they were sent. The question of the marriage of missionaries can only be settled by those most nearly concerned in the matter, and to them it had better be left. The work of unmarried women in missionary-fields is very important—indeed, indispensable. The difficulty in regard to their homes has been solved in late years by the plan of sending two or three together to make a home for themselves, and this plan has been found to be entirely practicable. Unmarried women hold high positions in our missions, and year after year the special difficulties attending their work are vanishing.

The missionary societies who take under their care both married and unmarried women are, in our judgment, wise. They find that all have a work to do—some in one way, and some in another. The opening of the zenanas of India to the missionary-women seems to have been the real starting-point of the women's societies in America. Whatever *woman only* can do, that woman must do; and in answer to the call from India women organized the first society. The *Women's Union Missionary Society* was organized in New York City in 1861. It has always worked independently of any mission-boards, and is composed of all denominations. The late president of this society, Mrs. Doremus, was justly termed the mother of missionaries. The organ of the society is *The Missionary Link*. Its home-workers are found in all parts of the United States, and its representatives in the foreign field in India, China and Japan, besides which it has schools in Greece and in Egypt. Of the special work of the society in this land (Japan), we need only mention the American home and the name of Mrs. Pruyn to bring it before the Lord's people at home.

Women's Board of Missions.—This society was organized in Boston in 1868, under the supervision of the American Board of Commissioners of Foreign Missions in the Congregational Church. The organ of the society is *Life and Light for Women*. Their foreign workers are in India, Africa, China, Japan, and, most of all, in Turkey, where the American

Board has been laboring for so many years, and with such marked success. This society is doing a great work in Japan. Its schools are in Ko-be, Osaca and Kioto.

A branch of the society just mentioned is the *Woman's Board of Missions of the Interior*, collecting the subscriptions and conducting the work of the Western part of the country, under the American Board.

The *Woman's Foreign Missionary Society of the Presbyterian Church* was organized in Philadelphia in May, 1870. The two magazines of this society are *Woman's Work for Woman* and *Children's Work for Children*. Its auxiliaries are numerous in Pennsylvania and the neighboring States, and its foreign work is in India, Siam, Syria, Persia, China, Africa, Japan, Mexico, South America, and among the Indians and Chinese of our own country. Its work in Japan is in Tokio and Yokohama, where it has under its care missionaries, single and married, a school in the latter place, and a part interest in the boarding-school at Tokio.

The *Occidental Branch* of the society was organized at San Francisco, Cal., in 1873. The ladies edit weekly one column of the *Occident*. The States and Territories around the parent society are still so sparsely settled that there are comparatively few auxiliaries, but we hope that more will be organized. They found a work waiting for them at their very door—the Chinese of California. Their "Home for Chinese Women" is doing a great work in bringing women and girls under Christian training and rescuing them from a sinful life.

The Ladies' Home and Foreign Board of Missions was organized under its present name in New York in November, 1870. It had formerly existed as a home society. Its organ is *Our Mission-Field*. Its foreign missionaries are in Syria, Persia, India, China, Siam, Japan and Africa. It has one school for girls partly under its care in Japan.

The Woman's Presbyterian Board of Missions of the North-west was organized in Chicago in December, 1870, the women of the Presbyterian Church separating from their fellow-workers in the Congregational Church. They unite with the society at Philadelphia in publishing *Woman's Work for Woman* as their organ. Their home-workers and auxiliaries are in the North-western States, and their foreign missionaries are among the Indians of North America, in China and Japan, in India and Persia, in Siam and Syria, and in South America.

The Woman's Baptist Missionary Society is in two divisions—the Eastern, organized at

Boston in April, 1871, and the Western, organized in Chicago in May, 1871. Its missionary paper is *The Helping Hand*. It has numerous home-workers, and Burmah has always been the special field of the Baptist Church since the days of Dr. Judson. It has also under its charge the Karen missions, Eurasian missions in Burmah, the Shan mission, the Telvogoo mission, also one to the Chinese in Siam and in China. It now has two missionaries in Japan—one in Tokio, and one in Yokohama.

The Woman's Foreign Missionary Society of the Methodist Episcopal Church was organized in 1869. It has at home over two thousand auxiliaries, and missionaries in India, China, Japan, Africa, Bulgaria, Italy, South America and Mexico. Its work in Japan is in Tokio, Yokohama and Hakodati.

The Woman's Auxiliary to the Board of Missions (Episcopal) was organized in 1873. It has a number of local societies throughout the different States, and missionaries in Greece, Palestine, China, Japan, Africa, and among the North American Indians.

The Woman's Board of Foreign Missions of the Reformed Church in America was formed in 1874. It has representatives in India, China and Japan.

We have thus glanced at the principal missionary societies in the home-land. They are like parts of a great planetary system—suns, planets and satellites all revolving around one centre, Jesus, the great central Sun—or like so many divisions of an army, under different banners, captains and generals, but all fighting for the King. What a mighty force it is! We in the field feel overwhelmed when we think of it. We can only pray God to give them grace and strength and wisdom as they need.

The papers and letters from our own society, the Woman's Foreign Missionary Society of the Presbyterian Church, show us how they work, and no doubt the others do their work in a similar way. Their object is "to promote an interest among Christian women in the work of foreign missions." The officers of the parent society consist of a President, Vice-Presidents, Foreign Corresponding Secretaries, Home Corresponding Secretaries, Recording Secretary, Treasurer and Board of Managers. In the committee-rooms of the parent society all the ends of the earth meet. Through the Home Corresponding Secretaries come the letters and reports from the auxiliaries throughout their boundaries, and through the Foreign Corresponding Secretaries letters from the missionaries in every country and from every clime.

In those rooms these reports and letters are read, plans discussed, action taken as to proposed work, and prayer continually made for the blessing of God upon all. And from these rooms come the magazines, in which missionary letters are printed, thus bringing every woman of the Church into close relationship with the missionaries, and to those busy workers in the field go letters full of words of comfort and cheer. Once a week the Executive Committee meets, while the Board of Managers has a regular monthly meeting, and once a month a general prayer-meeting for missions is held.

Auxiliaries.—" The object of these," says the second article in the constitution, "is to secure systematic contributions for foreign missions, and to disseminate missionary intelligence." Their officers are similar, except in point of numbers, to those of the parent society, and the auxiliaries are expected to report annually to the parent society. "The plan of many of these auxiliaries is to have monthly meetings of one hour, in which the promises of God are studied in regard to the evangelization of the world, with prayer and singing. The subjects recommended by the Assembly's Board are taken in order, and papers are written and facts and items given, letters read, stations traced on maps, etc. At these meetings the divine Master is always present, and often the hearts of the members burn within them. Think of the development and culture, intellectual, social and spiritual, possible to a band of Christian women steadily engaged in such a work, pursuing such themes and taking hold of omnipotent help for the perishing!" The funds are raised by each member paying a certain amount each month into the treasury, and a small amount for contingent expenses is often added to this by a trifling sum from each member.

Then the young people and children are brought into the work. "They are," writes one from home, "as of yore, especially forward and especially honored in crowning the King." In their mission-bands they hold meetings in which they have religious exercises, bring in information on the special topics of the month, hear letters read from missionaries or extracts from periodicals, present pictures, curiosities or anything adapted to shed light upon the customs of the country under consideration, introduce maps or charts to give the geographical features of the country, bring historical facts in regard to the same, and vary the exercises by relating incidents, reciting missionary poems, or adding any variety of entertainment that may contribute to the pleasure and instruction of the hour. The little magazine, *Children's Work for Children*, is expressly designed for them.

"The Presbyterial organization," says the pamphlet on that branch of the work, "is the combination of the local missionary societies existing in churches forming a Presbytery for co-operative work of foreign missions." The local societies are expected to send their delegates to the place where the meeting of Presbytery is held, and these delegates form a Presbyterial missionary society. This organization beautifully systematizes the whole work.

"A Presbyterial society, working systematically and feeling a responsibility for the cause within its own bounds, gains a thorough knowledge of the condition of each church in regard to missionary work, consults as to the general good, gives necessary information, increases the circulation of missionary periodicals and letters, encourages and strengthens weak societies, enlists interest, explains the best plans for systematic benevolence, and makes full reports through the secretary to the Board."

The interest aroused at the meetings is another blessing attending these organizations. It is earnestly recommended that the auxiliary societies, with "full accord," report to their Presbyterial secretary and remit funds to their

Presbyterial treasurer; which course greatly simplifies the work of the secretaries and treasurers of the parent societies.

The money from home comes to us in as direct a manner as possible, and with little or no diminution. The treasurer of the Presbyterian Board of Foreign Missions sends the mission treasurer drafts for the amount allowed to that mission. If any one has assumed the support of any special object in that mission, the money goes into the treasury of the Board, and helps pay the bill of exchange from which the sum contributed is drawn on the mission-field. Thus may any one see that the smallest contribution suffers no loss on its way to the field where it is to be used. Every mite goes into the treasury, and enters into the drafts drawn for the purposes of the work.

It is unnecessary to say anything more to meet the query so often anxiously put, "What is to become of my donation? Will it reach the object I have in view?" You may rest assured that your dollar will be faithfully applied according to your wishes. It will do its part in the great work; it is a unit among the thousands, and is as efficient as any of the rest. All this applies, of course, to the amount asked for in the estimates of the mission and allowed by the Board—not to outside ones sent irrespective of this arrangement. For such special provision must be made.

It is a good thing also that some one should be commissioned "to go from church to church, telling women about the missionary-field, forming societies among them, and urging them to come up to the help of the Lord, the help of the Lord against the mighty." This should be considered a part of the regular work, and compensation allowed to those thus employed. Returned missionaries can in this and in other ways still work for the fields they love that are far away; and if any can thus be induced to care and to pray, a great deal will be gained.

The annual meetings, when so many come together, are times when the friends who are interested in our work must take grand views over all the world. We out here have to be content with the reports of the secretaries, and with wishing ourselves there with them as they climb the mountain-tops. Oh, the views from thence must be grand and soul-inspiring! And then, too, the "hour of prayer," from 5 to 6 P. M. on each Sabbath, is something which commends itself to us.

I wonder sometimes if our constant cry, "Pray for us! pray for us!" does not weary those to whom we write. To call for the prayers of so many of God's people for one particular place is to ensure it a blessing. We feel more and more our dependence on God's favor and upon the power of the Spirit. Our school-buildings may be destroyed and our churches laid low, but the word of God, sown in the heart and quickened by the Spirit, "abideth for ever."

We can see from all this how a mutual relation is established between those in the field and those at home in working together, and together working with God. Wherever such relations exist, it is well to consider just what they are and what duties and benefits result from them.

It is hardly strange that, as the work grows more absorbing in the mission-field, my heart turns with ever-increasing interest to those at home who are engaged in it. I feel like eagerly questioning, "Do all attend the missionary meetings? Does every one take the magazines? Are you gaining anything spiritually from your labors? What is it that you are doing? What are you endeavoring to accomplish? Do you now know something of how it all looks to your missionary in the field?"

The new missionaries come out to us from you. It is so important that the *right* ones be sent, and so much harm may be done by the selection of those who are not fitted for the work, that the responsibility seems almost overwhelming. Therefore let the whole Church waken to a sense of this, and continually ask of God that the choosers may be guided to make the right choice. At the meetings of the auxiliary societies, when the women go up to pray, let them make this one subject of special prayer.

There are two ways in which women go out to the foreign field—as wives and as unmarried women, to teach in the schools or to do other special work. In the former case the choice does not devolve upon the societies, the missionary himself being the one to make the proper selection. But in the other instance, and the one which involves a great deal more, the matter of choice falls on the society. Looking over all the missionary lands or listening to a cry for help, they see that some one is especially needed for a certain field. Then an earnest, importunate prayer goes up to God for help, entreating him to send the right one. And how wonderfully those prayers have been answered those who made them can testify.

Or perhaps some one whose heart is burning with love for the heathen, and who feels the strong desire herself to go into the great white harvest-fields, makes an application to the society. They see in her one eminently adapted to the work, and they wish to send her. Then another necessity for prayer arises in regard to her proper field, the time for her to go, the means required. These are the subjects for prayer; the one who wants to go must *wait*, and the waiting-time is trying.

Let me say a word to such a one. You need to know almost *everything* in a foreign land; no knowledge can come amiss. I have needed to know how to make bread, and how to teach our servants all kinds of housework, and how to build fires. Once a man came to ask me to show him how to make a thermometer, which was quite out of my line of business. Let your waiting-time be spent partly in study, especially in study of the mission-work.

Some apply to the society for appointment who are considered unfitted for the work. Let not such feel harshly toward any one on this account. If you are not adapted to the work, you would only be a hindrance to the cause you love. Only let it increase your zeal to do what you can at home. Let the Lord see, if no one else does, that beautiful flowers of patience, humility and increased love grow up out of your disappointment.

With how great an interest must the Church

look on as one after another is chosen from the grand army to be sent to the outposts! The missionary having been chosen, the next thing is to provide the *outfit*. The servant of the Lord must be well equipped when she starts forth in the great work. It is necessary to be perfectly acquainted with the climate of the country. to which the missionary goes, that everything may be suitable. This makes a great deal of correspondence necessary on the part of those who have the missionary's outfit in charge. It is well to know just what can be procured to better advantage in the country to which she goes, or in what way expense may be saved.

It may seem strange that most missionaries who live in tropical or semi-tropical climates suffer as much with the cold as they do with the heat, and sometimes even more. The large, airy houses, with their verandas and many windows, are better adapted for the heat than the cold, and we grow very sensitive, so that when damp, rainy days come the cold is very penetrating and we need the comfort of thick clothing. Most of us wear thicker clothing here in winter than we ever need at home, except in regard to outside wraps. It is usually warmer out of doors than it is in the house. But there are certain seasons of the year when we cannot bear to touch woolen clothing, so that both very thick and very thin clothing is necessary for the Japan winter and summer.

The cabinet-organs which are sent by the societies are invaluable assistants in our work. We should hardly know how to get along without them.

When the missionary is ready to leave, those who are sending her forth assemble to talk about the country to which she is going, to speak of the work she is to do, to sing and pray together, and then to say "God bless you!" and "Good-bye." Those whom she meets along the way as she journeys toward the sea often desire to greet her, to encourage her and wish her all good things in the Lord, and some will accompany her "unto the ship" and watch until the gang-plank is lifted and the vessel is out at sea. All the Church will know about her going, because they will read the record in the missionary journal. And the missionary goes forth feeling that she has not only the presence of the Father, but also the tender, loving sympathy and the heartfelt prayers of his dear children. It is a blessed thing to go, and a blessed thing to help one in going, to do this God-given work.

We want to hear no expressions of pity, for we count ourselves the happiest of mortals.

Rather would we say, "Rejoice with us, O our friends, for the King hath called us to the front of the battle. He hath chosen us to go out to take possession of fair lands in his name. Our eyes shall see and our lips shall tell wondrous things. For hath he not said, 'I will not fail thee, nor forsake thee. Only be thou strong and very courageous'? 'This book of the law shall not depart out of thy mouth, but thou shalt meditate therein, day and night, that thou mayest observe to do according to all that is written therein, for thus shalt thou make thy way prosperous, then shalt thou have good success.' 'Have not I commanded thee? Be strong and of a good courage; be not afraid, neither be thou dismayed; for the Lord thy God is with thee, whithersoever thou goest.'"

Do not overestimate our sacrifice. But what we do for the sake of the salvation of souls and extending the dominions of our King, with the rest and blessing of his presence and the prospect of the certain sure reward, hundreds of others do for the sake of gain or fame, with no such Master to speak unto them "comfortable words," and with disappointment meeting them on every side. Read the history of the Spanish conquests, and especially the tales of the Roman Catholic missionaries, and you will see why we cannot boast. Here, in most troublous times, there have always been others to share the dangers and loneliness of our exile, and I have often wondered how they have endured them without our faith and trust in God our Father's loving care.

This leads me to say something to mothers of missionaries—those who have sons and daughters in the field. You give your children up to dwell far from you in heathen lands. It is a great sacrifice, and we wonder not at your sadness. But they go from you safe in the Lord Jesus, even the heart of the Father's kingdom. You know that at the most the separation is only lifelong, and that you have an eternity to spend together. You know that death, in whatever form it comes to them —whether by the sea or by fire or sword or pestilence—is only the King's messenger, welcome to them under any circumstances.

Do you ever think how many mothers are mourning their prodigal sons and erring daughters, wanderers from them in these foreign lands, from whom they never hear and who are treading the downward path? Those who labor in the hospitals can tell you something about this. Therefore grieve not for yourselves, but rather pray for the mothers whose sorrow is so deep and apparently hopeless.

And how often do we find that prayer for these wandering ones is answered!

Another thought: Let the women who go up to the meetings remember that the lands to which the missionaries are sent have been for thousands of years in Satan's indisputed possession, and that he is not going to give them up without a desperate struggle. Let them realize that the position is that of a little feeble band in the heart of the enemy's country, exposed to all the darts of the evil one. Then pray for us. We must have the presence and blessing of our God, else "how shall one chase a thousand, and two put ten thousand to flight?"

How eagerly you must watch for the missionary journals, that you may read the accounts of the battles going on in these distant lands—the great battles between Truth and Error, between Light and Darkness, between God and Satan! I think I can hear you saying to each other, "There has been a great victory in Persia;" "Soldiers are flocking to the standard of the King in India;" "Many in China and Japan have sought the shelter of the cross;" or, as you hear it from one place or another throughout the world, "A sinner hath repented, and we with angels rejoice." Dear friends, we need your prayers.

It is well that we are relieved from care concerning our support: we should not otherwise have time to devote to our work. And our salaries should be sufficient to enable us to live, with no burdens of debt to annoy us. We have burdens enough without that.

Our comfortable, pleasant homes are provided by the mission-boards. Thinking of this leads me to say something in regard to the missionary's home. Sometimes I hear sneering remarks about the way in which missionaries live, and persons at home receive wrong impressions concerning their houses and the number of their servants. It is best to look at the subject carefully and candidly, so that we may be able to answer any one who speaks in this way, or who has doubts on this subject. I do not believe that there is one of our missionary-circle, here or elsewhere, who would not cheerfully endure any hardship or toil for the sake of the cause, and a number of them could, if they would, tell tales of suffering from cold and pain and weariness, and even from hunger and thirst. But the missionaries do not go out to win a martyr's crown, but to do the Lord's work in the best, wisest and most efficient way.

There are two ways of working in the missionary-field. One is by establishing a strong centre and making homes; the other, by the itinerant system—that of going from place to place, without any certain dwelling-place, scattering seed as the missionary travels.

Native houses are not adapted to carrying on our work: they are too open and insecure. There are few who can endure the strain of living any length of time without relief, alone among the natives. Loss of health, of reason, and even of life itself, has been the result. And the natives do not understand or in any degree appreciate the sacrifice. We must bear in mind constantly one fact, and that is, the heathen cannot comprehend the idea of disinterested benevolence. They presume that there is always some selfish motive behind the apparent good-will.

Nor do we want to be dragged down to a level with the heathen in our manner of life; we want them rather to be raised to our level, and wish, therefore, to show them the beauty of Christian homes. They are attracted to the mission-houses, whose doors are always open to receive them, and we show the women our beds, which are elevated from the floor, and our more cleanly and healthful way of using sheets, and they see that our bath-rooms are in a private corner of the house, not, as theirs, in the most conspicuous part, their bathtubs often at the front door. We teach them the advantage of having the house less open and the apartments more private and all the home-life more isolated. The missionary's home is one of the refining things in a heathen land. But the houses must be adapted to the climate. We need them to be even larger, more open and airy, than those at home. And it is well that they look pleasant, with their verandas and large windows, and bright with flowers and sunshine.

Most missionaries come from refined homes, and can throw an air of refinement over the native houses, even the mud walls of Persian homes. Muslin curtains, prettily draped, pictures and little keepsakes, flowers and vines, make the home pretty and attractive without extravagance.

Missionary-women in heathen lands are very dependent upon their homes for all the pleasures they enjoy. Our work has no respite. We go on from month to month in the same routine, and, I often think, do not have enough of social enjoyment. The health of the missionary must be considered. Every year of added experience makes the missionaries more valuable in the field, and we do not want them to die or to go home. Our Boards do well, then, to provide us with pleasant homes.

But we often leave them and go out into the country and spend weeks, and even months, teaching the people and mingling with them—part of the year as itinerant missionaries, and part working from our strong mission-centre, sending out our native helpers, after patient instruction, and going with them often to superintend their labor.

In these lands we need very nourishing food: the system soon becomes enervated in these warm climates. In regard to the servants of the missionary, we often hear surprise expressed as to the number of them. Perhaps some even think that missionaries ought not to keep servants at all. 'It is necessary to have more servants here than we would need at home, for no one can labor much in these climates. Nor will one servant do more than one kind of work in this country. Our time and strength are too precious to spend in doing manual labor, which a small outlay will enable us to get natives to do. We came to do *missionary* work, and must be free to do it. So a number of servants is necessary, and it must also be remembered that each native servant is one more brought under the influence of the gospel. But if the economy of the matter be in question, it may be a conclusive answer to the objector that the expense of three servants here is barely equal to one-half the cost of one at home. I have often wished, however, that I could exchange my three or four servants for one good strong Irish woman.

Besides the things provided for us here, some things come to us from home. When we hear in Tokio that the steamer has arrived at Yokohama, we know that only a few hours will intervene before our mail will come, and we wait for the postman's call. How, think you, such words as these sound to us?—"If you can suggest any way in which the work you are doing can be aided by us, we hope you will do it. We rejoice in what God is doing for Japan." And one says, "We want to help you," and "I pray that you in Japan may have all the grace and wisdom and might that you need for every part of the work."—"It seems to me that many are praying all over the world as never before, 'Thy kingdom come.'"—"You are in the field doing the work of the Lord. You need first his blessing, without which the laborer worketh in vain, and you must also feel the need of help and encouragement from home."—"It seems to me that there is much earnest prayer for the Holy Ghost in our land." These are a few extracts from many letters. Do you not think such words strengthen us in these distant lands?

The magazines have their own special mission to us here. They enable the missionaries in all fields to become acquainted with each other. Often, in taking up new phases of the work, I have read what my sisters older in missionary-life have said in their letters concerning the same branches of the work, and have been profited. When the magazines come, particularly the one for children, portions of them are translated and read to our girls, and the result has been that they have formed a missionary-society themselves, and take up one country each month and prepare articles upon it, and pray for it especially. They have already learned a great deal about China missions, about Miss Dean's school in Oroomia, of Miss Fisk's life, and of Mrs. House's school in Bangkok. Our little children were much interested in the letter of "Leek," a girl in the Bangkok school, and began a quilt like the one she mentioned.

"Do the women of your country support missionaries in every part of the world?" asked a Japanese gentleman. "Oh yes," was the answer; "here is their book. Do you not see the letters in it from India, Siam, China, Persia and Japan? When will the women of your country do such things?"—"When this religion spreads through all the world."

You would like to see our Christian girls gathered for these missionary-meetings in a room in this great heathen city, with idols and idolaters all around them. It brings to my mind Paul's salutation to the Christian women of Rome: "Salute Tryphena and Tryphosa, who labor in the Lord. Salute the beloved Persis, which labored much in the Lord. Greet Mary, who bestowed much labor upon us."

Will the societies, auxiliaries and bands listen for a little while to some words from one in the field? We think we appreciate in some degree the difficulties and responsibilities of those who have the work in charge, the officers of our societies. We wish you had telescopes through which you might look at us, but, since you have not, we want our letters to be fair, impartial statements concerning the state of things here.

We wish to be very careful how we call upon you for help. But we are sure that the mere stating to you the difficulties which we meet is one way by which those difficulties may be overcome in great measure in the present and avoided in the future. Even when we are called to pass through the "fiery furnace," you will in some measure share our sufferings, but we shall all rejoice together at the full deliverance.

We are sure of your aid in every difficulty, of your sympathy in every experience, and of your joy in all our victories. But let us all remember that far above all Boards and committees are the eternal purposes of God. Great difficulties resolve themselves, or our Father gradually unravels them if we are only patient and wait.

The auxiliaries which provide the missionary's salary take her and her work as a special subject of prayer. Let them often write to her, expecting only an occasional answer in return. We are often pressed for time, but we want to let you hear from us, and will write when we can. Often, when great issues are at hand, we feel constrained to write directly to the parent society, but be sure that you are not forgotten by us.

In regard to the societies and bands who are supporting Bible-readers and the pupils in the schools, let me say something in regard to what is called "special work"—that is, the support of any particular person or child in a mission. No doubt it is pleasanter for you to feel that you have some particular person under your care. You want to hear of her, receive letters from her and know just what she is doing, and it seems right that you should do so. But when you take certain things into consideration, I am sure you will see how impossible it often is to give you such a special object, and how it may prove rather a hindrance than a help to the missionary in her work. For instance, a band has a little heathen girl in school here or elsewhere. It (the band) wants to know something about her, and this necessitates frequent writing on the part of the missionary; nor is it always easy to find something interesting to write concerning these apathetic little Asiatics.

But this is not the greatest difficulty, by any means. We are liable to constant changes—changes in our pupils, in our plans of work. What might seem best one month may look differently the next, or the child who might appear suitable at one time might prove to be one whom we could not keep, or we might find out things concerning her which would render any support from home unnecessary. Or the child might prove to be very naughty or dull, and we should not like to write such news home. And these things are not merely supposable cases. They are what have occurred under my own eye. One of our missionaries has said that she did not dare to write anything home about our fluctuating mission, for by the time it got back to her it was not true. Of course this applied simply to what are the mere incidents or contingencies of the work, the minor occurrences of the day.

I remember we once had a hearty laugh at one of our missionaries who began a letter by speaking of her "good teacher," and how fortunate it was that she had him, and had to end it by saying that he had gone she knew not where. I myself once wrote to one of the ladies' Boards, asking them to take charge of a woman whom I had in training as a Bible-reader, and when the ready answer came the woman was far beyond my reach, and I had only to write and say so.

We like the scholarship system much better, and sometimes we can keep one child on a scholarship for a long time, and thus give those who endowed it an opportunity to become acquainted with her. And we want to have the natives depend upon themselves, so that just as soon as we can dispense with the scholarship we may do so, or take one child off and put another in her place in rapid succession. We do not want what is designed as a help to become a hindrance to our work.

One specialty is the teacher employed by the missionary when acquiring the language. At first these teachers do little more than instruct us, but afterward we have them as helpers in various branches of our work. Their salaries must come from the Board. Another very important specialty is providing means for our journeyings for mission-purposes. Few of us can afford to pay this out of our salaries, and we do not go so often as we might were it otherwise. So one thing you can do is to provide means for the missionary to travel by jin-ri-ki-sha, ka-go, horse, camel, or even elephant, as the case may be.

Give your money regularly and systematically to the treasurer, and it will go to the parent society, and it will know what is needed and where it is needed. And do not cling to your "special work;" for if you can have any, I cannot. My plans and purposes are frequently broken off, and it only makes it all the harder for me when any one else is disappointed, especially if it be any of the young people or little children. We are glad the young girls and the boys are interested in our work, and the dear little children must know all we can tell them about our little ones.

You cannot give in the Lord's cause without receiving tenfold, and as you read of us in these missionary-lands you must realize your own privileges. Oh, church-women at home, what a mighty army do you seem to us! Surely every one in your land is taught of Jesus. You do not have to wait month after month to learn a strange tongue before you can begin to teach the heavenly language or the new song. You never had to see your pupils tremble before the death-penalty or come to you in danger of persecution. You do not need to hide your Bibles under your pillows, as I have done, because the volumes are so scarce. How rich you are in Christian literature! You can scatter it over all the land. If we had your numbers and your material, in a few days all Japan would know of the Lord. See that you rightly value and rightly use your privileges.

You are brought into close contact with other lands. Their geography, history and present state and progress grow familiar to you. What an education for your children, and indeed for yourselves! Is not your faith strengthened by what you see is being done in these lands?

Come, let us take these heathen women with us to the sepulchre. Point out to them the cross and the empty tomb. Ask the Lord to call each one by her name, and to open her ears that she may hear his voice and call him "Master." See her now bathed in the fountain, clothed in new garments, white and clean! Is it not a change? But stay yet longer. This is the "Morning Land." The grass is glittering with dew; the birds have only just begun their song; everything is fresh and bright. Come drink with these women at the very Fountain-head. See if the waters are not to your taste exceedingly pure and sweet. Perhaps some of you have forgotten somewhat your first delight in drinking of the water; perhaps some have gone too far away from the Source; the water may be mixed with something else. Let us all kneel and drink at the Fountain-head with our new-born sisters, heathen but a little while ago.

CHAPTER II.

"THE CHRISTIAN'S SHINING LIGHT."

> "With a pure clear light
> Jesus bids us shine,
> You in your small corner,
> And I in mine."

I SOMETIMES wonder how it is that many people have such crude ideas in regard to missionaries and the mission-work. In letters questions are often put which show us that friends at home are vainly trying to picture us in these far-off lands. They wonder how we are living and what we are wearing and eating and drinking, and seem to imagine that some great change has taken place in us as well as about and around us, and I feel like saying, "Dear friends, I am just myself; and my home is just as much like the one in our own land as we can make it; and we eat, drink and wear about the same things that we should at home; and the work seems all alike to me. It is only that I am *here*, and you *there*. You are to shine in your corner, and I in mine."

But I recall my own childish fancies about

missionaries as people going about in boats among islands, or teaching savages under palm trees—beings entirely different from ordinary mortals—and then I look about me, myself a missionary in this strange land, and smile to think how different it all is from anything I had imagined, and yet how much more is involved than all those childish fancies had conceived. And it is only now, after years in the field, when the surroundings have grown perfectly familiar to me, and the language is as easily spoken and understood as my own native tongue, that the similarity of the work here and as it is, or ought to be, at home impresses me, and I must go back to note the difference.

In the old days of pioneer missionary-life, in the times of isolation from our own countrymen and of dwelling among a strange people speaking a strange tongue, one could realize vividly the full import of the words which the Lord spoke unto Abraham, saying, "Get thee out of thy country, and from thy people, and from thy Father's house, into a land which I shall show thee." At night, looking up to the sky, full of stars as when the Lord called Abraham forth to look at them, and said, "So shall thy seed be," and then gazing down upon the pleasant land which we know is promised to the Son for his inheritance, the house in which we were living seemed turned into a tent, and we ourselves as Abraham dwelling in the "Promised Land," though having none inheritance in it, and yet, like him, rejoicing in the assurance that it should be ours. But not bidden, as was Abraham, to keep separate from the nations around us, we had come to tell the people of the Saviour whose day Abraham rejoiced to see; and fair though the land be in which as strangers we were now sojourning, yet faith taught us to look for a "better country," and we had come to point out to the dwellers here the way to that heavenly land. So we mingle with them to learn about their country and their character, their manners and customs, and, above all, to speak and understand their language. And to accomplish these things is the first great aim of the missionary.

We have found Japan a pleasant land in which to dwell, and the climate one in which foreigners can, under ordinary circumstances, live a long while without serious injury to the constitution. Earthquakes have rocked our homes and tempests have swept over us, but we have been kept from harm through all. We have traveled in the country, and have eagerly seized every opportunity of becoming acquainted with the character of the people among whom we work, that we may know how to deal with them. We Christian women who are here to labor among the Japanese women must know the natures of those with whom we come in contact. These women have always been kind and pleasantly disposed. Almost the first word I had to learn was *"Arigato"* ("Thank you"), and ever since that morning, a few days after we landed at Yokohama, when a woman on the bluff put a morning-glory into my hand, I have had to use that word constantly.

The women have shallow, undeveloped minds, with blunted ideas of truth and virtue, but they are capable of a high degree of culture, and work among them is very satisfactory in its results.

This constant contact with inferior minds, this continual giving out and receiving nothing in return, the feeling that years—even the best years—of our life are slipping away and we are gaining nothing intellectually,—these are among the greatest trials to which a missionary here is subjected. But we can afford to give when we work with One who gave his life for us "while we were yet sinners," and who now gives liberally to supply all our needs, asking only our loving service in return.

We familiarize ourselves with the manners and customs of the people by mingling with them. We take off our shoes, sit down on the mats and drink tea with them. We let bows and smiles and signs take the place of words at first. We greet kindly the little children, and find our way to the mothers' hearts through the babes. We watch them in the temples and in their gardens and their homes, joining with them as we can. In this way we learn the language. There is no way to learn how to speak a language but to speak it. We must use our vocabularies over and over until we see that the words we use are understood, nor mind if they are not right at first. We cannot learn the spoken language from teachers altogether—for in that way we should get a stiff form of expression—but we must listen to the people and try to talk as they do.

The Japanese colloquial is not difficult. The pronunciation is easier to us than that of French or German. The many forms of the language and the honorific expressions and euphonic changes are troublesome, but we soon learn to use them. We make many ludicrous blunders at first, but we profit by our own mistakes and try again. If any one asks us how long it took to learn the language, I have to say that I do not know, for we are always learning something new, and never feel that we have perfectly acquired the language. It takes years of residence in this country to be able to speak like a native, if indeed one ever does it.

As to the written language, it is well to learn as quickly as possible how to read the Scripture and the hymn-book, tracts, etc., which are published by the mission. In them all one set of characters is used, and they are not very difficult. It is well to read, or at least to know about, Japanese books, but one may take this leisurely, as it is not essential. The Japanese literature drains the mind without enriching it.

I wish I could impress upon every new missionary the importance of giving a year, or even two years, to study before she undertakes any special work in the field. Only those who have experienced it know what it is to be obliged to strain every nerve to understand or to be understood, and this while other cares are pressing also. If some time is devoted at first to study, it affords the new missionary an opportunity to become acclimated and acquainted with the people, and to learn exactly to what sphere of missionary-life she is best adapted, thus avoiding the troubles which arise from mistakes in beginning things not advisable or for which the missionary is not qualified. If too much time is spent on other things in the beginning, the language will never be really learned, and the consequence will be that the missionary will always labor at a disadvantage. "Learn the language! learn the language!" the old missionaries and all who know anything about the work will say to the new worker in the field. Spend your first energies on it, and while doing so study the people, learn the character of your fellow-missionaries; watch carefully their work, and then you will fall naturally into your proper sphere and find your work comparatively easy and pleasant.

The relations which the missionary as such sustains are three: (1) To the Board and the society by whom she is sent, (2) to her fellow-missionaries, and (3) to the heathen. The relation of the foreign missionary to the Board is that of "one sent" far off into the enemy's country by the grand army at home. They send us out well equipped for our work. They care for us when here by prayer, sympathy and money as we need. It is our duty, therefore, to send home reports of the land and the people, and of our own welfare and progress in the work. If we do not, how can we expect them to keep up their interest in us? How can they know wherein we require aid, or how to pray for and sympathize with us, if we do not tell them? They must follow us through our journeyings and our first experiences in foreign lands, and labor with us as the years go on and our work and interests broaden and deepen. And this makes letter-writing a duty. We are brought into correspondence with the foreign secretary of the parent society, with the secretary of the auxiliary that provides our support, and with the societies and bands that sustain scholarships in our schools, or Bible-readers whose work we superintend. Besides these, a number of letters come to us from others who wish to know something about our work or make inquiries about some particular branch of it.

As the parent society has all the work of the auxiliaries under its care, and the most important or interesting of the letters are published or in some way disseminated, much writing may be spared the missionary by sending all communications direct to the secretary of the parent society with whom she is in correspondence. Letters can be sent through her to the auxiliary societies or to individuals, or special items designated in the general letter to the Board will be copied and given to those who are specially interested. The secretary can thus relieve the missionary from too great a pressure of letter-writing.

But since this letter-writing must be done, it is best to consider the easiest way of accomplishing it; and I have always found it best to set apart a small portion of each day—perhaps only a half hour—for this purpose, regarding it as much of a duty as anything else, and in this way, without interfering with other things, I have easily kept up a large correspondence. It is well to note down little passing events which will be of interest to people at home, and to watch for everything which will add interest or value to our letters. Every one earnest in her work will throw her earnestness into her letters, and thus set on fire the hearts of the people at home.

When several missionaries are engaged at one station, what is called the "mission" is formed. Every member of the mission has his or her part to take in the work. There are mission-meetings once a month, when the state and progress of the work are discussed. For these meetings reports are made out and estimates of expense given, and plans for enlargement or change in work are examined, and if approved by the mission are sent on to the Board at home.

It is not always that the members of a mission agree in all things, neither are they always perfectly congenial companions. Nor is it expected that they should be such, for we come here unacquainted with each other, often with different tastes and opinions. Our imperfectly-sanctified human natures make us liable to err in many instances.

"Ye are the light of the world." "A city which is set upon a hill cannot be hid." Thus spoke the Lord Jesus to the disciples who occupied as missionaries the same position that we do. It seems to me that no Christians dwell on such high hills as do missionaries. When we assume the duties of our office we voluntarily go up into them, there to take a high position.

The eyes of the heathen are upon us. More than we think do they comment upon every action and word. When the city is divided, they know it; when the lights are dim, they know it. The eyes of those of our own land who sneer at our work are upon us, quick to see and glad to find anything by which they can gain some occasion for reviling or reproach. And the Church at home has high ideas in regard to what should be our self-renouncement and the consecration of missionaries, though ready to admit that we are but human. It is necessary, then, that there be not even an appearance of division in our city. And we who dwell therein, and those who come up to join our ranks, must be very careful to avoid all causes of dissension. We must see to it that each member has his or her appropriate work, and that there is no unnecessary interference on the part of one with another. And especially should Societies and Boards, as they send out new missionaries, be very careful to ascertain their characteristics in this respect, and to make such arrangements beforehand, if possible, that there be no trespassing upon or intrusion into the sphere already occupied by those who have preceded. Never should anything be allowed by which rivalry or jealousy may be fostered. Are they not all one, working for the same Lord, the same glorious end, and should strife or bitterness ever exist? "Let your light so shine before men, that they may see your good works, and glorify your Father which is in heaven."

The third relation of the missionary is to the heathen. To my mind, there are four distinct phases of "woman's work for woman" in the foreign field. The first is that of woman in the home. The Christian wife can show to the heathen that she is trusted by her husband and stands on an equality with him. One of the first things noticed by the people is that the wife walks *beside* her husband, and not *behind* him. We can show them that we do not need to blacken our teeth or otherwise disfigure ourselves as they do in order to render our husbands secure concerning us, nor do we need certificates from them to prove that we are not running away when we go from home for a few days.

There are so many beautiful things in a Japanese household in regard to the management of children and their obedience and respect to parents that a Christian mother needs to be careful that her own children are trained, in these respects, as well as those in the families around. But the infinite superiority of real Christian training can be shown to the heathen, and the beauty of a truly Christian household will not be lost upon them.

As a housekeeper there is much—very much—to be shown to the heathen—as, for instance, the advantage of regular habits and the value of time—and we can rebuke their indolent, aimless lives by our own better example.

No one need think that a missionary, in making the one great sacrifice, is free from all lesser trials, for we have here, just as housekeepers do at home, our own troubles with servants, and have great need of patience in this respect. When we first came here the servants knew nothing of our ways, and had to be taught everything. They did not know how to use a stove, and always wanted to kindle a fire under one hole and cook everything separately, beginning with potatoes early in the morning, setting them in a corner of the room to cool, and then putting on something else. They wanted to do everything down on the floor, spreading things around in all directions. They never stole anything of consequence, but would take wood out of the stove for charcoal. We have to do all the thinking and planning for them, as they have no idea of method in their work. The missionary housekeeper needs the prayers of her sisters at home for grace and patience in this part of her life.

Most of the unmarried ladies who are sent out have the charge of schools or are in some way connected with them. It is remarkable how mission-schools have been prospered. In Japan all our work has been developed from them. They were the beginning of the church.

The aim of the foreign teacher in the school is to train teachers and Bible-women and wives for native Christians. This means a great deal, and there is need for special prayer that the Lord will send the right ones into the school. This is our prayer: "Dear Lord, thou knowest the needs of this land; thou knowest thy gracious purposes concerning it. Send into this school those who will receive the truth and become truly enlightened, and thus be fitted in after-years to go forth to labor among the people."

The school-system here has become rather complicated, owing to the fact that English is so extensively used, and we had for a long time no native text-books. At first the girls came only to read English, and we translated it as best we could, but afterward we found that more was necessary, especially when boarders came into the house. So we have now an English department, in which only pronunciation is taught; translation classes, where a Japanese who understands English takes charge of the translation; and a Japanese department, which includes Chinese writing. Japanese teachers were not such strict disciplinarians at first as we desired, but they are learning better our style of teaching, and as native text-books are made they will be more extensively used. Music is also taught, and fancy-work.

Japan is said to be a paradise for teachers as well as for babies. The children are indeed docile and gentle, but still we have our difficulties. Sometimes we wish they had more energy, and we try to stir up a spirit of emulation among them. Long and hard has been the contest to make them give up their way of dealing by indirect means, and to have them come directly to their teachers with their wants and complaints, and to infuse a love of truth into their natures.

Frequent illness among the pupils has been one great difficulty with which we have had to contend. They require great care physically as well as mentally, and a teacher often has to play the part of a nurse. But as scholars they have some very good traits. They have great respect and reverence for teachers. They are studious to a fault. It is hard to induce them to take proper exercise and recreation. Their tuition-fee has always been paid promptly. They are neat about everything. Some are capable of a high degree of culture, and all repay their teacher for the care given to them. Happy years have been these spent in the mission-school.

Beautiful to the Christian woman is the next department of work for woman—that among the native women of the church. We see that they come to the Bible classes and to the church-services, and grow strong to walk in the narrow way. This includes the work among the O Ba sans—the old and feeble ones of the church—and also the leading and guiding of the baptized children, helping their mothers in training them, and exercising a watchful care over the little ones of the mission-school.

True, the work is often discouraging, it is with such feeble, faltering steps that they sometimes walk. And yet we have great happiness in this part of our work, for we can watch the timid ones grow strong and mark the development of their Christian character as they go on. Happy they who see, as we have been permitted to do in Japan, the first-fruits offered unto God!

Another part of the work is the sowing of the seed broadcast, in the distribution of the printed page, the word spoken to the individual, the meetings for instruction—like those in Gen-ske-cho—the work of the Bible-woman, the going forth to sow. We can pray, and those at home who are interested in our work can unite with us in prayer, that God will prepare the ground. Then forth to the work we go, carrying, as it were, seed-basket in one hand and sword in the other, for while we work we must also fight. In faith is the seed dropped, in sure reliance that it will be watched over by the Lord, to whom it is so precious.

We have considered the change of home, the relations and the duties of the missionary; now the qualifications for all this are but clear deductions. Since the missionary leaves her "country" and her "father's house," and goes to dwell among a strange people, speaking a strange tongue, being isolated from her own countrymen, she must be one who has found in God her home, in God her everlasting rest. I repeat, she must be one who has *found* rest, not one who comes expecting to find a rest here which she does not possess at home. For I know of some who have come to foreign lands thinking to gain in absorbing work relief from their own unrest. We do not find "absorbing work" at first. We have sometimes to wait long before we do find it, and the experience of most of us is that at home our time seemed more fully occupied and our work more important than it did here during our years of waiting before we could talk or before we found out just what our work was.

In the long journey, during the process of acclimation and in the endurance of discomforts falling to our lot in traveling through this land, we find a cheerful disposition is necessary, as well as good health. Travel in Japan is not so hard a matter as in some other heathen countries, as the Japanese are a cleanly people, and, with the exception of fleas (a disagreeable exception, to be sure), there are but few vermin. I have read, in one of the books of the missionary literature of Persia, a statement of the writer to the effect that he had seen ladies who had borne bravely many trials and much pain give way under this affliction.

Neither do we suffer from the thieving propensities of the natives as do the missionaries in other lands. We sleep quite fearlessly at night in the open houses, with all our baggage in straw baskets without lock or key. But we travel in jin-ri-ki-shas and ka-gos, and sleep on the floor, and grow weary without the accustomed luxury of chairs and tables, and we creep on hands and knees into the boats and cling desperately to the necks of natives who are carrying us through the water. And well is it if we can laugh at our discomforts and take pleasure enough in the natural beauties around us to compensate for all we may have suffered.

Since the missionary gains nothing, morally or intellectually, from those among whom she lives, she must go to her work with a good supply of both moral and intellectual strength. Abraham's strong faith, Job's patience, Moses' meekness, and all the histories of those "who through faith subdued kingdoms, wrought righteousness, obtained the promises," and of the women, also, who "received their dead raised to life again," are things familiar to us all our lives. Paul's missionary-life is ours for an example, and above all we can "look unto

Jesus," "who for the joy that was set before him endured the cross, despising the shame." "What do you do," said one missionary to another one day, "when you are tried by the hypocrisy, and sometimes the ingratitude, of this people?"—"I consider," was the answer—"I consider 'Him who endured such contradiction of sinners against himself.'"

And not only these, but the names of those with whom history makes us familiar, who have toiled and suffered and accomplished wonderful things, are "towers of strength" to us. So it is well that the missionary comes to her work acquainted with the history of the world, and with a well-balanced, well-regulated mind. We all know how this is attained only by a thorough education of all the mental faculties.

And well is it also, for the one who comes, to have means of recreation within herself. I love to see the missionary coming who is fond of flowers, of music and of beautiful scenery, or even of fancy needle-work; for I know how these things will help her in her isolated life. The question is often asked, "Does the knowledge of other languages help you in learning the Japanese?" It does not, in one sense, when the other languages are not cognate, but learning any one language always helps in another, as our minds are strengthened by the discipline of study, and we become accustomed to memorizing isolated words and to the transposition of sentences.

In order to find our way to the hearts of the people, a winning, kind manner is a necessity. One needs to be able to sit down with them on their mats, and to drink hot tea without choking, and swallow down unpalatable things without making faces. The Japanese food is not greasy, as is that of other countries of which I have read, and consequently to me was never actually distasteful. But I never could learn to use chopsticks.

Since the relation of missionaries to each other is one often calling forth much grace and patience, it is well that the missionary be one with no peculiarities to be humored. The mutual relation of missionaries brings out these personal peculiarities and idiosyncrasies in a very strong light. One long in the mission-field says, "There is always some dread in welcoming new missionaries. Sometimes they bring with them sorrow instead of joy. It is so important that they be well chosen— even chosen of God. Then they will be happy under all circumstances, 'working for God.'"

Therefore let the new missionary—one "chosen of God" and pointed out by him in answer to the prayers of the Church—go to her field prepared to *wait* to find out just what her place is, or to take that which is designated for her by the older missionaries, and, even if not satisfied, be still content to wait. And in the choice and occupation of her field, let it be with the spirit of Abraham, who said, "If thou wilt take the left hand, I will go to the right; or if thou depart to the right hand, then I will go to the left." The work is one—"you in your corner, and I in mine;" no rivalry, no discussion of diverse interests as such. Consider the words of John the Baptist in his deep humility: "He must increase, while I must decrease;" and the beloved disciple speaks only of *love*.

The missionary, then, needs patience, knowledge, faith, habits of method and regularity, so that one duty will not press upon another; and if she come as teacher, she should be acquainted with the best modes of instruction at home, and a good disciplinarian, or, what is better still, one who rules by love.

It is important that at least one in a school should have a good knowledge of music, and, indeed, every accomplishment can be made helpful in bringing scholars to the school, and so under our influence. Some knowledge of medicine is also a desirable qualification for a missionary. And in the Church we need those not easily discouraged, not disposed to find fault readily, and who will know how to utilize every spark of native talent. We need the very spirit of the Lord Jesus, who ever looked with pitying eye upon the "multitudes"—who loved the *people*. To me one of the most beautiful of all the gospel narratives is the one recorded in Mark vi. 31–34. The Lord had said to his disciples, "Come ye yourselves into a desert place, and rest a while," for "they had no leisure so much as to eat." But when they came to the "desert place," there before them were the "multitudes," and Jesus "was moved with compassion." How this comes home to our hearts as we are pressed and called on every side, and find so little leisure!

But just as the ears are sometimes opened to hear sweet melody in what at first seemed all discord, so, as the years of missionary-life go on and we come nearer to our Lord's side, following him in work among the poor and lowly, and going down with him into the depths of misery, are the eyes opened to see the exceeding beauty of the human soul. In our work we find the very essence of beauty, and a light has poured into our own souls which we never knew before. "If any one will do my will, he shall know of the doctrine."

These characteristics, these acquirements, these tempers of mind and soul, are not mere theories nor wild vagaries; they are just what we have felt ourselves to need in this land. Therefore let the one who possesses them, or most of them, consecrate them unto the Lord. Not all are really fitted for the missionary-work who may be devoted servants of the Lord.

> "With a pure clear light
> Jesus bids us shine,
> You in your small corner,
> And I in mine."

The heathen see the clear shining of that light. When D—— first came to the mission-house, she brought her idols with her, but long before any one spoke to her on religious subjects she threw them away: "I watched the Christians as they spent their time from morning until night in working for others, and I never saw anything like it before, so I threw my idols into the bay." O Ka san said, "I never knew anything like the care of these Christian teachers in the school. It is wonderful."—" Grandma," said little four-year-old Senki to old Hisa, " the love of the Christians is not like the love of the Japanese." And said one of the girls, "The love of the Christian is deeper than ours."—"We thought our teacher would be sick," said the girls, alluding to a grief of which they knew. But no; the teacher showed them that God was her strength and her refuge. Endurance in trial, courage in danger, self-forgetfulness in life, patience in sickness, triumph in death,—all these can be shown to the heathen by Christian women.

I wish to testify to the happiness of a missionary devoted to her work. There is no one happier in the world. And we who are here acknowledge that in the gospel we find a vigor, a freshness and a joyousness never before experienced in such degree. From the home-land come the evidences that some do depart from the faith, that some are doubting, that some deem themselves too wise for the gospel, but in our "Morning Land," in our "Sunrise Kingdom," we find rest and peace and strength and joy in Jesus. We are glad to be here.

CHAPTER III.

THE REGIONS BEYOND.

"Pray ye therefore the Lord of the harvest, that he will send forth laborers into his harvest."

LIFE here is earnest and practical. We have no time for theory or dreams. Day after day goes on in the same busy routine; every hour brings its own employment. There are little simple every-day duties in the house, the teaching and governing of children in the schoolroom, attending to some sick one's wants, or going out with Deguchi san or one of the girls to Gen-ske-cho, or to sow the seed elsewhere. And all this is sweetened and glorified by the fact that we are serving the Lord, and are receiving the "hundred fold."

But we are never so busy that we cannot often "lift up our eyes" to the hills far away; and on bright Saturday afternoons, when the week's work is done, we can take jin-ri-ki-shas and go to O-ji's fountains, or to Mu-ko-ji-ma's pleasant, flowery walks, or to Shi-ba's quiet woods, where no one would guess that we were in the heart of a great city. How many such hours we have spent there, when the sunlight trickled through the trees down upon the violet-beds and brightened the moss and fern and ivy!

In these times of resting there comes often a beautiful vision. A great wind has swept over Japan, and the idols have all been carried away—yes, even the beautiful images of Buddha have gone, or remain to be admired only as works of art. Instead of the pagan temples on the hills and in the villages and dotting the broad plains are houses dedicated to the service of the true God. The pilgrims have learned that neither on "this mountain" nor "at Jerusalem" need the Father be worshiped, but everywhere may he be found by those who call upon him "in spirit and in truth." They know of heights of holiness and wells of salvation higher and deeper than those of Fu-ji's top: "Beautiful upon the mountains are the feet of him that bringeth good tidings, that publisheth peace." In all the homes the word of God is read, and from them all prayer ascends. Every one speaks and understands the language of Canaan, and the "new song," which has been sung in such feeble strains only here and there hitherto, has now swelled into a grand chorus: "Hallelujah, hallelujah!

The kingdoms of this world are become the kingdoms of our Lord and of his Christ."

Shall my vision ever be fulfilled? Not by dreaming of it, surely; but this is the end to which we are to bend our energies. Then how must we go to work? It will never be accomplished by the foreign missionaries alone. We are too few in number and too weak in the flesh. Were our days as Methuselah's, or our strength as Samson's, or our numbers as the hosts of Israel, we might indeed expect to accomplish something. But our days are few and evil—few at the best, and made fewer still by the time we have to wait before we can go to work, and by the changes which come to us; and evil by reason of the infirmities of the flesh and the mistakes to which we, as erring human souls, are liable. And here in Japan our boundaries are restricted, and we may not go where we like.

Only a short time ago I was at Kanagawa, the little town opposite Yokohama. The emperor had just come home from a northern trip, and we watched the ornamented ships in the harbor and heard the guns which were fired in honor of his return. Then we saw him as he passed through Kanagawa in his open car. There was a great display of flags and the people were not wanting in demonstration, but they did not fall on their faces before him as formerly. After the car had passed, some of those in the hotel went up to the temple to worship. They had heard of Jesus, and some of them sang "Jesus loves me."

When the emperor had passed, we decided to go up the Tokaido to Tokio. Not since the days of railroading in Japan have we been over the old road between Kanagawa and Tokio. We passed many people on the road, and they all seemed as they did six years ago. We stopped at the old hotel where we always took dinner in the days of stages, but there was little sign of change there (except that no beggars were visible), and the people still knew nothing of God. We stopped at a temple and saw crowds going up to worship, and we went to Plum Ya-shi-ki and wandered about the beautiful grounds. There seemed no change in that part of the Tokaido, and we came home, sad and conscience-stricken, to devise new plans. And yet our work seemed fully up to our measure of strength.

Another day we went out in the suburbs of the city to the north and crossed the Sumida on a bridge, getting thus beyond the foreign limits. All was darkness there. On the way back we passed a little boy standing on a stone and talking to the setting sun. He did not seem to be praying, except as he repeated the words " *O Tento Sama! O Tento Sama!*" (" Mr. Sun"), just as they repeat "*Amida Dai Butsu! Dai Butsu!*" (" The Great Buddha").

How can missionaries ever boast of their work? No class of workers feel themselves more absolutely *nothing*. But our chief dependence is not on foreign missionaries, neither is it our object to fill Japan with them. It is rather to bring so large a force of native preachers, evangelical colporteurs, teachers and Bible-readers, both male and female, into the service that foreigners will no longer be needed, essential as their presence and their work are now, and will doubtless be for years and years to come.

I fear that when we pray the Lord of the harvest to send forth laborers into his field we think too much of the foreign missionary and not enough of the native helpers. The evangelization of a country depends upon *its own people*, and from them must the laborers come. The great white fields can be occupied in no other way. I would that all the Church of God would unite in earnest prayer to this end. Pray that India's sons and daughters may labor for India; that Persia's church-people may work for Persia, and the Chinese for China, and the Japanese for Japan; that in every missionary-land the hearts of the native Christians may burn with desire to carry the truth to the "regions beyond." But we deal not with theory and indulge not in visions; and comparatively new as this mission is, I think we can see that in the people which leads us to hope for great results—even that the grand consummation above described may be reached.

I do not wish to keep back from any one the discouraging features of the work. Some of those of whom we had brightest hopes have utterly failed us. Some have heard the gospel with joy at first, but are of those who have not root and soon are "offended." But that so many have persevered is more to be wondered at than that some have turned back.

Of the four Christians whom we found in Yokohama in 1869, old Baba (O Ba san) is dead. Kojiro and Ajiki have never, to my knowledge, entirely renounced their faith, but they are not working actively with any of the bodies of native Christians. But Ogawa, the elder, soon to be ordained a minister,* has through all times of sorrow and danger been faithful, and to-day is giving true evidence of his faith in his works. His is the "bright and shining light, shining more and more unto the perfect day." His wife has long been a mem-

* In 1878 pastor of a native church.

ber of the native church (Union), and they are united in the Lord. When he is ordained he will have the charge of native churches. Here is one at least who is ready to work well among his countrymen. But he is not the only efficient native worker. We have already noticed his association some years ago with the Yokohama elder Okuno, and remember their first missionary-tour together. In our church we have seen how soon it was organized, and even before that those who were baptized invited friends to hear quickly the good news of the kingdom.

At Toda san's, on the Ginza, at Chimura san's, in the vicinity of Shi-ba, at Iseki san's, in a distant quarter of the city, *sekiyo bas* ("preaching-places") were established. And all through the winter, in spite of wind and cold and storm, have the men gone out heartily to the work.

In Shi-na-ga-wa, a town in the suburbs, there has been preaching at the house of an old doctor who has a daughter noted in all that region for her filial piety. One bitterly cold day we all went out to a service near Hara san's "Willow Island." Two large rooms were thrown together, and they were filled with listeners. Some of the women sat far back and warmed themselves by the hi-ba-chis, but all could hear, and they listened attentively. The native evangelists have been far out in the country, and probably churches will soon be organized in the vicinity of Tokio with native pastors over them.

Our own church prayer-meetings are usually conducted by the Japanese. One of the licentiates preaches every Sunday in the church, and they are faithful teachers in the Sabbath-school. It is delightful to hear them giving in their reports at our monthly concerts, where each one tells where he has been, and with whom he has conversed, and how gladly the people have listened; and we believe they will gradually push forward until the truth is proclaimed throughout all the land.

But I think I hear some eager questioning about the women: "How are the women working? Will Japanese women take up with zeal the work for women in Japan?" Often we are tried by their shallow and frivolous natures and by the indolence which they show. Yet these very things, when they are in a degree overcome, make the power of divine grace manifest in them. The woman Deguchi san goes day after day to her work in the city, always refusing to ride, walking miles in the wind and rain and snow or in the summer heat. She comes home often, triumphant in her joy, to tell how gladly this one or that one has listened or has become a believer. She knows where every child in the school lives, and if one is absent more than two days goes to find out the cause. She does a great deal of copying, being a good writer, and is always busy. Often at night, when the house is quiet, I hear her voice in prayer.

Old Hisa, under careful direction, although weak in some respects and often trying, has kept patiently at her work month after month. She and Deguchi san went out in the country to O Rin san's house one cold day, walking eight or ten miles on a bad road, and teaching the people all the evening. Fifteen people assembled to hear.

I have great hope, too, of our girls. They come to school in weather that would keep many a child at home in our country. The little ones are brought on the backs of servants. Never once, in all the days of apprehended trouble from the ya-cu-nins, have they all at the same time kept away from school. Every Sabbath some one—often a number of them—has been here, even in most troublous days. At the time of the first baptisms among the scholars we saw evidences of great strength of character, and they have been earnest, consistent Christians ever since. Their attendance at church and Sabbath-school seems no forced thing.

One of the pleasantest hours in all the busy week is that one on the Sabbath evening when the others go to church and I am left with the little ones to have a talk about the services of the day and to hear what they have to say about the sermon. Their prayers are simple, child-like petitions, and their faith is beautiful to witness.

The Christian girls take turns in conducting the morning devotions in the school-room, and even the little ones lead in prayer. But some extracts from letters will give an idea of what religion is to them, better than anything I can say. "I pray to God for you every day," writes one to her absent teacher, "and our heavenly Father will hear the prayer of your dear friend." One, whose mother was sick, writes: "I could not go to church on Sunday for a long time. Every day I live in the house quietly, and it seems as if I had lost my dear friends, and I seem to live alone among the heathen people, but it is not so. We have the great Friend, and he will help us when we are weak and lead us when we wander. He loves those who love him. I am very happy when I think that I love him, and he blesses me all the time. My hope is in Jesus Christ."

"I heard a strange story," says another. "It is that in a city of Shiushiu twenty-four men became believers without any teaching. Some one got a Chinese Bible, and they read it and thought about it, and they discovered that there is one God, who made heaven and earth, and they became believers. This is a proof that God has blessed my country.

"I went to church on Sunday. The minister preached about faith, and it was very interesting. Now I am thinking about faith every day. How precious and how important faith is! All things which are done on the earth are by God's will. I must try to break any chains that bind me. I am glad that you have a class of young men on Sundays. I hope at last they will become Christians and our brethren. I pray for you and for those whom you teach on Sunday.

"To-day is Friday, and it is very pleasant weather, but a little wind blows. To-day's prayer-meeting was very interesting, and O I-ne san led; and she talked about 'Love your enemies.' The older girls talked about verses which they chose themselves, and the little ones recited. Our teacher asked us to bring, each one, one girl to the Sabbath-school. Almost all of the girls have led one or two girls to the Sunday-school. Sometimes I '*catch*' boys and girls on the way, so the Sunday-school is very large. All of the girls are poor and dirty, with babies on their backs. We have no power to lead them, but God can show us how. I am very glad to see them come to the Sunday-school. Now we must try to love them. Last Sunday, Miss Nui and Miss I-ne received baptism. And now our little O I-ne san has become a member of the Church of Christ in Japan, and we all rejoice.

"I must try to be hopeful and cheerful. Sometimes the way which we are traveling seems dark by reason of weakness in heart or disease of body, but Christ is our Light in the way. A Christian's life is not always peaceful. God has not promised us so. Jesus says, 'Take up my cross daily and follow me.'"

These letters are written in English, plainly and intelligibly, showing proficiency and skill in the use of our language.

These extracts will serve to show something of the hearts of these girls. I believe that, with all their apparent frivolity and running after things new and exciting, the Japanese are patient and endowed with great powers of endurance. May we not, with the evidences already given, look forward to a bright day for Japan, when the country will be filled with laborers from their own land?

And this brings forward in strong light the

self-abnegation of the foreign missionary. Our place is to bide, as it were, *behind* our work, to be constantly putting the fields which we have ploughed and sowed into the hands of others to reap—to make no name or fame for ourselves, but to seek to be "nothing."

"One soweth and another reapeth," saith the Lord. And to what end? "That both he that soweth and he that reapeth may rejoice together." Then again I beg all the Church of God to "pray therefore the Lord of the harvest that he will send forth laborers into his harvest;" and while you pray, remember from whence those laborers must come—*principally* from the people themselves. I repeat it: on *native workers* depends, under God, the chief and abiding success of missionary-work.

One object in each separate field should be to make it as independent as possible of the foreign missionary, and to reduce rather than increase the expenses of the Board at home. We must be careful, therefore, how we give our help. If self-denial and a sense of need are the life of the Church and the soul of prayer with us, so it is with the heathen. They must be trusted to depend upon their own resources, to build their own churches, take care of their own schools and support their own pastors. *And they can do it.* Do not let us imagine that the heathen are going to sit still to be converted. We care not for numbers, except as interesting statistics in comparing one year with another, for they may be doubled, trebled, quadrupled, in a year. Give the gospel to one, and that one may be the instrument of leading thousands to Christ. So let us pray, so let us direct our work, that all missionary-lands may soon be filled with laborers from among their own people.

CHAPTER IV.

"*THE LORD SHOWED HIM ALL THE LAND.*"

"So they went up to the mountains to behold the gardens and orchards, the vineyards and fountains of water.

"The pilgrims therefore went up to them (the Shepherds), and asked, Whose Delectable Mountains are these?

"*Shepherds.*—These mountains are Emmanuel's land, and they are within sight of his city."

THE time comes when the laborer in the harvest-field can go forth to work no more: strength fails. Then it is as if the angels of God carried the weak and suffering one up to an exceeding high place—so high that we can look down over all the land upon the sowers and reapers that are yet at work; so high that we can almost look into heaven and stretch out our hands to take our crown. I fear that we down in the harvest-fields, busy with our own work, do not often enough take views from high places. If we did, there would be less danger of growing narrow-minded or selfish in our work.

It is very important—indeed, necessary to our success—that we attend diligently to our own portion of the field, but in digging and ploughing, in planting and sowing, and in watching the ripening grain, we sometimes keep our eyes down too long, forgetting to climb to heights from which we can look over all the land. We can go up at times of missionary-meetings and conventions, and we can ascend smaller hills every week at our prayer-meetings, when we speak to each other of our work, and ask, "Is it thus or so with you?" Let us as from a mountain take a view of Japan, which we are now seeking to win for Christ.

The empire of Japan comprises a group of islands lying to the east of China, Corea and Siberia. Of these islands Niphon (or Hondo), Yeso, Kiusiu and Shikoku are the chief. Besides these, there are thousands of smaller isles, some of which are nameless, or merely numbered, while others, such as Eno-Shima and Miajima, are famous throughout the whole land for the rare beauty of their scenery. The combined area of the islands is estimated at one hundred and fifty thousand square miles, and the population at thirty-three million. The country lies mostly between thirty and forty degrees north latitude, and embraces quite a variety of climate. In the North snow covers the ground during most of the winter, while in the South the change from winter to spring is scarcely perceptible.

The origin of the Japanese nation is not certainly known, nor is it necessary to discuss it here. There seems to be a general impression among themselves that they are Mongolian; in which they are no doubt correct, but whether purely so, without admixture of other blood, is questionable. They are not an inventive people: their minds are rather receptive and imitative. Whence they obtained their ideas originally no one certainly knows, but they have gone on for hundreds of years living in the same low wooden houses, eating the same food, using the same implements and utensils, and cutting their clothes after the same fashion, without any apparent desire for improvement. But when foreigners, after much difficulty, had once gained access to the people and were permitted to make homes for themselves in some of the ports, the whole nation ran eagerly after our Western science and civilization; and so rapid have been the changes that all the world has looked on with amazement, while to us who are here it seems as though a century of change had passed over the land in but a few years of time.

I am not aware that any great change has

been made in the political divisions of the country or in the general policy of the government with regard to its own internal application, but there are evidences of progress which deserve special notice.

The agricultural department (*Kai-ta-ku-shiu*) has done much to improve the fertility of the soil, and the introduction of foreign seeds, bulbs and slips has proved that Japan is capable of bearing fruits and vegetables equal to those of our own land. Delicious pears have been raised, and strawberries, currants and gooseberries are now abundant and good in Tokio and Yokohama, while tomatoes and other once-foreign vegetables are raised in perfection. Some of the chief experiments of the Kai-ta-ku-shiu have been in the island of Yeso, which lies to the north, and a great deal has been done toward reclaiming its barren soil, as well as that of other islands.

The Japanese government has met in a timely manner, and solved, what is so puzzling a problem just now in some other lands—"What shall be done with the tramps?"—by sending the beggars of the empire to the island of Yeso, where all who are able-bodied are compelled to aid in the agricultural labors of that country. The result is that you may travel the empire over and not meet with a regular beggar or tramp—a marked contrast to what existed when we first came here. Beggary was then a profession.

There is some talk of new grasses being introduced in order that proper pasturage may be afforded for sheep and cattle. The exceeding coarseness and roughness of the native grass have precluded the possibility of raising these animals in any number, and the strange anomaly presents itself to a foreigner traveling through that otherwise beautiful country, that neither sheep, cow, goat, nor even pig, can be seen in all the land. Now, however, we may perhaps have our old desire realized in seeing sheep feeding upon the hillsides and cattle grazing in the valleys.

The railroads of Japan are two; or, more properly, there is but one railroad, finished at each end. So far as now completed, this line connects the eastern seaport of Yokohama with Tokio, and the south-western port of Kobe with Osaca and Kiyoto. It is expected—at least, hoped—that the railroad will be completed down the whole length of the To-kai-do, thus connecting the two capitals and the two great seaports of the island of Niphon. The railroad "stations"—as called by the foreigners and Japanese here—or depots are fine foreign buildings, and the greatest care is taken to prevent accidents, people not being allowed to cross the tracks when a train is anywhere in sight.

The telegraph is in operation all through the empire.

The school-system of Japan has undergone a complete change in late years.* Besides the Kai-sei gakko, or imperial college, at Tokio, and the academies connected with the governmental departments of engineering, mining, agriculture, army, navy, etc., there are at certain points in the empire what are called Eigo gakkos, where English is taught and foreigners employed. There is a lack of system and a crowding of studies in these schools which we regret, but hope that in time these errors will be rectified. There are normal schools through the country, where scholars are taught as in the one at Tokio. The system has been given them by an American, and they have graded Readers, object-cards and maps prepared expressly for them. Teachers from all parts of the country come to Tokio and study the system there. Other open ports have become centres of learning, and thus the children throughout all

* There is now (1878) a regular bureau of education connected with the government, and great pains have been taken, by special embassy and other means, to investigate the methods and appliances of other countries, with a view of incorporating what is in their opinion good in them into their own national system.

the empire are being taught much more thoroughly and wisely than were their fathers and mothers.

The school-buildings are mostly of a partly foreign style. We were surprised by their number and neat appearance as we traveled through the country. Many Japanese young men are studying medicine with foreign physicians; at U-ye-no is a fine hospital. For educational purposes in science, law and medicine, as well as for the general benefit of travel, Japanese students are frequently sent to America and Europe.

The expediency of beginning a school expressly for the education of the blind is being discussed. It is greatly needed.

The normal school for girls in Tokio was opened in the fall of 1875. The empress herself was present. The first girls' school, opened in 1872 in connection with the Kai-sei gakko, is still in existence. Five girls were sent to America in 1872.

Books of all nations, on all subjects, are being translated. We hope some one will be raised up in Japan who will reduce the language to a system, discarding in large measure the Chinese, but this work does not yet seem to have received much attention.

Newspapers are being circulated very generally, some in easy colloquial, as the *Ichi nichi shimbu,* or "*Daily Gazette,*" in Tokio.

Prison reform has occupied the attention of the government to a considerable degree. In some places, even, the missionaries have been allowed to go into the prisons. Whipping has been prohibited. The heads of criminals are no longer exposed on the highways, nor are barbarous modes of punishment resorted to —at least, so far as we have opportunity of knowing.

The currency has been changed. Now we have the *yen* (dollar) and the *sen* (cent), and so fifty sen, twenty sen and ten sen, the decimal currency having been generally adopted.

Japan has a regular standing army. The vessels of war are but few and the naval force is as yet insignificant. Both military and naval schools have been established, and are carried on with thoroughness. Foreign officers have been at the head of these, but are now being gradually displaced as native ability comes to the front.

In looking upon the people, it is interesting to observe how far these foreign innovations have affected them individually or as families in regard to language, houses, food and dress. In many parts of the empire, and among many of the people, we notice no apparent change as yet, but here and there, especially in the open ports and at the seat of government itself, we discover considerable difference. As new objects have been brought before them and new ideas introduced, they have required new words, and have generally drawn upon the Chinese language for them.

Many of the Japanese are now building houses partly in foreign style, although they usually prefer to live in the Japanese part of the establishment. We may see in almost every house in Tokio something foreign, tables, chairs or pieces of drugget, which they find more comfortable in winter than their own mats. The natives are beginning to use meat and milk to some extent, quickly recognizing their nourishing qualities.

Many of the men appear in foreign dress, but there is little change in women's apparel. Some of the costumes of the men, half native and half foreign, look very curious, and it is odd to see some with bath-towels around their necks as comforters, and coolies wrapped up in bed-spreads. But such incongruities are disappearing. One great advance in civilization is that the coolies are obliged to wear clothes, and no longer appear in an almost nude state—at least, this is the case in or near the great cities. They have, or pretend to have, in their bath-houses separate apartments for men and women, and the people now usually dress before they go out on the streets.

The old Yoshiwarra system—the jo-ro-reis—has been virtually abolished. These women are not supported or countenanced by the government, as formerly, though in some parts of the country too much indulgence is still shown.

We think that, amid all fluctuations, changes and mistakes, progress in Japan is marked and sure. As missionaries, we do not care to Americanize or Anglicize the people, unless as a natural development. Indeed, we are very careful in our girls' school to have, so far as practicable, everything in native style, that we may not educate them away from their own people.

I shall never forget how I was struck, one day, picking up a Chinese copy of the *Pilgrim's Progress,* to see in the cuts Christian as a Chinaman with a long cue. I think I always had an idea before that Christian was an Englishman. Happy for the world is it that "Christian," either as a Japanese or Chinese or Hindoo, or as a citizen of any country, without changing his clothes, food or distinctive habits of life, may journey on the heavenly way, and at last find entrance through the gates into the city.

The seven open ports of Japan—Yokohama, Tokio, Ko-be, Osaca, Niigata, Hakodadi and Nagasaki—are interesting to us chiefly as missionary centres, and as such we will briefly view them.

Yokohama.—This city is still the great seaport of Japan, and has the largest foreign population, which last fact is, alas! in nowise of any advantage to the missionaries. For here, as in all other missionary-lands, we must admit that the hardest thing we have to contend with is the ungodly conduct of our own countrymen, and of those who come as the representatives of other nominally Christian nations. The Japanese understand no distinctions at first. They call us all Christians; and the lawlessness, recklessness, intemperance and licentiousness of American and British seamen, as well as those of other countries, bring continual reproach upon the cause of Christ in this land. And many other foreigners, by their disregard of the Sabbath and shameful conduct in many respects, prove sad hindrances to our work. What an impetus might be given to the work if only the representatives of the two great Christian nations who speak the same language would by their lives and by their expressed sympathy aid the missionaries in their work!

But we have found among the foreigners

outside of our missionary circles many warm and sympathizing friends whose whole course has been most kind and helpful, and some who have proved themselves true lovers of God and earnest promoters of Christ's work in this land.

Mission-Boards.—The mission-boards represented in Yokohama are the Reformed (Dutch), the American Presbyterian, which occupied the field about the same time as the Reformed, the Baptist, the Methodist, and the Woman's Union Missionary Society.

The Reformed Board has six missionaries in Yokohama. The first native church was organized under the name of the Union church, the converts being those who had been under the instruction of both the Reformed and the Presbyterian missionaries. There is a large girls' school under the care of this Board.

The American Presbyterian mission is the only one which has its buildings in the settlement, the buildings of the other missions being on the bluff. On the compound are two mission-houses, a dispensary, which is used also as a chapel, a school for boys, and a Sabbath-school room, besides a building used for a girls' day-school.

Of the medical work done in connection with this mission too much cannot be said. It is only necessary here, however, to mention the name of the noble veteran in that department, Dr. J. C. Hepburn, whose labors have been so unremitting and crowned with such wondrous success. His name and his work are known in all the churches. The *Dictionary*, which has been of so much use to all foreigners, is the work of this same member of the Presbyterian mission.

Besides the meetings in the dispensary, services are held in a house in the native city on Sabbath evenings. The number of missionaries belonging to the Presbyterian Board is seven.

The Baptist and Methodist missions are at this date comparatively new. The missionaries are learning the language and teaching.

The "American Home for Girls," under the auspices of the Woman's Union Missionary Society, is a centre of light and influence known and felt through all the country round about Yokohama and Tokio. Besides the Japanese, Eurasian and destitute children of all nations there find a home and receive loving care. A newspaper in Japanese for children is published by this society.

The work which is carried on among foreigners in the hospitals and on ship-board, and the temperance movement, deserve special mention and consideration.

But the great work conducted at present in Yokohama is the translation of the Scriptures as a whole. This is done by the labor and under the supervision of a committee chosen from all the Boards. They have nearly completed the New Testament, and will soon begin on the Old.

I cannot turn away my eyes from Yokohama without taking one glance at the cemetery where our missionary dead are sleeping. The first who was laid there was the little daughter of a Baptist missionary, and for a long time she slept alone. Then, by a strange, sudden calamity—the bursting of the boiler of a little steamer in which they were traveling—two members of our own mission, with their little "Eddie boy," were taken from us, leaving us dumb with amazement and sorrow. Only a few days before, we had had our last excursion together, going in a house-boat up the river Sumida. As we stopped and moored the boat for a time near Adzuma Bashi, the natives gathered around, and Eddie's papa lifted him to the top of the boat and said that he should be a missionary. We saw them late Saturday evening, bade them "Good-night;" their carriage turned the corner, and they were gone from our sight until in-the better country we shall bid them "Good-morning." The little infant of three months, the only surviving member of the family, was soon after taken to America, where he now is with his grandparents.

A little missionary baby who never saw the light was next laid near them, and a missionary brother from China found his resting-place under the same trees which overshadow their graves. Then one of the brightest of our mission-band in Tokio, of the Scotch Presbyterian Mission—one who had labored with us scarcely one year—went home after only a few days of illness. Her last message to the Japanese was, "Tell all these people that I did want to teach them about their Saviour." Her baby-daughter followed her in two short weeks, and was buried in the same grave. Then a beautiful little daughter of friends in the Methodist mission closed her eyes to this world, and she too was laid to rest in the cemetery at Yokohama. These are our missionary dead. Pleasant were their lives—sweet is their memory.

Many foreigners now sleep here, a large number of whom died from violence or found a watery grave. Kind hands have placed a monument in a prominent spot in memory of those who perished in the Oneida, an American war-vessel that collided with the British vessel, the Bombay, in 1870. One of them, the assistant-surgeon of the Oneida, young Frothingham, had greatly endeared himself to the foreign missionaries by his kind sympathy and timely help. He was a teacher in the Sabbath-school while the vessel lay in port.

Tokio.—Tokio, our city of the plain, the centre of political, literary and scientific life in Japan, is also one of its finest centres for missionary-work. The great drawback here is that the Concession is small and all the missionaries are obliged to live on it. In some instances missionaries, by taking charge of schools in some way nominally under Japanese care, have been allowed to live in the city; but the government is becoming more strict rather than more lenient on that point, and it is feared that all will be driven into the Concession.

The mission-boards represented in Tokio are the American Presbyterian, the Scotch Presbyterian, the Methodist, the Baptist, the American Episcopal, the Church of England and the Society for the Propagation of the Gospel (English). All of these missions have churches or preaching-places and schools under their care.

In connection with the Scotch Presbyterian mission is a large dispensary. The American Presbyterian has one large school for girls, the Methodist one, and the Scotch Presbyterian one.

A union has lately been formed of all the churches of the Presbyterian family, Scotch and American (including the Reformed), in church-work and organization among the natives. The missionaries of these Boards, with their native helpers, make a large and efficient force.

On Sabbath-days now all over the city people can be seen going up to worship. From one place and another comes the sound of an organ, and the voices of native Christians ascend to God in prayer and praise. The Bible is in many a home, and, better still, its truths are written on many hearts.

It is proper to state that the Greek Church has a mission and a magnificent building, reckoned among the finest in the city. A number of Roman Catholic priests are here, and the Sisters have a school for orphans.

Ko-be.—This beautiful little seaport lies at the entrance to the inland sea in the south-eastern part of the island of Niphon. The land rises rapidly from the bay, swelling into high hills back of the city. These hills make Ko-be the great sanitarium of Japan. The foreign settlement here is quite large, and some of the buildings are very fine. The city is connected by a railroad with Osaca and Kiyoto, the distance being forty miles.

The principal attraction of Ko-be is the waterfall. There are two falls, the upper and the lower. The Japanese think their *O Taki* a wonderful thing.

The mission-work in Ko-be is carried on almost entirely under the auspices of the American Board of Commissioners for Foreign Missions. The missionaries and native helpers move down toward the southern part of the island and to Shikoku. The girls' school in this mission is large and flourishing; pupils come from all the country round about. Many of them are members of the native church. A newspaper is published by one of the members of this mission. In regard to the work among the women, which is very encouraging in Ko-be, one of the missionaries writes: "Two of the women have been down twice lately to Akashi to stay a few days, with apparently much success from their work. One woman from there was up here to-day, and said she did not really understand much about Christianity until those women came. 'Now,' she says, 'a few of us women down there have been thinking that, since women have so much more patience than men, we must get together between the Sabbaths, and if we can't get anybody to teach us we must study together and try to get ready to teach these blessed truths.'"

Osaca.—This city, like Tokio, is on a plain, but there is no bay, and the summer heat is oppressive. It is a city of bridges, some of which are really wonderful in their construction. The mint, where the new money is coined, is in this city. The railroad-station and the city-hall are fine buildings.

The castle, with its magnificent masonry, is the principal object of attraction in Osaca. When we visited it, two years ago, we were escorted through by a soldier, and looked with wonder at the huge stones and high battlements from which we gazed upon the city. On the Concession are many fine buildings, and a river passing through it makes it pleasant.

The mission-boards represented here are the American Board, the English Church and the American Episcopal. The mission-work for a time was very slow, but considerable impetus has been given to it lately. There is a girls' school in connection with the Episcopal mission, and one under the American Board. This latter is not a boarding-school, the ladies preferring to devote most of their energies to outside work among the women.

Kiyoto.—This is not an "open" city, but missionaries are allowed to live here. Sometimes a little apprehension is felt concerning the permanence of the mission, which belongs to the American Board, but as yet nothing has occurred to interrupt the labors of those engaged in the work. It is a very interesting station, being in former times the very centre of paganism.

It is a gay city, too, as we who have seen the people going up to the theatres and watched the gay crowd at their *Susume* can testify. Never shall we forget the brilliant scene which we witnessed there one night. Little platforms were built right over the shallow but rapid river which passes through the city. The platforms were lighted by lamps and torches, and on them people were gathered for entertainment. Eating, drinking, dancing with hands instead of feet, and singing were the principal amusements. It was an exceedingly gay, animated scene, and we enjoyed looking upon it from the bridge so much that we joined the crowd and sat down on one of the platforms to eat watermelon and drink tea.

One of the first at Kiyoto who became interested in the truth was a woman, now the wife of Nesima, a native Christian educated in America. We noticed her on a boat going from Kiyoto to Osaca. She had an English Bible in her hands, and was going to Osaca to study with one of the missionaries. She is a woman of great strength of character. The missionaries are about to put up a building for a girls' school. So this great centre has the gospel given to it also.

Niigata.—This city lies on the Sea of Japan, to the north-west of Tokio. Foreigners are allowed to live in any part of it, but it is not yet occupied very strongly by any mission-board, although the Scotch and American Episcopal Boards have stations there, and we have good accounts of the progress of the work. The journey is made overland from Tokio. Many Bibles have been sent to the missionaries there.

Hakodadi.—This city is on the island of Yeso, which lies to the north of Niphon. It is a cold, rather barren, country, but lately has been much improved by the efforts of the Ka-ta-ku-shiu. Steamers run between Hakodadi and Yokohama. On the island is a volcano.

The people are somewhat rough, being mainly uncivilized *Ainos*, who are considered the aborigines of the country, and convicts and tramps from the other islands. Some of the Ainos have been in Tokio, and attempts are being made to civilize them.

In connection with the Ka-ta-ku-shiu, there has been in Shi-ba a girls' school for the children of the Ainos, which it was proposed to remove to Yeso. Whether this plan has been carried out or not I cannot say; but we hope that before long there will be schools for girls in Yeso.

Two mission-boards have stations in Hakodadi—the Methodist and American Episcopal. Accounts of work are interesting, and the following extract from a letter will tell of a work done outside of the missions: "We have heard of Dr. Clarke's work in Sapporo, Yeso. He has just gone home, after a year spent in getting the agricultural college started. He was president of the agricultural department in Amherst College, Massachusetts; was told when he came, by the Christian teachers in the Kai-sei gakko that he must not expect to teach Christianity in connection with his work: it would not be allowed. But he took some Bibles with him, and on his way up, being accompanied by Gen. Kuroda, in command of that department, he inquired if he might teach the Bible. The general said 'No'—not that he supposed it was a bad book, but the government did not tolerate Christianity yet, and he could not allow the Bible to be used in the school.

"Shortly afterward, on Gen. Kuroda's remarking that Dr. Clarke was to teach morality, the doctor replied, 'I cannot; you have forbidden me the only text-book I know.' The matter was dropped there, but again and again it came up, until Kuroda said, 'I do not know as much about text-books as you do; you must select your own. Only teach morality.'

"So the Bibles were put into the hands of the sixteen young men—picked men from the Kai-sei gakko—and without comment they were required to commit to memory portions selected from the Old and New Testaments, until finally they began to ask questions which Dr. Clarke was glad to answer, and a Bible class was speedily formed. The result, so far as appears now, Dr. Clarke thinks, is that the sixteen young men are all Christians; and even if the Bibles are taken away, they have the word hidden in their hearts."

Nagasaki.—No one who has seen it will ever forget the beautiful entrance to the landlocked harbor of Nagasaki, in the island of Kiusiu. High islands rise out of the sea, conspicuous among which is Shimabara, the rock from which the Christians were thrown in the old days of persecution. Nagasaki is all shut in by hills. We felt as though we were treading on historic ground as we wandered through *Desima*, where the Dutch were confined so long and suffered such indignities for the sake of trade, being the only nation which would submit to Japanese terms. Here is the new Methodist chapel. The Methodist and the Reformed are the only churches which have stations in Nagasaki. The houses of the missionaries, on the hills, are very beautiful, but the climate is much warmer than in Tokio. The work progresses more slowly there, as the people seem more prejudiced.

These are at present the great mission-centres of Japan. From them go forth the laborers, both foreign and native, to all parts of the land. Around them, in the little villages and larger towns, are native churches and preaching-stations, and new ones are constantly being formed.

The missionaries have been on the Ha-ko-ne Mountains, and the children there sing "Jesus loves me." They visit Nikko's beautiful temples and teach the word and leave Bibles and tracts. And in the summer vacation, when they leave their homes and go out into the country or by the seashore, they gather in the children, and through them interest the parents.

Is not the view from over the mountain-top full of hope and cheer? What seemed, down below, like broken plans, frustrated purposes, shattered hopes and grievous disappointments, up here are seen to be only parts of God's plan in scattering the truth over all the land.

CHAPTER V.

SAI-O-NA-RA.

> "Let the fiery, cloudy pillar
> Lead me all the journey through."

"Whether it was by day or by night that the cloud was taken up, they journeyed. Or whether it were two days or a month or a year that the cloud tarried upon the tabernacle, remaining thereon, the children of Israel abode in their tents and journeyed not; but when it was taken up they journeyed."

UNCERTAINTY and change are amongst the most trying things of missionary-life. We must hold ourselves ready for constant meetings and partings, for continual comings and goings. We in Japan live right on the very highway of travel to the Orient. One of the privileged duties of our life is the entertainment of missionaries going to and from their stations. Right glad are we to welcome them when they come or sympathize with them as they go, for leaving the work is the hardest trial of the missionary. Some we only see once; we bid them "Godspeed," and they go on their way; but our lives are enriched by them all.

Then the time comes when for us too the fiery, cloudy pillar is lifted and we must "arise" and go elsewhere. I wonder how it was in the Hebrew camp during that wonderful journey through the wilderness into Canaan? When the cloud rested for "one year," did they forget that they were only travelers, and did they try to make a home for themselves in the wilderness? Were their tent-pins ever driven so deeply in the sand that they had trouble in taking them out? or were they always ready to strike their tents and march away? When the cloud was lifted at night, was there much hurry or confusion in the camp? Did the people complain when they left Elim's fountains and palms, and were their mouths filled with murmurings when they encamped by Marah's bitter waters—when they knew that at any moment the cloud might be lifted and they permitted to journey on? "Dear Lord, thou knowest how hard it is to leave the warmth and shelter of the tent to journey forth into the desert."

How like is our journey to that of the children of Israel through the desert! Clearly as Hebrew women saw while in their tent or on their march the mysterious pillar, now resting, now going before the mighty host, so can the child of God whose eyes are fixed upon the pillar of his providences fully know when to journey on and when to tarry. Yet how much better off are we than they! True, the same One was with them who is with us, but they knew him only afar off and as the "Angel" —the "Angel of the covenant"—while to us he is Jesus, the crucified, risen Saviour, Emmanuel, Christ the Lord.

I have had a long talk with Takejiro. He is under Christian influence, and is thinking seriously of becoming a Christian himself. The woman Hayashi and her two little boys are in a northern province with the husband and father. She sent her farewell by a letter, with a picture of herself. She has been ever a comfort and a help to us since she joined us. Before her husband returned to Tokio last summer she was troubled a little, and begged that we would pray that he might not be angry with her for uniting with the church. This simple request was gladly complied with, and she came to Sabbath-school, smiling and happy, to tell us that he was not angry, but was coming to church himself in the afternoon. She whispered in my ear as she was leaving the room, "I wish to work for God."

Deguchi san and Mitsuye san have been my companions in a distant province of the South. The latter has been a devoted nurse through a long illness. These people are most faithful to those they love. The little O Nui san, who wrote to tell of her baptism, is the sister of O Shi-ge san. The father had known of his eldest daughter's baptism for a long while, and though not manifesting anger refused permission to O Nui san at first. But they all prayed (and prayer is a real thing to them), so that at last O Nui san's request for baptism was granted, and she and O I-ne san were baptized the same day. The latter's Christian character is developing beautifully, says her teacher. Does any one remember the tiny child of six years whom we first saw asleep upon her pallet in the little house near Gizo bridge? The "young rice" has been carefully watched and tended.

A very large proportion of the girls who have been members of the school from its beginning are either professors of religion or still under Christian influence; and we leave them all working—all the native Christians in every school and every church that we have known. And still the number increases, so that we can scarcely tell accurately the number of native Christians, churches or schools.

O Ka san came to say "Good-bye." She had in her hand a beautiful piece of crape, her parting gift to O I-ne san's teacher. "You are going home," she said, and then sobs choked her utterance. How I wish that I could go away knowing that her feet too were walking in the way to the better country! But we shall still hope and pray that the mother may be led by her daughter to Christ.

The girls came from Tokio to Yokohama to say "Good-bye" before the ship sailed. The parting was sad, for we knew not for how long it might be. But we sang our little hymn together that we had sung so often in the school and church at Tokio:

> "Jesus loves me, loves me still,
> Though I'm very weak and ill;
> From his shining throne on high
> Comes to watch me where I lie.
>
> "Jesus loves me! He will stay
> Close beside me all the way;
> If I love him, when I die
> He will take me home on high."

Then the girls knelt together whilst O Chiye san prayed; and we parted thus strong in the faith of the Lord. O Tama san crept back to the bedside after the others had gone, and said, "We have sung that hymn and prayed that prayer. I shall never forget it—never!"

Feb. 28, 1877.—A bright morning has broken over Japan. Earth, sea and sky are glorious in the winter sunshine. The great steamer is moving rapidly. The engines are working, the sails are spread, and around us fly the sea-gulls. We are "homeward bound."

But our eyes are not turned toward the home-land to-day. They are fixed upon the fast-receding shores of Japan—fixed upon Fu-ji, all white and glittering. Nearly eight years ago, as the rays of the early sun brightened those beautiful islands, I said in gladness "*O hayo!*" —"Good-morning!" And now the blest morning of a new life has spread its cheering light over the land just waking from the spiritual sleep of centuries, and still I may say "*O hayo!*" as the Sun of righteousness ascends to meridian height. May darkness nevermore come over Japan! May its light shine "more and more unto the perfect day"!

But as parting from earth precedes the entrance into heaven, so must I say "Good-night" where but a short time ago I said "Good-morning." Yes, to the country I love I must say "*Sai-o-na-ra*"—"Good-bye"—if it must be so. If never to see thee again in this life, when we wake from sleep may we meet thy people again and mingle our joyous "*O hayos*" with glad "Hallelujahs"!

THE END.